SOCIAL POLICY FOR THE TWENTY-FIRST CENTURY

SOCIAL POLICY FOR THE TWENTY-FIRST CENTURY

New Perspectives, Big Issues

BILL JORDAN

polity

First published in 2006 by Polity Press

Polity Press
65 Bridge Street
Cambridge CB2 1UR, UK

Polity Press
350 Main Street
Malden, MA 02148, USA

ISBN-10: 0-7456-3607-1
ISBN-13: 978-07456-3607-8
ISBN-10: 0-7456-3608-X (pb)
ISBN-13: 978-07456-3608-5 (pb)

A catalogue record for this book is available from the British Library.

Typeset in 10.5 on 12 pt Sabon
by Servis Filmsetting Ltd, Longsight, Manchester
Printed and bound in Great Britain by TJ International Ltd, Padstow

For further information on Polity, visit our website: www.polity.co.uk

Contents

Part III Global Social Justice: The Big Issues

List of Tables

Acknowledgements

I would like to thank David Held for persuading me to write this book, and for steering me to its present form.

I am also grateful to Michael Breuer, Martin Seeleib-Kaiser, Gordon Jack and Charlie Jordan for stimulating conversations and suggestions before and during the writing of it. Sarah Jordan kept me up to date with developments in France, and sent me several items of literature, as well as contributing to many of the ideas and discussions in the book.

As often before, I am indebted to Gill Watson for typing and tidying up the script, often from a considerable distance.

Introduction and Themes
of the Book

In the new century, three big issues increasingly confront the social policies of governments. Can their efforts to improve their citizens' well being be reconciled with the needs of the poorest populations in the world? Are they rooted in a convincing version of their own domestic social order? And are they sustainable over time, given finite resources? These issues have also surfaced in the deliberations of international bodies, such as the G8 and the European Union (EU).

In none of the affluent First World countries have coherent policies for addressing these questions yet emerged. For example, France and Germany still have generous welfare states, but they seem less able to respond to the challenges of an integrated world economy than they were twenty-five years ago. They suffer from low rates of growth and high unemployment, and risk becoming backwaters of introverted self-protection unless they undertake painful restructuring.

Their welfare states provide an attractive way of life in these countries, but stand accused of being handicaps to competition with China, India and the post-communist countries of Central Europe. Their electorates have registered fears over such pressing future questions as the further enlargement of the EU, free movement, immigration and fair trade with external states, especially those of Africa.

By contrast, the Anglophone countries (the USA, the UK, Canada, Australia and New Zealand) appear more resilient in the face of global market forces, and hence better able to stay in the mainstream of world economic and human development. But they have experienced greater inequalities between their citizens, and have adopted more restrictive, targeted welfare regimes. While the leaders' model for the world economy has prevailed, under the hegemony of the USA, its benefits for the poorest populations, and its ecological sustainability, are still unproved.

Furthermore, it is in the Anglophone countries that doubts about how well-being is linked to the social order have most explicitly surfaced. Individualism, rivalry and conflict have created a culture of insecurity and policies of enforcement and incarceration. The world development model has generated foreign policies which – in the Middle East and Central Asia – have alienated large groups and led to civil and international strife.

In this book I shall argue that it is time for social policy, as an academic discipline, to address these issues directly. It is very strongly associated with the period after the Second World War when welfare states were created in the First World countries. These, through their measures for social justice between citizens, seemed to balance capitalist dynamism with the protection of human capacities, and were seen as models into which state socialist regimes might evolve, and towards which developing countries might aspire.

However, they have not, after all, created a durable synthesis between freedom and security, because they did not take proper account of the three issues identified above. What Karl Polanyi (1944) called *The Great Transformation* – the movement towards unifying the whole planet as One Big Market – has continued to reshape the collective landscape worldwide. As the set of institutions in which the social life of the industrialized economies had become embedded, welfare states were now the targets for transformation, and the social policy community was associated with their defence. In this sense, it became part of a movement for conservation rather than change.

I shall argue that the current intellectual frameworks and research agendas of social policy tend to inhibit the exploration of these big issues. They fail to analyse the interactions between the various parts of the world's economic system or the interdependence between populations. Hence they do not reveal the factors which influence development and well-being. Nor do they show how the policies of First World governments affect the options open to those of developing countries.

This book draws on perspectives and analyses from political and social theory, economics, psychology, migration studies and international relations in an attempt to do better justice to these issues. While national governments remain important actors, and nation states are often taken as the units of account, I shall give equal attention to the purposes and strategies of international organizations, business corporations and ordinary individuals and households, using case examples from all over the world. Above all, I shall show that these purposes and strategies are now often global in their reach, and that this has important implications for national social policies.

Social policy, globalization and well-being

I am not claiming that social policy analysts have failed to address the consequences of global economic integration. But they have done so in terms primarily of the responses of national governments to pressures on welfare systems rather than the opportunities and constraints of a new set of relations between affluent, newly industrializing and developing states.

Since the publication of Esping-Andersen's *The Three Worlds of Welfare Capitalism* (1990), a central question for social policy research has been how generous welfare states were created and sustained. Scholars have refined his classification of 'welfare regimes' and clarified their relationship to 'production regimes' (Huber and Stephens, 2001). They have tested their adaptability under conditions of globalization (Scharpf and Schmidt, 2000a and 2000b), and they have measured the extent of retrenchment in their provision of benefits and services (Pierson, 2000).

By 'generous' welfare states, these authors mean that their redistributive systems sustained large transfers of income, resulting in relatively equal final outcomes, and that their public services supplied high levels of employment and provision. The leading examples come from Northern Europe, with the predominantly Christian democratic regimes of Germany, Austria and the Netherlands achieving the first of these criteria, and the Scandinavian social democratic regimes attaining both. By definition, this form of analysis treats each society as a closed system of transfers and exchange of services. It cannot take account of such phenomena as transfers abroad, remittances by immigrants, or international trade in human services. It also cannot analyse the impact of government policies on the well-being of populations in other countries or regions.

Comparative social policy studies do address the ways in which such welfare regimes are 'embedded' in 'production regimes' (the relationships between enterprises, banks, labour organizations and government in each state). They aim to show how the combined configurations of welfare-state and productive institutions sustain internal levels of investment and employment in each of the regime types (Huber and Stephens, 2001, ch. 4). But they cannot capture the dynamics of international finance and production and their relation to the overall transformation of social relations and human capacities worldwide.

Above all, these methods do not provide ways to evaluate the dominant model of world economic and social development. They focus on how national governments reform their institutions; global markets supply the context for political struggles in which adaptations must be compatible with international competitiveness. They neglect the linkages between, for example, the incomes gained by pension funds in the USA and the UK from investments in China and India, and the sustainability of industrial and commercial expansion in those countries. In so far as the dominant model of world development relies on a benign dynamic between the savings of pensioners in those affluent countries and the wages of workers in newly industrializing ones, issues of justice and ecology depend on the explication of these links.

Social policy theory and research in these traditions has uncritically adopted assumptions about human well-being from social and economic theory – assumptions which are now being challenged within those other social sciences. It has not set out to investigate the impact of transformations on qualitative aspects of well-being, relying instead on the proxies of income and consumption.

For example, the sophisticated work of Iversen and Wren (1998) on the role of service employment in balancing fiscal prudence with income equality is an impressive extension of the insights that have been gained through this tradition. But the service economy which has come to prevail in all First World countries is a very diverse mixture of private and public, high-wage and low-wage, male and female employment. I shall show that theory and evidence on the nature of services, and their contribution to individual and collective well-being, is notable by its absence.

What psychological research is beginning to indicate is that well-being rests on a combination of intra-personal and relational factors; intimacy, friendship, membership and solidarity are all aspects of this balance. So the emphasis on individual self-responsibility in citizenship and individual choice over public services, which are central to Third Way models in the Anglophone countries, potentially underestimate the collective elements in well-being. I shall analyse how a theory of services might supply the missing features in a qualitative analysis of policy outcomes.

Overall, I aim to develop an approach which can take the whole world as its unit of account, and can assess the coherence of the current programme for promoting global human capabilities, in relation to the big issues identified at the start of the book. But this also involves a re-examination of the basic assumptions about welfare which drove the post-war transformation – notions of citizenship, community and civil association.

Reciprocity and interdependence

Fundamental to the current model of world development is the reciprocity between affluent and poor economies in the realization of human potentialities. This is derived from a global market in which capital always seeks its most efficient use and workers are drawn into employments which offer the best wages. George W. Bush, Tony Blair and the World Bank subscribe to the principle that all populations benefit from a dynamic which reduces the costs of goods to consumers, and raises the incomes of all the factors of production, through international investment and trade.

But the reciprocal advantages for citizens of rich and developing countries rely on very complex networks between financial institutions, industrial corporations and governments. These international processes create links between the fortunes of individuals on opposite sides of the planet. The social policies of each state must take account of the complexities of these interdependencies.

For example, despite its role as economic superpower and world hegemon, the US government relies on loans – from Japanese savers, and from the trade surplus of the Chinese economy – to sustain its programme of expansion. George Bush's policies for cutting taxes on the rich and privatizing social security schemes, and for maintaining high levels of employment, earnings and consumption (as well as military interventions in Afghanistan and Iraq), are dependent upon financial flows from these Asian giants, and therefore upon their social programmes.

The Chinese government was able to instruct its central bank to buy hundreds of billions of US government bonds because of the extraordinary transformation of its economy, which enabled it to sell such volumes of manufactures to the USA. Having reversed the development strategies of the Maoist period, for twenty-five years the new regime has pursued a hectic expansion, based on the creation of huge 'Special Economic Zones' for manufacturing as the driver of export-led growth. In turning its southern coastal belt into the 'workshop of the world' – producing two-thirds of the world's microwave ovens, half of its clothes and a third of its computers – the Chinese government has lifted about 270 million people out of poverty.

But it has ruthlessly controlled the flow of migrant workers from its hinterland, and allowed huge regions to decay in rural backwardness or rusting, state-owned industrial plants. In 2003, an additional 800,000 citizens joined the ranks of those in abject poverty, earning less than 15p per day (Watts, 2004, p. 7). Those migrants who are allowed to enter the prosperous coastal region provide cheap labour for the sprawling new factory sites and for the construction of glittering city developments. New arrivals from rural provinces are not only paid far less than settled workers; they are also visibly smaller and thinner, and often work in appallingly unsafe conditions. Yet their earnings allow them to send substantial remittances back to rural kin, whose incomes are only a quarter of those of urban families.

The Chinese authorities' choice to make loans to the US government, rather than make systematic attempts to develop this hinterland or to redistribute the gains from growth of nearly 10 per cent a year, was therefore a strategic one. For the first five years of the century, they calculated that it was more advantageous to finance the purchase of China's exports by US consumers through these loans rather than to broaden its industrial development or equalize citizens' incomes. But the revaluation of the Chinese currency in July 2005 signals that they may be reconsidering this strategy. It suggests that the authorities may in the longer term be switching towards holding a mixture of Japanese, European and US currencies and bonds. This would threaten existing US government programmes, but could boost the economies of Japan and the European countries.

Of course, the rapid expansion of manufactured exports would not have been possible without investment in the Special Zones from all over the developed world, channelled through entrepreneurs in Taiwan and Hong Kong. Now the more affluent residents of these zones have the chance to travel abroad, as business people and as students. So large are the numbers studying in higher education in the English-speaking countries that there is now strong competition between the USA, Australia and the UK (where there were 32,000 such students in 2004). These global flows drive the restructuring of universities not only in these countries, but also in the European states which seek a share of this lucrative 'market'.

Meanwhile, residents of the poorer Chinese provinces seek to move to the affluent zones, even without the official 'passports' they require; these illegal internal migrants are periodically rounded up and removed by the police. Others migrate abroad; certain provinces now have established traditions for this strategy, and 'bridgeheads' of settled migrants in Europe, North America and Australia (Pieke, 2002). These transcontinental movements of population call forth social policy interventions, for instance in the UK. They have provoked measures on asylum, on clandestine entry (as in the deaths of fifty-four Chinese men in a container from the Netherlands in 2001), and on regulation of migrant labour (as with the deaths of cockle pickers in Morecambe Bay in 2004).

In the USA, the savings to consumers from buying manufactured goods from China, compared with the costs of producing them at home, are estimated at $100 billion since the start of the economic reforms (Watts, 2004, p. 7). The availability of such goods – because of the Chinese government's loans to its US counterpart – facilitates restructuring of the US labour market. It allows the Bush government to accelerate the transition to a service economy. Because of the sustained spending boom, jobs expand in retailing, leisure, and personal and domestic services (low-paid work taken mainly by women), and in higher-paid finance, business, media and professional services.

In the US presidential elections of November 2004, this enabled President Bush to fight off the challenge of John Kerry, who sought to represent the interests of traditional blue-collar workers in declining industrial areas, as well as those of ethnic minority groups. Bush could defend social policies directed at making the workforce adaptable and 'flexible', and at reinforcing tough conditions around social assistance programmes (Standing, 2002). The trade deficit and the consumer boom allowed the transformation of whole communities in the USA. For instance, the city of Bethlehem, Pennsylvania, once a major producer of steel for the US industrial sector, has now been transformed into 'Christmas City, USA' – a mixture of a kind of homage to its biblical name and a theme park commemorating its foundation in 1741 by Moravian protestant refugees (BBC Radio 4, 2004a).

Thus the social policies of the Chinese and US governments are interdependent and rely on mutual support, which is threatened by the revaluation of China's currency. But of course these reciprocities are multilateral; so the Chinese authorities' decision to break its peg to the US dollar and link its value to other currencies, including the Euro, will affect those countries' economic relationships with each other, as well as with itself.

The US business sector still invests more in the member states of the EU than in China, and this massive flow of investment is reciprocal. Businesses on both sides of the Atlantic find it advantageous to establish production sites, making cars and other high-value, high-tech products, on each other's territory, thus saving transport costs and obviating various other barriers.

However, the flow of investment from the USA to Europe is arguably of greater importance to sustaining the social policy strategies of European governments than the flow in the other direction. To take the example of Germany, the leading economy in the EU, its 'social state' still relies heavily on sustaining skilled employment for men in the industrial sector. Germany is still the world's largest exporter, with a trade surplus of $196 billion. It has adapted its institutions far more slowly than has the USA or the UK; under pressure from global market forces, the German government has until very recently increased social insurance contributions rather than reduce unemployment benefits or pensions. As a result, wage levels among skilled workers have been maintained, but the workforce in these industries has shrunk alarmingly and little new employment in other sectors has been created. Germany needs to sustain its traditionally strong industrial base while it tries to adapt to new global conditions, and the investment it attracts from the USA is important for this strategy.

However, the costs of maintaining the 'European Social Model', epitomized by the German corporatist system, do not fall solely upon Europe's citizens. The EU puts up many barriers to trade with countries from outside its borders, and especially trade in agricultural products. The Common Agricultural Policy (CAP) is a programme which has hitherto subsidized this form of production, but will in future give income to farmers themselves; it is the largest single programme in the EU's administration. It serves to disadvantage producers, especially in Africa, who could otherwise supply many European consumers at far lower costs. Taken together with the subsidies and other barriers in the USA, all this contributes massively to the poverty of farmers in that most disadvantaged continent.

In this section I have introduced some of the broader perspectives from which social policy will be analysed in this book – perspectives which are of immediate relevance for a new generation of researchers and students. On the one hand, we all nowadays behave as if we believe that the integration of the world economy benefits all its inhabitants. Not only do we buy products sourced from all round the globe and invest (either directly, or through our pension funds) in companies in many different lands. We also take holidays in exotic places, work abroad, and sometimes own a house or apartment in another country. In their 'gap years', or after graduating, students often travel round the world, either purely on vacation or to volunteer in projects for development or social support.

On the other, there are growing doubts about whether the global economic order will lead to greater justice and equality among the world's populations. Military conflict, and especially regime change for the sake of markets and Western-style democracy, has provoked fierce resistance. Evidence of some less developed countries 'catching up' with affluent ones is balanced by other data showing the poorest falling further behind (World Bank, 2001, pp. 51–5). Climate change threatens the sustainability of growth strategies. Large numbers of young people are drawn towards anti-capitalist and global justice movements, mobilizing against the forces which drive economic integration. This book will attempt to clarify the issues, the dynamics and the ethics of these disputes.

The structure of the book

In seeking a framework for these enquiries, and exploring these issues, I shall draw on the work of several recent social policy analyses which have started to break the mould of the welfare-state tradition. One of these is Bob Deacon's *Global Social Policy* (1997), in which he considers the strategies of the International Monetary Fund (IMF), World Bank and World Trade Organization (WTO), along with other international bodies. The journal of the same name extends this dimension of social policy research.

In part I of the book, I shall include this perspective in an investigation of global human development, and an evaluation of the current model, sponsored by the US and the UK governments. Starting from the tsunami which struck the coastal strips of countries along the Indian Ocean rim on 26 December 2004, I examine the scope for social policy within this region (the most promising in the developing world) under this model (chapters 1 and 2). I also discuss how the reciprocities and interdependencies described in the previous section enable and constrain further development within the new global division of labour (chapter 3).

This approach builds on the work of Ian Gough and his colleagues in their *Insecurity and Welfare Regimes in Asia, Africa and Latin America* (2004). In East Asia, the traditional role of extended families as sources of savings and redistribution survived the transition to postcolonial industrialization and urbanization. Using export-led growth, strongly sustained by the financial sector, and attracting investment from the developed countries, these societies achieved impressive improvements in educational attainment and life-expectancy, despite very low public transfers for income maintenance. The financial crisis of 1997–8 and the intervention of the IMF and World Bank (Stiglitz, 2002, ch. 4; Gough, 2004) illustrate the impact of international finance, imposed liberalization, and the evolution of the global development model.

The aim of the analysis is therefore to clarify the dialectic between the internal institutional configurations of societies and the strategies of international organizations (including banks and businesses). In some cases – for instance, most of the Latin American countries – debt-laden and crisis-ridden states, with quite substantial expenditures on social and health insurance schemes and universal, publicly funded education, were forced to liberalize foreign trade and capital markets, to reform public finances and to restructure public services as conditions of loans from the IMF and World Bank (Huber, 2002). Under the orthodoxy of the Washington Consensus (1980–2000), they were required to switch towards export-orientated economic development strategies (Edwards, 1995), leading to deregulation of labour markets and increased poverty and unemployment. This has increased reliance on market suppliers of services, but also on the extended household as a source of income transfers and mutual support (Barrientos, 2004, pp. 124–52).

However, Latin America has recently emerged as a source of resistance to this model. Neither President Lula of Brazil nor President Chávez of Venezuela is opposed to globalization; they seek to redistribute its benefits among the poorest of their citizens. The continent has spawned movements to redefine the relationship between global finance and local populations, such as the revolt by indigenous people in Bolivia, demanding the return to public ownership of that country's oil and gas resources (Gott, 2005).

The analysis of this dialectic must also take account of the governance and social relations prevailing in the poorest states. In Africa, the decline in development and well-being, with wars, civil conflicts and the HIV/AIDS pandemic, reflects the failure of post-colonial governments to protect and harmonize their populations, as well as the failure of international agencies. Where there are few successful entrepreneurs or well-structured labour markets, where much activity consists of coercive or violent seizure and extortion, theft or begging, and where the public sector employs soldiers, bureaucrats and professionals on low salaries who require other sources of income, individuals tend to rely on the patronage of the few who are connected with capitalist firms or government office, and have grown rich, often through corruption (Bevan, 2004a, pp. 97–8; 2004b). Yet in spite of all this, some international programmes, such as the UN World Health Organization's for eradicating measles and polio, have been rather successful (see pp. 255–6).

To do justice to this diversity of social relations, it is necessary to include the actions and strategies of informal community systems, non-government organizations (both local and international) and social movements. This goes beyond the concept of 'welfare regimes', already stretched in Gough et al.'s analysis (Davis, 2004, p. 258). It also addresses the impact of international trade in commercial human services, such as health and education. The interactions between business and government strategies in the First World countries, and social policy transformations in the industrializing and developing states, will be extensively analysed in chapters 5 and 6.

In the second part of the book, I shall turn to the transformation of the affluent states within the global order – their transitions into service economies, with large financial sectors, relying on investments all over the world. These restructurings were embraced by the Anglophone countries in the 1980s but have been more slow and painful in continental Europe, and especially in Germany, which made heavy weather of reunification after 1989 and is one of the last to adapt its welfare state (Bleses and Seeleib-Kaiser, 2004).

One part of this transformation involves a shift away from class-based political struggles, towards new cleavages and mobilizations. Research has indicated a reduction in the differences between party political programmes over social policies (Huber and Stephens, 2001); some authors go so far as to suggest that all European debates now revolve around versions of the 'liberal-communitarian' model which evolved under Third Way governments in the USA and the UK in the 1990s (Seeleib-Kaiser et al., 2005).

In chapters 7 to 10, I analyse the implications of this shift for social relations, policy and governance – to greater 'flexibility' and 'work-based welfare' in the labour market and income maintenance (chapter 7) and to more self-responsibility for citizens and the transformation of public sectors, encouraging them to make choices between such facilities (chapter 8). All this entails a polity in which all members are encouraged to be adaptable, mobile and 'independent', and a civil society with many associations and activities, creating 'responsible families and communities', with important implications for women's roles (chapter 9).

But these transformations in social relations have raised many doubts about the new order. In chapter 10, I focus on the research finding that, in these affluent First World countries, 'subjective well-being' or 'self-assessed happiness' no longer reliably rises with increases in national income per head of population. Psychologists have compared data from many countries over several decades and found that, although rich people are everywhere happier than poor ones, citizens of the rich states feel no better than they did thirty or forty years ago (Kahneman et al., 1999). Economists now accept that the formula for improved well-being which has worked for the previous 200 years – individual liberty, a market economy and consensual government – no longer holds, once average per capita income reaches $15,000 a year, at current prices (Frey and Stutzer, 2002, pp. 8–9; Layard, 2003a, 2005).

This should focus social policy's attention on collective units – the family, community and polity – which have been identified as crucial for self-assessed happiness (Myers, 1999; Argyle, 1999; Helliwell, 2002). In the UK, Tony Blair was sufficiently impressed with the research evidence to give a press conference on 7 March 2005, in which he appeared alongside other ministers to announce a commitment to sustainable development and improved well-being, and government research into establishing a national index (*The Guardian*, 2005a).

This gives rise to the first of the big issues to be tackled in the third part of the book – the question of how to root social policies convincingly in society's order (Jordan, 2004, 2005). Are the institutions constructed out of individual choices, and which enable autonomy and mobility compatible with sustainable improvements in the well-being of all citizens? In particular, if the liberal-communitarian model emerging from Third Way programmes becomes the dominant one for social policy, what forms of community can provide a viable form of membership and belonging under conditions of globalization (Putnam, 2000, 2002)? This will be the main concern of chapter 11.

In the analysis of these issues, the role of services (both public and private) is crucial for balancing individual freedom with communal conviviality. In chapter 12, I show that social policy lacks a coherent basis in economic theory for assessing these questions – for instance, debates about the respective merits of commercial, faith-based or state services in education and welfare provision. As the political mobilizations for democratic decisions over these issues shift towards values and morality – as in the re-election of George W. Bush in 2005, and to some extent in the lead-in to the UK general election in May 2005 (*The Guardian*, 2005b) – social policy needs a better methodology for evaluating the contribution of services to well-being.

In chapter 13, I return to the issues of reciprocity and sustainability between affluent and developing states in the world economy. I argue that it is time for social policy analysts to link their work with that of political theorists, who are increasingly concerned with the possibility of global governance, to address issues of interdependence in an integrated world system (Delanty, 2000; Dryzek, 1999; Held, 2004). This analysis should explore issues of cosmopolitan citizenship in a world of mass migration and the political bases for global social policies.

Finally, I shall turn to the big questions about how to reconcile the demands of social justice among members of a diverse and unequal world population with the requirement for sustainable use of finite natural resources, and the needs and rights of future generations. In chapter 14, I shall develop the work of those who are challenging the 'productivist' assumptions behind welfare states (Offe, 1992;

Gough, 2004), including Tony Fitzpatrick's stimulating critique of the Third Way model, *After the New Social Democracy* (2003). In particular, I shall examine the scope for trade-offs between the claims of those of generations still to be born, considering the case for new forms of redistributive policy within national and global systems (Fitzpatrick, 2003, ch. 7).

A 'non-productivist' programme, which recognizes the value of care, the contribution of culture and the importance of context, might reconcile technical advance with a more just and less rivalrous set of economic and social relations. This book provides new perspectives which contribute to the possible emergence of such a programme.

Part I

Social Policy and the Global Economy

Section 1A

Human Development and Redistribution

1

New Models of Human Development

On 26 December 2004, tsunamis caused by a massive earthquake off the north-west coast of Sumatra devastated the coastal strips of states around the Indian Ocean. Over 220,000 lives were lost, including those of about 10,000 European tourists, and 5 million people were made homeless. The tragedy reminded the world of its interdependence in an integrated global economy, and evoked unprecedented charitable contributions, as well as government aid, to Indonesia, Sri Lanka, Thailand, India and Malaysia, the countries chiefly affected.

However, it also illustrated the shortcomings of international institutions in the face of human need. As the United Nations mobilized relief, and individual states came forward with specific supplies, there was confusion, duplication and even rivalry. The United States claimed a leading role in organizing the response, demonstrating its president's disdain for the UN; and there were criticisms of the Indonesian government in particular, because of its military operations in the province most damaged and its inadequate co-ordination of relief efforts.

The whole disaster could serve as a parable for the dilemmas of social policy in the age of globalization. Confronted with the plight of millions made destitute, and the destruction of hospitals, schools, transport and the whole infrastructure of people's lives, the Indian government insisted that its emergency services (which had experienced several natural and man-made disasters on a similar scale) were adequate to the tasks. But all the other states affected appealed for foreign assistance, without clear principles about how to combine this with their own resources. The international effort, while expressing the generosity of peoples, was disorganized and fragmented.

None of this should be surprising, given the limited scope for social policy intervention of the international institutional system, and the limited reach of principles of social justice. Despite the penetration of foreign finance and industrial investment into this region, and the expansion of trade and tourism, neither in terms of organizational structures nor in the programmes and strategies for development were there comprehensive arrangements for meeting human needs. Each country had been pursuing its own very different pathway, independently of all others, trying to harness powerful economic interests from the affluent world, to combine them with its resources, and to equip its workforce to serve their purposes. But most of the dead and displaced were poor women, children and fishermen, making their living on the margins of these economies.

Furthermore, orthodox social policy analysis throws only a partial light on the issues confronting these countries, because of its focus on the decisions faced by governments with fixed resources to distribute among finite populations. In this perspective, the aims of social policy are to achieve efficiency and equity in the use of these resources. The objectives are to redistribute income, wealth and power in such a way as to sustain freedom and work incentives, to support adequate living standards, and to maintain social integration (Barr, 2004, pp. 4–12). Although social justice may be defined very differently depending on whether a libertarian, liberal or collectivist theory is adopted (ibid., ch. 3), with a few exceptions, such as Gough et al. (2004) and Deacon (1997, 2003), these analyses address the issues from the standpoint of the government of an industrialized society, with established civil and political rights and security of property, able to achieve economic autonomy and a balanced budget in its relationship with others. In other words, society is theorized as a system of co-operation among its members which is self-sustaining, and social policy as the means by which citizens' well-being is optimized.

This set of assumptions does scant justice to the diversity of the countries affected by the disaster, or to their relations with each other and the wider world. When the UN helicopters were flying low over the Andaman Islands to check the extent of the devastation, they were assailed by a volley of arrows fired by an indigenous tribe. These people have preserved their way of life, largely through their suspicions of and hostility to the Indian administration's representatives. Rather as the wild animals throughout the region seemed to suffer very little loss of life, they might have sensed the oncoming tsunamis, and moved to higher ground (BBC Radio 4, 2005a).

At the other end of the scale of development, Malaysia and Thailand are comparatively successful newly industrializing countries, which achieved very rapid rates of export-led growth in the 1980s and early 1990s. In Thailand particularly it was the tourist industry, where so many winter visitors from Europe were taking their holidays, that was badly hit. Yet any analysis of these countries' projects for recovery from the disaster, and for restoring the well-being of their citizen-victims, would need to take account of the economic crisis which afflicted South-East Asia only seven years earlier. It was these countries, and the model of rapid expansion they had all adopted, which proved vulnerable, as the links between financial and industrial sectors which had sustained their export drives were revealed to be shakily founded. The crisis illustrated how the welfare of populations throughout that region were connected through strategies for attracting investment from, and selling manufactures to, the First World states. Like the tsunami round the Indian Ocean, the Asian financial crisis hit all shores, and linked all fates.

On opposite rims of the disaster area, India (a huge and diverse democracy) and Indonesia (a very large, predominantly Muslim country, with a history of corrupt military rule) represented important economies in the processes of global transformation at the start of the new century. In both, the massive supply of potential industrial and service sector workers from rural regions made them potential rivals to China in the race for development and growth; but each had chosen a different pathway. Finally, also diametrically opposite each other geographically were Sri Lanka, a democracy torn apart by civil war, but with a long tradition of good-quality health and education services, and Burma, a secretive and closed military dictatorship, shunned by international human rights organizations, yet attracting investment by international firms. Refugees and migrant workers from Burma were among those who died in Thailand.

In this chapter and the next, I shall use these countries to illustrate the main elements in my analysis of social policy developments in the new century and to introduce the main themes of this part of the book. They supply a case study in the connectedness of the four levels of strategic action which are the perspectives of my approach to interdependence and reciprocity. They also illustrate the growing disparity between indicators of economic growth and indicators of human development (Deacon, 1997, ch. 2). Some of the developing countries of the world have achieved rapid rises in national income per head of population without corresponding improvements in the health, education and welfare of their citizens. Others have recorded substantial improvements in the latter aspects of human development, which have outstripped their economic performance (UNDP, 1993, p. 104; 1995).

Accordingly, the United Nations Development Programme set out in the early 1990s to design a measure of human development which took account of criticisms of the assumption that gross domestic product

(GDP) could reliably be used to indicate progress and improved well-being (UNDP, 1993). GDP records market transactions and omits activities and exchanges (such as subsistence farming, exchanges within families and communities, and the care given within families) over which no money changes hands. The Human Development Index includes longevity and knowledge, indirect measures of Sen's (1985) 'capabilities'. Attempts have also been made as far as the UN's indicators are concerned to factor in political freedom (UNDP, 1992).

All this poses a new set of questions for social policy analysis, which are not really addressed by the orthodox welfare-state tradition. Globalization has implied that governments which wish to harness the resources of multinational corporations and benefit from the expansion of world trade cannot effectively pursue policies which drive down the profits of the business sector, increase the share of their national incomes going to wage and salary earners, or protect large parts of their workforce from competitive forces. But they do still have scope to build up the 'human capital' of their citizens (their physical and intellectual capabilities), partly because these are of value to firms which employ their labour power. To what extent do they also have scope to equalize incomes, life chances, opportunities and resources among these populations, given the competitive pressures of their situation under globalization? These first two chapters will use the examples of these countries to try to answer this question.

Post-colonial development and social policy

In his excellent *Global Social Policy* (1997), Bob Deacon focuses on the role of international organizations such as the IMF, World Bank and WTO in the development of social policy worldwide. While this book seeks to take account of this dimension of globalization, it starts by analysing the institutions and programmes of states like those affected by the tsunami in the light of the strategies of transnational firms, and of their own populations. The models of development now sponsored by international organizations (World Bank, 2001; Stiglitz, 2002) presuppose a dynamic between commercial forces and human resources, and try to influence the policies of governments through the conditions attached to grants and loans. This chapter uses the countries of that region to illustrate the variety of national responses to this set of factors and the dynamics of change, starting from their colonial legacies.

The twenty years after the Second World War represented a formative period for these countries, during which they threw off colonial rule by European states (with varying intensities of political and military struggle) and established autonomous regimes. That era was characterized by low levels of international movements of capital and of trade – well below those of the early twentieth century – but powerful economic interests still bound them to their former rulers, through established plantations, trading companies and production sites. Both the mainstream economic theory of the time (Lewis, 1954a; Heckscher, 1950 [1919]) and the critical Marxist analyses of uneven development and the dependency of the former colonial countries (Mandel, 1972; Frank, 1979) saw their reliance on agriculture, mining and the export of raw materials as structurally determined; they differed only in their assessment of the advantages of this for the former colonies.

However, the other feature of that period, the Cold War between liberal democracy in the USA and state socialism in the Soviet Union, gave these countries some room for manoeuvre in their social policies. Liberation struggles and post-independence reconstruction allowed them to court the USSR, and to play it off against the USA, as a source of support and assistance. India and Indonesia in particular became the leaders of a non-aligned group of states seeking to deal even-handedly with both superpowers, and to gain advantage from their rivalries.

At the same time, all these countries had substantial communist movements within their own polities, owing allegiance either to the USSR or to China, which their governments had either to include in the political process (as in Indonesia) or to suppress. This required governments to compete for the loyalty of their citizens with open or covert internal political forces, mobilizing for radical redistributions of land and other assets. In several countries, and some Indian states, this strongly influenced social policy in the direction of extensive programmes for the improvement of health care and basic education for the whole population.

For example, in Sri Lanka (which won its independence from Britain in 1948), the government immediately embarked on providing health and education services to reduce infant mortality and preventable illnesses, and to achieve universal literacy among citizens (see pp. 44–7 below). So successful were these programmes that soon the life-expectancy of children at birth, and the rates of adult literacy, were on a par with those of many far richer countries, and well above those of others with faster rates of economic growth (see table 1.1). At the same time, the government of the Indian state of Kerala achieved similar success with its health-care and education programmes (see pp. 36–7) – as, of course, did that of communist China

Table 1.1   Social indicators, 1993–4

Country	GDP per capita (US$)	Life-expectancy at birth (years)	School recruitment (5–14) (%)
Kerala (India)	400	73.0	n/a
Sri Lanka	600	73.0	82
China	500	71.0	88
Malaysia	6,140	70.0	75
Brazil	4,720	65.5	91
Gabon	3,750	54.5	n/a
France	16,050	76.5	100

Sources: Sen (1999, fig. 2.1); World Bank (2002, table 2.12).

under Mao Tse-tung. These were examples of what Amartya Sen has called 'support-led' development (Drèze and Sen, 1995; Sen, 1999, p. 46).

In the developed First World countries, we are currently debating how to pay for the health-care and education systems which sustain high life-expectancies and literacy rates. How then were such poor countries able to afford services of these standards? As Sen points out, health care and education are labour-intensive but – if they are provided at a good basic level – use relatively little equipment. In a low-wage economy, the relative cost of these services is rather low, so the policy decision to pursue these goals did not involve major sacrifices of other opportunities (Sen, 1999, pp. 46–8).

The choices about priorities made in the aftermath of independence (in the 1950s and early 1960s) were fateful for the subsequent pathways to development of the states in this region. India as a whole did not make the same choices as Kerala, instead introducing a more sophisticated, technological and hospital-based health system (beyond the means of the majority of the population), and neglecting basic education in favour of universities and colleges (Sen, 1999, p. 42). This was one of the factors in the persistence of massive inequalities in Indian society and the much later spurt of economic growth there (compared with China). As Sen points out (ibid., p. 43), as a democracy, India was far more successful in dealing with famines and natural disasters than China, whose first, unsuccessful bid for industrialization (the Great Leap Forward) led to the deaths of 30 million people. But political freedoms did not equate to improved social citizenship and human development.

Indeed, to understand the evolution of social policy in this region of the world, it is important to set aside the Anglophone view of the links between citizenship and social rights (Marshall, 1950, 1970). In that tradition, citizens gained first civil and then political rights before – as an aspect of democracy, and largely through the mobilizations of working-class political parties and trade unions – they were granted access to education, health care and social security. In Asia generally, and particularly in Malaysia and Thailand among those countries on the Indian Ocean rim, the model of Japan was far more widely followed. There, standards of education among the general population were higher than in Europe at the time of the Meiji restoration (the mid-nineteenth century), before industrialization started, and over a century before democracy was imposed after its defeat in the Second World War (Gluck, 1985). Even under an autocratic regime, in which ordinary people had neither civil nor political rights, the rulers introduced what are now called 'social investment' policies (Giddens, 1998), developing the human resources of their populations *before* economic growth took off (Sen, 1999, p. 41).

Similarly, in the period after they won independence, first Singapore and then Malaysia and Thailand followed the lead of Japan, South Korea, Taiwan and Hong Kong in establishing high-quality basic education and health-care services when they were still poor economies; they also introduced land reforms, which gave their rural populations a basis for economic security. All this occurred in political conditions which were far from democratic, and amid considerable political conflict and civil insecurity.

But if these policies set in place the human capital which enabled the 'Asian miracle' of economic development to happen, it was globalization – and especially the emergence of transnational corporations as the new form of capitalist firm – which supplied the means for the explosion of growth. It is to this process, and its influence on social policies, that I turn in the next section.

New structures and strategies for large firms

The 'Asian miracle' not only provided an alternative to the model of welfare states which emerged in Europe, North America and Australasia in the immediate post-war era. It also supplied global capital with new opportunities for transforming production processes, deploying labour power, and integrating the world economy. And this was in large part a response to the constraints on expansion and profitability imposed by welfare states in the affluent developed countries. It was to escape labour market regulation, environmental planning, taxes and social security contributions that companies began to evolve strategies for relocating more labour-intensive activities of mass production in less developed economies, and combining these with research, development and high-tech production in their First World bases. Hence it was in good measure the policies of those governments which established welfare states that provoked transnational innovations, and in turn led to new modes of social provision which have influenced welfare-state reform programmes.

In the models of economic development which prevailed in the immediate post-war period, it was argued that predominantly rural economies like India, Indonesia and Malaysia could trade most advantageously with developed economies by specializing in products such as foodstuffs, cotton, rubber, minerals and other raw materials. Because land and labour power were in plentiful supply, but capital was scarce and expensive, they would do best to exchange these for manufactured products (Heckscher, 1950 [1919]). Eventually, their plentiful supply of peasant workers would provide the basis for industrialization, as had happened in Europe in the nineteenth and early twentieth centuries (Lewis, 1954b). Although the forced industrialization of the previously backward and impoverished USSR under Stalin challenged their orthodoxy, the example of failure, famine and mass suffering in China during the Great Leap Forward (1958–61) served as a warning; and the economic dominance of the former colonial powers was used to reinforce this political message.

All this complemented the institutions for income redistribution and public services which were central to welfare states. Cheap raw materials fuelled the rapid reconstruction and industrial expansion of the West European countries after the end of the war. In continental Europe, the first phase of this process relied on generous supplies of available labour from refugees and migrants, displaced during the conflict, and by the communist coups in Central and Eastern Europe (Kindleberger, 1967). In the second phase, it involved recruiting unskilled labour from former colonies (the Caribbean and the Indian subcontinent in the case of the UK, North Africa in that of France), or from the Mediterranean (Portugal, Greece, Spain, Yugoslavia, Turkey) in those of Germany, Belgium and the Netherlands (Böhning, 1972).

In these ways, European welfare states were able to combine very rapid economic growth with a regulated labour market, high industrial wages, and pensions and unemployment benefits which replaced these wages at a high rate – for their male citizens, at least. What is today known as the 'European Social Model' was at least partly constructed on the dependence of former colonies and less developed regions on trade with these prosperous states, and on workers who came as 'guests' and did low-paid tasks. The main variations in this model concerned the Scandinavian states, which redistributed the highest proportions of national income, gave the most generous social services in kind, employed most women and paid them the best salaries, but used least foreign labour power; and the Anglophone countries, which had lower male industrial wages and less redistribution through benefits, and spent less on *public* health provision (Esping-Andersen, 1990; Higgins, 1981).

In relation to later processes of globalization, it is important to recognize that industrial companies were not coerced or harried into these arrangements; they found them very advantageous. Historical research has shown that, between 1950 and 1979, in the world's thirteen major economies, real national income per head and the stock of capital grew far faster (at 3.4 and 6.8 per cent respectively) than in any earlier period since 1820 (Glyn et al., 1990). It paid firms, in the industrial sector in particular, to invest in national systems for economic and social management. In the German model, for example, the employers' federation, along with that of the trade unions, participated with representatives of the state in planning investment, wage rates and output for the economy, and in administering social security funds. These forms of 'corporatism' applied in the Scandinavian countries also; labour market regulation, minimum wages, pension contributions and redistributive policies were all negotiated jointly in these ways.

Only in the UK, where finance capital was always dominant over its industrial counterpart, and in the USA, with its strongly liberal traditions of enterprise, were these arrangements never successfully formalized. This was also partly because UK and US companies had the largest stocks of overseas investments, stemming from the British empire and the global role of the USA. Their bankers and industrialists therefore had least to gain from purely national economic planning and regulation.

In accounts of how the transformation of the world economy began, the 'oil price shocks' of the mid-1970s are often seen as a turning point, when the strategies of firms and governments were altered because Middle East oil producers began to co-operate to limit supply and raise prices. However, the fundamental strategic shift had begun almost a decade earlier. As full employment was achieved in the First World countries, new reserves of rural labour power were no longer available for industrial expansion, and trade unions became stronger, the pace of growth of all these economies in the post-war era began to slow. Profits declined, the share of wages in national income rose, investment fell, and companies began to look for opportunities abroad (Mandel, 1972).

The changing patterns of industrial investment and production worldwide reflected this transformation of the structures and strategies of large corporations. Up to this time, US companies had invested heavily in European subsidiaries, and in Japan. Now both these and German firms began to develop production sites in the Mediterranean countries and in the Middle East, while US, German and Japanese companies invested in South-East Asia. UK corporations' share of overseas investment worldwide fell; the value of the stock of German companies' foreign investments rose from $3 billion in 1967 to $19.9 billion in 1976, while those of Japanese firms increased from $7.5 billion to $19.4 billion in the same period (Hood and Young, 1979, table 1.4, p. 18). By 1971, multinational corporations, comprising a mixture of capital from an affluent First World state and indigenous capital, but controlled from centres in the former, were producing more commodities outside their base countries than the total value of world trade (Tugendhat, 1973, p. 21).

As a result of these shifts, growth rates of economies such as Spain, Greece and Turkey in Europe, and Singapore, Hong Kong, South Korea and Taiwan in Asia, were considerably faster (at around 5 per cent) than those of states in Western Europe and North America, and this dynamic of change did not stop at this point. For example, while Japan's rapid growth in the 1950s was based on the mass production of cheap goods and on drawing workers from the countryside into the industrial sector, this quickly changed in the 1960s into producing more high-value, high-tech commodities by more capital-intensive methods. Japanese firms diversified production, relocating their factories for less sophisticated goods in Korea, Hong Kong, Singapore and Taiwan. As wages and other costs there began to rise, firms in Japan and in those countries moved on to Malaysia, Indonesia, Thailand and the Philippines for mass production. Hence the economies of the countries on the rim of the Indian Ocean were shaped by the strategies of multinational corporations which emerged in the mid-1960s.

In addition to this new dynamic of growth and change providing opportunities for development, there were also international pressures on all countries towards lowering barriers to the free movement of capital and products. Under a new Washington Consensus (Stiglitz, 2002), from 1980 the IMF and the World Bank, and later the WTO, pursued concerted policies to promote competitive markets and create an integrated world economy. So the last wave of countries to join the ranks of newly industrializing economies, including Malaysia, Thailand, Sri Lanka (see pp. 44–7) and Indonesia as well as much of India, were being forced to compete with each other for foreign investment, and for shares of the global market in manufactured goods, under conditions very different from those in which the First World countries had been able to establish their welfare-state regimes.

However, as has already been noted (p. 25, above), this did not eliminate the scope for social policies which were redistributive of incomes and assets, or which improved the health, education and welfare of citizens. Nor – despite the Washington Consensus – did it result in a single, standardized model of economic and social institutions for all the countries seeking to accelerate development. In the next section, I shall examine the range of measures for redistribution and the enhancement of capabilities which were still available, and how the various governments of the region sought to use the possibilities allowed them.

National governments in the world economy

From the time when the new structures and strategies of large banks and industrial corporations were first recognized, some theorists argued that the 'golden age' of welfare states was over, and that the newly industrializing and less developed economies had no immediate prospect of protecting their populations from global market forces. For example, Charles Kindleberger, basing his analysis on new patterns of US business investment abroad, concluded that 'The nation state is just about through as an economic unit. Two-hundred-thousand-ton tankers . . . airbuses and the like will not permit the sovereign independence of the nation state in economic affairs' (1969, p. 207).

The reason why Kindleberger adopted this stance, right at the outset of the globalization process, was that he recognized that – once finance houses and business firms began to break free of the agreements under which they had participated in national economic and social management (see pp. 26–7) – there would be relentless pressure for free movement of goods, money and technology. This did in fact occur, as described above, making nation states court banks and corporations for their favour, instead of binding them to contracts with their trade union federations and citizens. Competition between nation states, under the aegis of international organizations committed to promoting free movement and trade, would create a global economic environment in which wages would vary according to the demand for, supply and productivity of workers (and not according to national agreements); and investment would flow to wherever after-tax profits were most attractive (and not to where it had been allocated under national economic plans).

In other words, the world economy would be run as if all markets were perfectly competitive; in principle, it would act like a national economy with one capital market and free movement of raw materials and products. However, two of the factors of production, labour power and land, would be immobile – absolutely so in the case of the latter. Hence, in an integrated global economy, the labour market would be segmented, with each country's workers as a closed sector and each territory under a separate jurisdiction which sought to optimize the development of its land.

The ideological basis for the Washington Consensus was that this model of the world economy worked to the benefit of those populations which were least advantaged by systems of national economic management and social protection. In a new version of an analysis first put forward by Adam Smith (1776), the IMF, World Bank and WTO argued that competitive markets in all products would raise real wages, because employers would have incentives to hire more employees until the sale value of the last unit of output equalled its cost to produce. In theory, this would favour post-colonial countries, which had been kept in a state of underdevelopment in special trading relationships, and unorganized workers, who lacked the protection of those whose unions had done deals with national governments. If the model worked, both poor countries and poor workers should be enabled to catch up.

But the Washington Consensus model was also meant to discourage governments from trying to adopt redistributive policies or seeking to give their citizens economic security (see pp. 33–5 below). It saw such actions as misguided and counterproductive. In the first place, with free movement of capital, taxes and social insurance contributions which aimed to redistribute to the poor would simply lead those with mobile resources to move them out of the country. Indeed, professionals and highly educated citizens might well seek to leave, legally or illegally. Trade unions, struggling for higher shares of national income, would damage their members' interests if they forced profit rates down; international investors would just turn elsewhere.

All in all, therefore, the model portrayed the redistributive policies characteristic of welfare states as perverse; national polities were no longer closed systems of co-operation, and attempts to capture the benefits of 'social partnership' (in the European tradition) turned them into 'leaky buckets' (Okun, 1975). The gains to the poor were more than offset by losses to the better off, and they in turn would seek to move their assets elsewhere. The militant rhetoric of the new model, particularly in the era of neo-liberal ascendancy (the governments of Margaret Thatcher in the UK and the presidencies of Ronald Reagan and George Bush senior in the USA), put orthodox social policy on the defensive. Theorists sought to demonstrate how welfare states survived, in Europe especially, rather than to show how they might be further widened and deepened (Pierson, 1991; Leibfried and Pierson, 1994).

Conclusions

In this chapter, I have introduced the perspectives adopted in the book, and traced the origins of the current relationship between international financial and trade organizations (IMF, World Bank and WTO) and national governments in the developing world. This provides the basis for the analysis of the scope for social policies of redistribution and human development in the next chapter.

The Washington Consensus, between these organizations and the US Treasury, imposing financial and trade liberalization and the restructuring of fiscal regimes and public-sector agencies, will be analysed in detail (with case examples) in chapters 2, 4 and 5. It reflected the model of world development favoured by neo-liberal economic and political theorists, who argued that social institutions of all kinds should be based on the choices of free individuals (see chapters 7 to 10). These theorists were strongly critical of the regimes created in post-war welfare states and in many post-colonial administrations. They claimed that autonomous individuals, competing in markets, could reliably improve their own well-being, and that of their societies. Indeed, this was the only way to reconcile freedom, prosperity and good governance.

There was nothing new in these ideas. They were derived from the Enlightenment philosophers of the late seventeenth and the eighteenth century (chapter 7). They underpinned the mainstream economic theories of development of the leading theorist, W. Arthur Lewis (1954a, 1954b), who applied the model first outlined by Adam Smith to the successive breakthrough to rapid growth of manufacturing and agricultural productivity of new waves of national economies (see pp. 25–6). As we have seen in this chapter, some of the Indian Ocean rim countries illustrated this process.

Indeed, the East Asian model for achieving the breakthrough, export-led growth, was probably the oldest in the world. Archaeologists in Cyprus have recently uncovered the site of a Bronze Age 'industrial estate', containing a number of 'factories'. It was clear that this site, on the coast, was used to mass produce commodities such as perfume for export (probably to Crete). Industrial-sized jars for olive oil indicated the scale of the operation (BBC World Service, 2005a). So the model now used by the Chinese authorities (pp. 5–7) was first developed at the dawn of European civilization.

But this seems to put social policy on the defensive. By returning to an earlier model of economic development, and insisting that human development could best be achieved within this, the Washington Consensus appeared to be aimed at restricting the scope for interventions to improve well-being and raising quality of life. In the next chapter, I shall investigate the theoretical basis for social policy activity in this model.

2

The Scope for Redistribution and Social Justice

In the previous chapter, I traced the origins of the Washington Consensus, and how this was applied to post-colonial societies in the South and East Asian region of the newly integrated world economy. In this chapter I shall consider the scope for social policies under this model for economic development, and how the strategies of governments interacted with those of individuals and households, in the same region.

There were many respects in which the model was unrealistic, both in terms of its optimistic prospectus for greater equality through free markets worldwide and in its pessimism about measures for redistribution, social protection and public services. In the first place, those countries in South-East Asia which had already made the transition to newly industrializing status before the model had become the basis for a global programme of the IMF, World Bank and WTO had achieved many of its goals by very different means.

First Japan in the 1950s and 1960s, and later Taiwan and South Korea in the 1970s and 1980s, had not allowed free trade or free capital movements; they had managed trade and imposed capital controls. They directed their industrial expansion to the manufacture of exports, and subtly (or crudely) limited imports. In Japan, as late as 1978, manufactured imports made up only 2 per cent of GDP, compared with something nearer 15 per cent in European countries. South Korea, the world's third largest producer of cars, imported only 4,000 such vehicles in 1995 (Singh, 2000, p. 4).

Indeed, despite the best efforts of the IMF, World Bank and WTO, it was this model which most strongly influenced the next wave of newly industrializing countries, including Malaysia, Thailand and, of course, China. All tried to create institutional links between their financial sectors, their government ministries and both foreign and domestic manufacturing companies, which promoted export-led expansion, by steering investment towards these industries. They also found ways of limiting imports of such goods. Indeed, the Chinese authorities were so successful in their negotiations with the World Bank that they persuaded its officials of the value of their strategy. In his influential book *Globalization and its Discontents*, the Bank's former chief economist praised the Chinese government's insistence on careful 'pacing and sequencing' of the liberalization of its capital markets and trade arrangements (Stiglitz, 2002, pp. 59–70). In other words, China had the economic muscle to hold out for its version of the South and East Asian model, against the pressures of the Washington Consensus, and actually managed to divide the World Bank from the IMF, bringing that consensus to an end. But the IMF's insistence on capital market liberalization had by then brought about the financial crisis of the whole region (1997–9), which affected Malaysia, Indonesia and Thailand very adversely. This will be analysed in chapter 4 (see pp. 73–7).

The Chinese authorities were adopting this growth strategy as a radical change in direction from the policies of the Mao era. As we have already seen (pp. 3–5 and 24–5) export-orientated industrialization was facilitated by the huge gains in education and health achieved in the earlier period. But Malaysia, Thailand and Indonesia were developing their programmes for enhancing 'human capital' at the same time as seeking rapid growth. They were also making decisions about how much redistribution to attempt, and how much inequality to tolerate. In his revisionist version of the global model, Stiglitz acknowledges that these countries were more successful than others in Latin America and Africa precisely because they departed from the IMF orthodoxy, and devoted resources to health and education and to redistribution for the sake of equality, stability and solidarity (Stiglitz, 2002, pp. 79–80).

Using the scope for these measures afforded by the success of their economic strategies, Malaysia and Thailand in particular were able to achieve much in these fields (see table 1.1, p. 24). The policies of the IMF, as well as those of the World Bank, now recognize the importance of primary education, especially of girls, for economic as well as human development (Sen, 1999, pp. 190–200). But these achievements have proved fragile in the face of pressures for rapid liberalization (see pp. 47–8). As Stiglitz notes, 'overly stringent "adjustment policies" in country after country forced cutbacks in education and health: in Thailand, as a result, not only did female prostitution increase but expenditures on AIDS were cut back; and what had been one of the most successful programs in fighting AIDS had a major setback' (Stiglitz, 2002, p. 80).

However, these arguments do not prove that there is similar scope for social policies of human development and redistribution under the strictly competitive conditions of the global market model, nor do they explain the variations in success (both economic and social) in the states on the Indian Ocean rim. I will turn to these issues in the next section.

Redistribution in a competitive environment

Suppose that we accept the assumptions of the Washington Consensus model – that the world functions as a single competitive market, with free movement of the factors of production except labour and land. In other words, we accept that the 'Asian miracle' of the 1980s and early 1990s was a one-off case, and – despite the modified version of the model now adopted by the World Bank (2001) – will be impossible to replicate in other regions. How is it possible to demonstrate that redistribution for the sake of greater equality and social justice is feasible and desirable (i.e. that it will not simply create the 'leaky bucket' phenomenon – see p. 30)?

The distinguished economist Samuel Bowles set himself this challenge, adding the specific provisos that the proposed policy measures should be viable in small economies as well as large ones, and under democratic systems of government (Bowles, 2000). His conclusion was, broadly, that measures which increased the productivity of labour at low cost were highly advantageous, and that the scope for them arose from two sources. The first was that trade union activity which promotes workers' self-discipline, solidarity, participation and loyalty, enhancing work effort based on a sense of fairness rather than insecurity and employee surveillance, can induce higher productivity and gains in both employment and wages (see also Bowles and Boyer, 1990). The second is that government provision of both health and education services and unemployment benefit can increase productivity, employment and wages by more than the cost of supplying these services. These institutions are all complementary; workers consider it worth going to school and looking after their health if employment is relatively secure and a subsistence income is guaranteed during spells of unemployment (see also Blanchard, 2002).

In addition to these institutional arrangements, the government might regulate employment (through minimum wages legislation and severance payments requirements) in order to restrain competition between workers and reduce damaging rivalries. Bowles showed that

policy differences in these areas might account for the very large variations in the rise in real wages in manufacturing industry worldwide –
by as much as 16 percentage points *per year* on average, between 1970
and 1992 (Verhoogen, 1999; Bowles, 2000, fig. 5). During these
twenty-two years, real manufacturing wages grew by an average 8 per
cent per annum in Taiwan and South Korea, and fell by the same percentage in Tanzania. But significantly only in India, among those countries on the Indian Ocean rim recorded in the statistics, did these wages
decline during the period. Furthermore, although there was considerable variation in the extent that productivity gains were reflected in
wage increases, all the Asian countries – including (marginally) India –
managed to capture growth of value added in real wages, with Taiwan
and South Korea again the leaders, and a number of African, South
American and Middle Eastern countries failing to achieve this (Bowles,
2000, fig. 6).

But there is another potential source of productivity gains in countries on the cusp of rapid development. The other immobile factor of
production, land, was very unequally distributed at the end of the
colonial period, with most landholdings in the hands of a few very
wealthy owners. Reforms and redistributions which transferred holdings to former tenants, or gave them security of tenure and a greater
share of the fruits of their labour, could improve agricultural productivity and lead to more efficient use of land resources. Such reforms
and redistributions were characteristic of South and East Asia; Bowles
notes that these could be counted with Nordic wage-equalization policies as instances of how welfare-enhancing gains in productivity and
efficiency were achieved in open economies.

A good example of this refers back to the case of the Indian state of
Kerala (see pp. 23–4), which defied the national trends to achieve large
improvements in literacy and life-expectancy in the post-colonial
period. Because Kerala was a state in a huge democratic country, its
government could not impede the free movement of factors of production (including labour) across its boundaries; it also had limited
scope for legal and fiscal variations from the national rules. However,
through land reforms, Kerala (along with West Bengal) substantially
redistributed income and improved the situation of the poorest sector
of the population (Ramchandran, 1996; Besley and Burgess, 1998).
Because Indian national law forbade the transfer of land to tenants,
under these reforms their share of the crop was increased from the traditional half to three-quarters, and they were granted security of tenure
if they supplied a quarter share to landowners (Bowles, 2000, p. 20).

These factors also help explain the variations, both in growth of
national income and in increases in human development, between

countries on the Indian Ocean rim. In particular, they account for the relatively poor performance of Indonesia, a very large country in terms of land and population, and exceptionally rich in natural resources. From 1955 to 1965, under the leadership of President Sukarno, and with the participation of the largest communist party in the world outside the USSR and China (the PKI had 3 million members in the early 1960s), Indonesia was one of the leaders of the non-aligned states (see p. 23). Then a military coup, led by General Suharto, and widely believed to have been supported by the CIA, over-threw this regime and led to the mass killing of those suspected to be communists (Pilger, 2002, ch. 1). Suharto initiated a programme under which mineral rights, land and industrial assets were divided up among multinational corporations (ibid., pp. 41–2); Indonesia also took large loans from the World Bank, and became a 'model pupil' of its development plans. During the East Asian financial crisis of 1997–8 Indonesia was among the states most adversely affected, and Suharto fell from power in the midst of the catastrophe – disgraced as a corrupt autocrat and the perpetrator of human rights atrocities in East Timor and other provinces.

Under Suharto, the Indonesian authorities did not use any of the scope for human development or redistribution identified in this sec-tion. This can be seen from the statistics on the period. In the 1960s, life-expectancy for men and women was 47.5 years, compared with 55.1 for men and women in East Malaysia and 64.8 for men and 66.9 for women in Sri Lanka. By the early 1990s, it had risen to 60 in Indonesia, but 70.1 in Malaysia and 73.5 in Sri Lanka. Secondary school enrolment (as a percentage of all eligible children) rose from 55 per cent in 1980 to 71 per cent in 1998 in Sri Lanka. In Malaysia the comparable figures were 48 and 98 per cent. In Indonesia, no figure was available for 1998, but the proportion in 1980 was only 29 per cent (World Bank, 2002, fig. 2.12). As a clear indication of the exploitation of Indonesian workers, real wages in manufacturing grew twice as fast in Malaysia as in Indonesia (Bowles, 2000, fig. 5), despite the fact that labour productivity grew twice as fast in Indonesia (ibid., fig. 6).

Above all, land, other assets and income were not redistributed under the Suharto regime; instead, an elite grew immensely rich and corruption among officials was rife. In all, foreign debt amounted to $262 billion in 2002, 170 per cent of gross domestic product (Pilger, 2002, p. 45). Failing to win the loyalty of its citizens, or to create sol-idarities between them, the regime faced a number of independence movements, most notably in East Timor and Aceh (where the earth-quake and tsunami struck). These conflicts were expensive, and further reduced the scope for improvements in human well-being.

Meanwhile, India experienced a belated period of rapid economic growth, finally reaping the benefits of its legacy from the colonial era – far higher rates of adult literacy at the start of the period, and a highly educated middle class. India's growth spurt, based on a variant of the Asian model but focused on financial services, communications and information technology, has finally come about despite enormous inequalities and a far lower overall rate of human development than its great rival, China (Deacon, 1997, tables 2.1 and 2.3).

Globalization, social policy and human development

What conclusions can we draw from all this evidence, from the countries on the Indian Ocean rim, about how globalization has influenced human development? Is it possible to generalize about the interactions between multinational corporations and banks on the one hand, and the governments of developing countries on the other, and on the role of international financial institutions? Is there a new model of human development (or more than one), and what are the lessons for the affluent First World states?

The first point to make is that these countries have since the 1970s all pursued pathways which are very different from welfare states, in any of their post-war varieties. The far more competitive economic environment in which their institutions have evolved precluded the social protectionism which characterized European welfare states in particular. Because gains in human development had to be won through improved productivity rather than at the expense of profits, and in higher wages rather than higher social benefits, these new institutions promoted adaptability, resilience and self-reliance rather than security and stability. This applied to the provision of public services as well as to income maintenance; in the Asian model families and communities were required to be adaptable and resilient and to support each other (Gough, 2004, pp. 177–8).

Although all this was quite different from the thinking which characterizes the orthodox social policy analyses of the welfare-state tradition, it was in line with developments in the philosophical theory of justice. This now accepts that human well-being cannot start from guarantees that individuals' situations will not be worsened; people are vulnerable because they have plans and projects which may go wrong, and because they are prone to disease and accident, and are mortal. So justice should be about equality of opportunity rather than outcomes; people should be equally free to achieve rather than prescribed equal achievements (Ackerman, 1980; Van Parijs, 1995; Sen, 1999). They should have access to equal resources for their projects rather than having their welfare equalized by the authorities (Cohen, 2000; Dworkin, 1981, 2000). All of this presupposes something more like the new Asian model(s) than like welfare states.

However, this does not necessarily imply that the new approach to human development and justice is less radical than the old welfare-state version. After all, if no one must be allowed to be worse off, this might imply that the privileges of the rich and powerful are protected. In fact, continental European welfare states did rather little to redistribute vertically; they largely consolidated inequalities of wealth and power. By contrast, the redistributions of land which occurred in many Asian countries transformed the life chances of poor peasants. Several of them also achieved greater equality of incomes than prevail in the affluent states.

Insecurity and vulnerability are, of course, built-in features of competitive markets. Efficiency is achieved because there are rival producers, and new entrants may always introduce new products, techniques or organizational innovations. All firms may experience brief periods when they enjoy economic 'rents' (returns higher than those available under perfect competition, because of a monopoly on a new invention or method, for example). However, free markets will soon erode these and keep pressure on all to adapt and change. It is a well-known criticism of the European welfare state, and particularly the German model of 'social partnership', that it gives all interest groups a stake in the existing institutional structures and none any incentive to reform them (Scharpf, 1997). What was a great strength, in terms of solidarity in the post-war period and industrial growth in the 1960s and 1970s, has proved rigid and unadaptive under competitive pressures. Above all, it has constantly protected the earnings of the (shrinking) industrial workforce and maintained high replacement rates of unemployment benefits; the consequent rise in social insurance contribution rates has made it very expensive to hire new workers. All this is only just beginning to change (Bleses and Seeleib-Kaiser, 2004).

However, it is obvious that all human beings need a certain degree of security and protection in order to function well. Humans have a longer period of dependency in childhood than other animals; they are poorly adapted to lone survival, even as adults, because they lack the swiftness and ferocity to capture prey, or the capacity to live for long on the most readily available vegetation (grass and leaves). So they have always relied on systems of co-operation in ever-larger groups and communities. In a sense, social policy is always about the current stage of collectivization of these issues (Swaan, 1988), and democratic governments seek optimum security for their citizens through their choices. If they create too much insecurity and strife among populations, they face rebellion; if they make the economy too rigid and unadaptable, they will be replaced by reforming forces.

The issue of optimum security was raised, in a very tragic form, by the earthquake and tsunami disasters. Poor fishermen, poor women and children in coastal communities were already vulnerable in economic terms. They had few resources to fall back on and were not insured. The governments of countries on the rim of the Indian Ocean were unprepared for the scale of the calamity, but some performed better than others in their response. The Indian government was experienced in mobilizing the resources of a very large economy and focusing them on the areas affected; this was part of India's democratic tradition (Sen, 1981). Sri Lanka, Thailand and Malaysia benefited from international assistance, and organized relatively efficiently to deal with the aftermath. Indonesia, by contrast, was far less quick and efficient in its response, and many lives were probably lost unnecessarily. Very little is known of what happened in Burma because of its closed and secretive regime.

In the final chapters of the book, I shall return to this issue of optimum security, and how social policy can address it, for the sake of justice. I shall ask what new institutions might provide forms of income security and resource redistribution which would not damage adaptability and resilience. This involves looking at what measures can give people opportunities to develop their capabilities, while leaving them free to take up these opportunities in their own ways.

In the next section, however, I shall turn to the ways in which individuals and households have responded to the new models of development in the Asian countries analysed so far. What strategies have they adopted, and with which consequences (both intended and unintended)?

Strategies of individuals and households

So far, this chapter has considered the interactions between strategies of corporations and governments within a framework of regulations and policies set by the IMF, World Bank and WTO. But the other perspective adopted in this book is that of individuals and households. How did they respond to the transformations of their countries' institutions and economies analysed above?

At the start of the post-colonial period, the vast majority of the populations of the countries on the rim of the Indian Ocean were peasants, working for subsistence on land they did not own. As late as the early 1970s, over 60 per cent of the active workforces of all these states were in the agricultural sector, with the exceptions of Sri Lanka and Malaysia (Kidron and Segal, 1981, chart 40). However, a huge change in employment structures and living environments was already under way in the region. Between 1950 and 1975, urban populations grew by over 200 per cent in Sri Lanka and Thailand, and by over 100 per cent in India, Burma, Malaysia and Indonesia (ibid., chart 49). There was widespread urban upheaval or strike action in industrial centres at least once in India, Burma, Thailand and Java (Indonesia), and three times in Sri Lanka (ibid., chart 65).

By 1994, the processes of industrialization and urbanization had transformed all these countries, as can be seen from table 2.1.

So, despite land reforms and redistributions in many of these economies, the predominant movements of population were from country to city, and of employment from agriculture to industry, as Lewis's model of development postulated (Lewis, 1954a). In a sense, the experience of this region was a speeded-up version of the industrialization and urbanization of the USA and Europe in the nineteenth and early twentieth centuries. By 2015, eight cities in the countries on the Indian Ocean rim are expected to have over 8 million inhabitants; Bombay is projected to have 26.3 million, Calcutta 17.3 million, Jakarta 13.9 million, Bangkok 9.8 million and Madras 9.1 million (Giddens, 2004, fig. 18.2).

The dominant strategy of individuals and households in this region was therefore to move to industrial city life for the sake of higher wages, and a lifestyle based on greater individual freedom, more material possessions and less reliance on kinship and communal ties. But, unlike the Chinese authorities, who kept strict controls on internal

Table 2.1   Workforce and residence, 1994

Country	% of labour force in agriculture	% of population urban	GNP per head (US$)
India	n/a	27	1,100
Sri Lanka	45	23	850
Burma	69	27	n/a
Thailand	60	30	2,210
Malaysia	19	54	6,130
Indonesia	52	36	880

Sources: Giddens (2004); World Bank (2002, tables 1.1 and 2.3).

movements of population, their governments were unable to supply the urban infrastructures for these new inhabitants. This is most graphically illustrated in the 'megacities' listed above, all of which have fringes of shanty dwellings, and informal economies through which those on the margins of the official and commercial systems survive (Castells, 1996). The newest migrants and poorest inhabitants are likely to have large families, so this is a youthful population, needing education, training and support. It represents a challenge for city governments – managing huge and diverse populations, with substantial groups of mobile, global economic agents as well as this influx of poor rural migrants, and attempting to integrate them both socially and economically (Borja and Castells, 1997).

But in addition to these movements within countries there has been a large growth of migration between states of the region. In the 1970s, such migration was still taking the form of refugees fleeing the conflicts in Vietnam, Laos and Cambodia. Over 150,000 such refugees entered Thailand from those three countries in that decade, and a further 75,000 fled Vietnam for Malaysia (Kidron and Segal, 1981, chart 32). But there was very little *economic* migration between the states.

All this changed in the next two decades, as individuals and households began to recognize the demand for new workers in other states, and the differentials in the rates of growth of the various sectors of these economies provided new opportunities for gains from migration. Our analysis of the scope for social policies to improve efficiency and equity (pp. 35–8) assumed that populations were immobile; this is no longer the case in this region. There is now a recognizable 'migration system' in South and East Asia, similar to ones that exist in other regions of the world (Fawcett, 1989).

This new phenomenon illustrates another dilemma of national governments in relation to the strategies of individuals and households. As well as trying to manage the sustainable growth of the economy and a fair distribution of resources, they must create solidarity, loyalty and a commitment to the common life of citizenship if they are to retain its most potentially valuable inhabitants (Jordan and Düvell, 2003, ch. 5). This is a matter of political culture (democratic participation, strong civil society, active community) as well as economic rights. As we have seen (pp. 20–1), these states, with the exceptions of India and Sri Lanka, were late developers in the fields of civil and political rights, especially Indonesia; and Burma is still a military dictatorship.

There may be several reasons why countries develop high rates of emigration. Being poor and backward, but having a large rich, developed neighbour (as in the case of Ireland and Britain in the nineteenth century, or Poland and Germany in the late twentieth century), is one such situation. But another is either that the political culture encourages such emigration (as is the case of the Philippines) or that citizens develop 'exit strategies' (seeing movement within the country or abroad, rather than collective action and political participation, as the way to improve their life situations) as their habitual responses (Jordan and Düvell, 2002, ch. 10).

A third possibility is that the particular configuration of a state's social and economic policies results in a highly educated and trained workforce, but with low pay and poor employment prospects within the country. This has been the case in the post-communist countries of Central Europe since 1989, resulting in high rates of emigration (Jordan and Düvell, 2002, chs. 4, 5 and 10). It has also been the case in India, where large numbers of the best qualified academics, professionals and technicians go to work in the USA, the UK and Europe. The 'brain drain' phenomenon (Bhagwati and Wilson, 1989) is particularly likely to occur in countries with successful higher education systems but low rates of economic growth, as was the case in India until the late 1990s.

India and Sri Lanka (see pp. 44–7 below) are now part of global migration systems, India because of its size and skilled labour force, Sri Lanka as a result of political turmoil and an asylum movement. They also send substantial numbers of less skilled workers to the oil-rich Middle Eastern states. But the other countries have become part of a regional migration system, in which Japan and the first wave of newly industrializing countries drew in workers to meet shortages of unskilled labour (Jones and Findlay, 1998). Japan itself, South Korea, Taiwan, Hong Kong and above all Singapore (a city state with 100 per cent urban population) all attracted migrants to take low-paid industrial and construction work; they also recruited female domestic workers from the Philippines. Workers are granted contracts, negotiated through private recruitment agencies (ibid., p. 9).

Migration theorists have argued that population flows tend to follow the reverse direction of pathways of direct investment from abroad (Sassen, 1988, 1998). This pattern seems to have occurred in the region, as most corporate investment has come from firms based in Japan and newly industrializing countries (Jones and Findlay, 1998, table 4), and most trade also takes place between them. In addition to Tokyo, Hong Kong, Jakarta and Bombay are becoming 'global cities' (Sassen, 1991), with cosmopolitan populations, acting as headquarters for transnational companies which produce and recruit worldwide.

Malaysia has become a net *importer* of labour power, mainly from Indonesia, Thailand, the Philippines and Bangladesh. But Thailand, still a net exporter of workers, also recruits from Burma and Cambodia (Jones and Findlay, 1998, fig. 1). Increasingly, individuals and households see working and living abroad as an option to be considered among their strategies for improving their standards of living, as flows of economic migrants rise from year to year – both through regular channels and irregularly, by clandestine means, or disguised as tourism or study abroad.

Such strategies challenge national governments in several ways. Are foreign workers and their families to be given rights to employment protection, health care, education and welfare services? How are their wages, salaries and employment conditions to be regulated? How are the social diversity of populations and the possible tensions between migrants and indigenous groups to be managed? Can the social benefits of education and training of citizens be captured by encouraging loyalty to their country of origin, or as remittances from work abroad stimulate the home economy, and sustain settled families? These issues will be further analysed in chapters 10 and 14.

All the strategies outlined in this section stem from the spontaneous choices of individuals and households. But forced migrations, the legacy of the colonial liberation struggles, are not things of the past. Indonesia, for instance, has generated flights from political persecution and human rights abuses because of its suppression of internal independence movements. And the conflicts in Sri Lanka have brought about global dispersals of that country's citizens, which will be the topic of the next section.

Case study: Sri Lanka

The case of Sri Lanka illustrates the links between social policy, globalization, political strife and transnational population movement. In the post-colonial era, the government adopted 'support-led' policies which proved unsustainable, leading to an economic crisis. A new administration then switched to an export-orientated strategy for rapid economic growth, under the terms of a loan from the IMF. This led to civil conflict, a suspension of political rights, and eventually a civil war against the minority ethnic Tamil Tigers in the north of the country. That in turn has led to the mass exodus of asylum seekers to India and Europe and North America.

Sri Lanka's social policies after independence in 1948 represented an attempt to create a welfare state, but took account of the country's stage of economic development. Sri Lanka had been a democracy since 1931, and had embarked on many of these policies before independence; parties competed with each other in terms of welfare programmes.

Table 2.2   Social indicators, Sri Lanka, 1946–73

	1946	1953	1965	1973
Adult literacy (%)	58	65	72	n/a
School enrolment (% 5–14)	41	58	65	78
Life-expectancy (years)	43	56	63	66
Infant mortality (per 1000)	141	71	56	46

However, the Indian Tamils, who had been brought to the country by the British to work in plantations, and who enjoyed relatively high status and incomes under colonial rule, fared badly under governments which represented the interests of the Sinhalese majority (75 per cent of the population).

In focusing on programmes for human development, the Sri Lankan governments devoted substantial proportions of national income to health (2.5 per cent in 1971/2, on current account), education (over 5 per cent) and food subsidies (8 per cent). It was subsequently acknowledged that these programmes achieved among the highest gains in human development in the world.

A World Bank assessment in 1980 concluded that 'Sri Lanka's social indicators relative to its income were the best among 59 countries' (Isenman, 1980); a subsequent analysis showed that it was 'exceptionally successful in protecting the poor from the worst effects of falling consumption' (World Bank, 1982, p. 28).

In 1977, Sri Lanka faced an economic crisis because of slow growth, failure to adapt and an adverse balance of payments; the government fell in a general election, and the new administration turned to the IMF for a loan, promising in return to reform institutions and initiate a completely new economic strategy. The IMF's conditions for the loan amounted to the adoption of the model which had been successful in South Korea, Taiwan, Hong Kong and Singapore, but without the protection for new industries – export-led growth, attracting investment from abroad, devaluation, but also removal of foreign exchange controls and import restrictions. It also insisted on the elimination of food subsidies (to be replaced by targeted 'food stamps' for the poor) and the dismantling of public-sector corporations (Rupesinghe, 1986, pp. 229–30).

These events were a kind of nightmare version of what had happened in the UK in 1975–6, and Sri Lanka continued to provide a distorted mirror image of the British experiences. The Wilson government, too, had had to go to the IMF to ask for a loan, and to promise restructuring and government spending cuts in return. This was followed by public-service union strikes and civil disorder (the

Winter of Discontent, 1978–9), the fall of the Callaghan Labour government, and the election of Margaret Thatcher's Conservatives. Her programme for embracing global market forces and limiting the scope of the public sector in turn provoked the inner-city riots in the summer of 1981 and the Miners' Strike of the mid-1980s. Protest action on the streets was contained by the use of riot police, and there was new legislation to curb trade union collective action and civil demonstrations.

In Sri Lanka, the dismantling of the welfare state was far more radical and proceeded much more quickly. Food subsidies were cut from 7.5 per cent of GDP in 1977 to 3 per cent in 1982. Government spending on health was reduced to less than half its level of the early 1970s, and education to less than a third (Rupesinghe, 1986, pp. 231–3 and table 15.2). Infant mortality rates rose by 29 per cent, and undernutrition among the child population became widespread (ibid., p. 235). Real wage rates fell, but inflation was rampant, as subsidies were removed. Export-orientated production did expand, and the rate of growth accelerated, but income distribution became markedly more unequal (ibid., pp. 234–5). Women joined the labour market in large numbers in order to make up for shortfalls in household incomes; other women travelled to the oil-rich Middle East states as domestic labour – 100,000 in 1983 (ibid., p. 236).

Far more serious than these changes for the longer term were the conflicts generated. Inter-ethnic violence erupted in 1983, and was followed by the suspension of many civil and political rights and a massacre of Tamils. Gains from the economic reforms were quickly lost through the costs of the civil war which ensued. The export-led model proved difficult to adopt in a democracy with a pre-existing welfare state, strong trade unions and ethnic cleavages. This was all the more marked because Sri Lanka was given no scope to protect either its fledgling industries or its poorest citizens; this fed resentment among Tamils, leading to protest and retaliation.

The tragedy of Sri Lanka since this time has been the continuing flow of refugees out of the country, and particularly of educated Tamils from the northern region. Almost twenty years after the conflict started, there were still over 120,000 Sri Lankans living abroad as refugees and asylum seekers. Of these, over half were in India, but the rest were spread across Canada (10,000), France (15,000), Switzerland (13,500) and the UK (10,500) (UNHCR, 2001, table 6). Although some were returning, there were still over 1,000 new applications in the UK each quarter in 2003 (UNHCR, 2003, table 3).

Sri Lanka is renowned as a tourist paradise. When the tsunami struck, there were many European tourists on the coast, though most escaped injury or death. The fate of Sri Lankan democracy, and its welfare state, illustrates the ambiguities of globalization, the Washington Consensus and the new model of human development. Unlike the case of China, Sri Lanka's democratic political system did not allow it to use authoritarian methods to switch from a support-led strategy to an export-orientated one. Although it had a clear start on Malaysia, Thailand and Indonesia in terms of human development, and was ahead of India also, the IMF intervention was disastrous. Unlike the UK, which changed direction more gradually under Margaret Thatcher, and was able to absorb the conflicts caused by her transformations within the political institutions of liberal democracy, Sri Lanka suffered blows to human rights and human development. For the citizens of the poor countries of the world, social policy is often a matter of life and death.

Conclusions

These first two chapters started with the disaster on the coastal fringes of the Indian Ocean on 26 December 2004. They took these countries as illustrations of the opportunities and constraints of the integrated world economy, the role of multinational business corporations, the policy framework of the international financial institutions, and the strategies of individuals and households.

At the time of writing this, it is not clear whether the catastrophe has changed any of these factors in the development of social policy in that region, or further afield. It seems unlikely to alter the strategies of banks or businesses, because these follow a logic of profit. This logic has brought greater prosperity to Malaysia and Thailand in particular, and lifted millions out of poverty. But it has also brought exploitation and squalor to Indonesia and has failed to rescue Sri Lanka's poor.

The policies of the World Bank in particular have changed considerably since the Sri Lankan debacle. But the accountability of national governments to financial institutions has not. As we shall see in the next chapter, this lies at the root of the constraints on social policy, and limits the scope of nations to help each other as well as themselves.

This is important, because – in the wake of the tsunami disaster – there was, however briefly, an apparent change of heart among some of the leaders of some of the affluent countries. Spurred on by the generosity of their citizens, they began to canvass the suspension or cancellation of debt payments from poor countries. Gordon Brown, the

UK's Chancellor of the Exchequer, toured Africa, trying to negotiate taking over a share of the debts of some of these to the World Bank. But to make a real difference the change would have to go much further than this, because of the way credit and debt are structured worldwide. This will be analysed in detail in the next chapter.

We have seen that the Asian model of social policy addresses human development, adaptability and resilience in more direct ways than welfare states did, and has some impressive achievements. But it stalled in 1997 with a financial crisis; and the Japanese economy has stagnated for a whole decade (Gough, 2004). The rise of China is ambiguous also, because its achievements have involved prolonged authoritarian rule, deep social divisions, and an absence of basic liberties (see pp. 5–7).

However, it is possible that the tsunami catastrophe might mark a turning point. Natural disasters have, on occasions, changed political cultures and social policies. For example, the earthquake which destroyed much of the city of Kobe in Japan in 1995 brought about a re-evaluation of many aspects of Japanese society. Although there was a history of very serious earthquakes, about every sixty years, in Japan, and one was long overdue, the authorities were unprepared and responded very slowly. The military awaited orders; the local officials were ineffective, especially in organizing a force of tens of thousands of young volunteers, who flocked to help in the rescue efforts. The Japanese public recognized that their complex and sophisticated network of public agencies was not, after all, a guarantee of security or efficient action (BBC Radio 4, 2005b).

As a result, the Japanese public saw the need for a stronger civil society, with more voluntary associations and civic participation. Perhaps it was the sight of the local criminal mafia running a soup kitchen for homeless survivors, before the city authorities had made any such provision, which brought about this realization.

International action in response to the tsunami catastrophe has demonstrated the potential for global action. In the next two chapters, I shall analyse the links between the different levels of organization identified in this section.

Section 1B

How the World Works

3

Explaining the New Global Division of Labour

On 15 January 2005, the British comedian Dawn French, who plays the Vicar of Dibley in the BBC TV series, led a delegation of real-life women clergy to present a petition for debt relief and aid to the developing countries at 10 Downing Street. A new movement, Make Poverty History, was campaigning in the wake of the Asian tsunami disaster, and hoping to follow up the public response to the needs of destitute and homeless victims with pressure to address poverty worldwide (BBC Radio 4, 2005c). The campaign was carried forward by Bob Geldof in May and June, culminating with the Live 8 concerts urging the G8 summit at Gleneagles to address poverty in Africa.

In this chapter and the next, I shall aim to show that these issues of national debt and individual destitution can best be understood in terms of the global financial system and the new relations of production it has created. What the Make Poverty History campaigners are in effect demanding is a reversal of the present global structure of accountability, in which business corporations and governments must justify their strategies and policies (now called 'business plans' even if they consist of the provision of health care, education and welfare services) to banks, insurance companies, pension funds and, ultimately, the IMF and the World Bank (see, for instance, IDA, 2001). They are claiming, implicitly if not directly, that such decisions should be made according to human values and political priorities, not the return on financial loans.

Because the dynamics of these relationships are seldom made explicit, my analysis aims to set these out, and show how they differ from the relationships which were taken to underpin welfare states. In the post-war period, because it was reasonably realistic to assume that each nation state was a self-contained system of economic co-operation between its citizens, the goal of government was to manage potentially damaging and wasteful conflicts of interest between the classes – *rentiers*, who lived on their income from financial loans or the ownership of land and houses, *capitalists*, who owned buildings and machinery and produced goods and services for consumption, and *workers*, who earned wages and salaries. These conflicts of interest were seen as underlying the emergence of two totalitarian political systems: state socialism (which called itself communism), in which the one-party government took control of all financial instruments and productive resources in the name of workers; and fascism, in which a self-appointed group claimed to override class interests in the name of a national, ethnic and spiritual destiny, and used a mixture of capitalist and socialist instruments of rule, while suppressing all other forms of political mobilization.

Welfare states were direct responses to these totalitarian systems, which had polarized world politics in the middle of the twentieth century. They aimed to use democratic means to resolve conflicts, restrain economic competition, and redistribute the benefits of more co-operative relationships between the classes. They drew on the theories of the economist John Maynard Keynes (1936) to show how the state could, by its management of interest rates, taxation, redistribution, investment and public spending, smooth out the 'cycles' of inflation and deflation, boom and bust, which had afflicted liberal democratic versions of capitalism. In this way, financial, business and trade union organizations could be drawn into systems which allowed reliable economic growth, and citizens could have their human development needs met through social security, health-care, education and welfare services financed out of contributions from all the three elements in the 'social partnership'.

In the first two chapters, we saw how the welfare states established in North America, Europe and Australasia in the post-war period ceased to satisfy the requirements of financial and business interests in these countries, and how they subsequently evolved strategies for earning higher returns through relocating mass production in newly industrializing countries such as Malaysia, Thailand, Indonesia and, eventually, India (see pp. 25–6). This in turn required a transformation of productive organizations in the affluent First World countries, and of their welfare-state institutions, to take account of the new global division of labour in an integrated world economy.

What happened through these processes was that the class relationships of the nineteenth and early twentieth century, which shaped the politics of the affluent countries, and the strategies of individuals and households, have been replaced there by new relations of power and production. As most of the physical work of manufacturing, construction, mining and agriculture has shifted to the developing world, citizens of the First World countries are in a different relationship with each other, and with those of the newly industrializing and less developed countries. A global elite of staff in financial, business and administrative organizations moves freely between all these states, striking deals, planning outcomes, superintending the processes of production, and maintaining the links in the world's economic system. The research, development and finance for these activities is still located in the rich countries, as are most of the shareholders.

During the era of welfare states, the goal of social policy was to reduce the disparity in life chances between members of the classes, and to create opportunities for people of ability to move into positions of responsibility, where they could make a full contribution to prosperity and progress. In effect, the aim was to make far less significant the distinctions between people with money and property, people with productive resources, and people who earned a weekly or monthly pay-packet. What has happened is that these distinctions are now blurred in affluent societies, at least for mainstream citizens. Most own, or aspire to own, their own houses. Many have pensions or shares, and hence (in effect) a property income. Compared with the post-war era, more are self-employed, and more run small enterprises; far fewer do manual work. Men's and women's jobs are more similar, and their pay is more equal. Most do service work and change jobs more frequently.

However, all this disguises the fact that class interests and conflicts have been globalized rather than reconciled or abolished. Much of the income which the citizens of affluent states earn from their pension rights or shareholdings comes from investments in companies which produce in China, Indonesia or Brazil. Much of the debt which the movement Make Poverty History was seeking to relieve is owed to banks in the USA, the UK, France and Germany, which also make personal loans to their homeland citizens, and pay interest on their savings. The new division of labour, credit and debt makes many in the First World mainstream into part-time rentiers, holding part of the Third World's debt in their personal portfolios.

So when the UK Prime Minister, Tony Blair, made a speech a few days before the petition was presented by Dawn French and her colleagues, in which he defined his government's aim as to 'increase personal prosperity', he was largely endorsing these relationships (*The Guardian*, 2005c). The 'personal prosperity' of UK citizens has been growing in large part because of the good returns which British banks and businesses have been getting on their loans and investments in the newly industrializing and less developed countries of the world. It was therefore ironic that his colleague and rival, the Chancellor of the Exchequer, Gordon Brown, was simultaneously in Africa, seeking to take over part of the debt of some of the world's poorest countries.

Under Third Way governments in the USA and the UK, Bill Clinton's and Tony Blair's treasuries have also become the departments administering tax credits for low-paid workers and their households (see pp. 77–80). Just as financial institutions now sit at the apex of the global economy and make the conditions under which credit is given to businesses and governments, so too, in these pioneers of the new model of social policy in the First World, finance departments of states now dispense credits to those citizens whose access to bank credit is very limited. So it will be these government ministries which will in turn have to decide how to balance their dispensations to poor countries and to their poor citizens. Finance is the dominant interest and decision-maker, at home and abroad.

At the level of individuals and households, the mainstream populations of the USA, the UK and other liberal welfare regimes such as Australia (Pusey, 2003) and New Zealand (Kelsey, 1995) rely less on public services of social security (state pensions and benefits), and more during their working lives on mortgage companies, credit cards and bank loans and in retirement on occupational and private pensions. All these link their fates to those populations in the indebted countries of the developing world who produce most of the technological gadgets and household appliances they use, and much of the food they eat.

The role of financial organizations in social policy

In one sense, therefore, the new division of labour, credit and debt reflects a return to the economic relations of the nineteenth century, but it is on a global scale. Then a very small group of financiers and landowners in the UK, Europe and the USA funded manufacturers and merchants in their home countries who, supported by armies and administrators, also established mines and plantations all over the world to supply raw materials in exchange for processed goods. Now loans from financial centres, deriving ultimately from the property and savings of whole nations, channel funds into huge industrial zones in China, India or Brazil, using materials from all over the globe. Both the financial operations and the manufacturing activities have been dispersed throughout the world, and now employ millions of workers in former colonial dependencies. But the fundamental relationships between the functions of rentiers, capitalists and workers remain similar.

This would have surprised those who sat down to design the new institutions for the world economy at the end of the Second World War. The most influential figure among that group, the British economist John Maynard Keynes, was a sophisticated, cosmopolitan liberal. Although he is justifiably represented as one of the main architects of the national systems for economic management which were the bases of welfare states, he was equally a founder at Bretton Woods in July of 1944 of the International Monetary Fund (IMF) and International Bank for Reconstruction and Development (later known as the World Bank). What would have surprised (and somewhat disappointed) Keynes is not that the global economy has been integrated into a single system, but that it is, in effect, run by financiers who create credit and collect interest on debt, and not by governments and a politically accountable IMF, on behalf of electorates dominated by working-class parties.

Keynes, like the institutions he helped to create, saw the world economy as a single system, and any subdivision of entities within it as essentially artificial. The model which he developed in his *General Theory of Employment, Interest and Money* was intended to rebut the neo-classical explanation of mass unemployment, the scourge of the interwar years. In that account, the supply of labour always created its own demand, if wage rates were sufficiently flexible. Keynes sought to prove that it was possible to have 'an insufficiency of effective demand' for goods, and hence for workers, if capitalists' investments for production did not use up all available funding (ultimately derived from savings) because the rate of profit was falling.

In terms of social policy, Keynes wanted to be able to argue that *someone*, under these circumstances, should be in a position to fund more investment, and get consumers to spend more. Increased consumption would help, because it would improve the prospects of higher profits. So building more schools, hospitals, transport systems and social housing (investment in the infrastructure) would relieve unemployment and stimulate consumer goods production; and providing decent unemployment benefits would be good for the economy. This was exactly the opposite of the orthodoxy of that time, which argued for higher taxes and cuts in spending on public projects, cuts in benefits, and cuts in wages.

However, Keynes was very ambivalent about who this 'someone' should be. Because his model of the economy was, in the classical tradition of Adam Smith, the whole world, it would have made most sense if it had been a benevolent international committee. Given the political realities of the day (competing nation states, with protectionist programmes, rearming for conflict), he reluctantly adopted these as his units of account (Keynes, 1957 [1936], p. 37). This meant that his generalizations about 'aggregates' (of money supply, labour and demand), of key importance in his theory, were all made at the national level.

This did not imply that he thought this was the most desirable level for policy-making. He added his policy conclusions to the *General Theory* as appendices, the final one of which was called 'Concluding Notes on the Social Philosophy towards which the General Theory might Lead'. He argued for higher government spending on 'public works' and on redistributive measures to make incomes more equal.

My main reason for outlining these aspects of Keynes's theory is to contrast his analysis of decisions about 'aggregates', for the sake of full employment, maintaining wage rates and equalizing incomes, with the model which now prevails. Although Keynes had doubts about whether political authorities were suitable for these tasks, he was very clear that financiers (bankers, fund managers, landowners) were not. Without directly advocating the public ownership of these institutions, he thought that his model would lead to 'the euthanasia of the rentier, and consequently the euthanasia of the cumulative oppressive power of the capitalist to exploit the scarcity-value of capital', simply by lowering the rate of interest.

> Interest today rewards no genuine sacrifice, any more than does the rent of land. The owners of [finance] capital can obtain interest because capital is scarce, just as the owner of land can obtain rent because land is scarce. But whilst there may be intrinsic reasons for the scarcity of land, there are no intrinsic reasons for the scarcity of capital. (Keynes, 1957 [1936], p. 376)

In many ways, the IMF was a better expression of Keynes's principles, and the workings of his economic model, than a democratic national government (accountable to lobby groups and the electorate) could be. The IMF was set up, as a technical system under expert guidance, to provide loans to governments threatened with recession which could not afford to take the steps necessary to increase aggregate demand (Stiglitz, 2002, p. 12). This was a form of collective action at the global level, to make markets work better and smooth over imbalances of trade between countries, stabilizing currencies through 'international settlements'. Keynes thought that interest should be paid on credit as well as debt. He wanted the IMF to act as the benevolent committee of the world economy, creating a supply of funds which would promote growth and employment, replacing the role of banks, finance houses, and those who lived from property incomes of all kinds.

It is important to recognize that the thinking behind the British and European welfare states largely accepted these assumptions, which would be regarded as revolutionary today. The state, acting in the name of the 'common will', ought to be able to eliminate the role of the 'functionless investor' by making capital readily available to businesses at low interest rates. This 'socialization of investment' would proceed gradually, through co-operation between government and private initiative; the 'instruments of production' themselves could remain in private hands, so long as the government could use its powers 'to determine the aggregate amount of resources devoted to augmenting the instruments and the basic rewards of those who own them' – i.e. profits (Keynes, 1957 [1936], pp. 377–8).

These views were by no means heretical at the time. For instance, Harold Macmillan, later to serve as Conservative Prime Minister of the UK (1957–63), thought that all industrial investment should be in the hands of a public National Investment Board, with the sole exception of new speculative enterprises, for which there should be a stock market (Macmillan, 1938, p. 261). But they were not shared by economists in the US Treasury, whose influence limited the role of the IMF in the international economy and worked towards the preservation of world financial markets, which were dominated by US banks and funds.

In order to understand how social policy is made in today's integrated world economy, why welfare states did not lead to the 'euthanasia of the rentier', and why Tony Blair should define the aims of a 'progressive, reforming' UK government in terms of 'personal prosperity', we need to analyse how finance capital shaped the new global division of labour, credit and debt. Why was the Keynesian model of the world economy discredited, and what replaced it?

The neo-liberal model and the Washington Consensus

It was a long set of steps from Keynes's model of national and global authorities, acting as the clearing houses for investment funds and trade accounts throughout the world, to Tony Blair's vision of a society founded on 'personal prosperity' (one he shared with Margaret Thatcher, Ronald Reagan, Bill Clinton and both George Bushes). In order to understand the path between these points, and how it affected social policy, we need to trace the rapid decline of the model which sustained welfare states and the rise of a resuscitated older model of the roles of individuals and governments, based on an entirely different conception of how money and property informed the allocation of productive resources.

Keynes's idea of 'aggregates' (the sum totals of money, machinery, workers and so on, in any jurisdiction) was echoed in models of welfare states. For example, William Beveridge, a friend and disciple of Keynes, argued that 'it must be the function of the state in future to ensure adequate total outlay and by consequence to protect its citizens against mass unemployment, as definitely as it is now the function of the state to defend the citizens against attack from abroad and against robbery and violence at home' (Beveridge, 1944, p. 29).

Given this condition, and state-funded secondary education, a heath-care service covering all citizens, and child benefits, there were clear contingencies which individual workers, employers and the government could join together to insure against – unemployment, industrial injury, sickness and retirement (Beveridge, 1942, p. 120). This confidence was based on aggregating the number of men and women in full-time employment (but treating married women as dependent family members) and balancing their social insurance requirements against the aggregate contributions of the three partners. It was the 'magic of averages' rather than the individual prudence of each worker, or the risk assessment skills of an insurance company, which could achieve this result.

For all the variations between subsequent versions of welfare regimes (see pp. 66–7), this basic model supplied the fundamentals of all the European systems of social citizenship. By the 1970s, Scandinavian social security schemes had higher rates of contributions and benefits than continental Christian democratic ones, which in turn had higher rates than UK, US and Australasian or Japanese ones. The rank order of government spending on public health care and education was slightly different; for instance, the US government spent proportionately more on education, but much less on health care, than some European countries (Esping-Andersen, 1990). But they all relied on Keynesian aggregates for their principles of regulating wages, managing investment, redistributing income and providing for contingencies.

As we saw in chapter 1, by the early 1970s, multinational corporations had already burst out of their post-war reliance on national settlements with trade unions and governments; they had begun to invest, produce and trade worldwide (see pp. 26–8). Financial institutions were funding this diversification, and also the policies of newly industrializing countries, which aimed to channel this strategy into export-orientated production in their territories (see pp. 33–5). When the Israel–Egypt war of 1972 led to a steep rise in world oil prices, the Keynesian model of economic management became vulnerable. Inflation, a long-term feature of the system, escalated, and growth slowed or reversed. The IMF and World Bank abruptly dropped the role they had taken since 1944 and switched to a new one, reflecting the new thinking in the US Treasury (the Washington Consensus). They insisted on lower deficits and higher taxes and interest rates as conditions on loans to governments. 'Keynes would be rolling over in his grave were he to see what has happened to his child' (Stiglitz, 2002, p. 13).

The economic theories behind this shift deserve to be explained at this point, because they still supply the fundamentals of the strategies of the IMF and the World Bank, of the US and UK treasuries, and hence of the finance ministries of most governments in the world. Continental European administrations have been far more reluctant to give up a perspective on economic policy based on aggregates, or modify the institutions of their welfare states in line with the theories. But the strategies of firms and individuals everywhere have been deeply influenced by the shift, and – as we shall see in part II of the book – even people's sense of their own identities, projects and commitments rely on the assumptions of the new model. When Tony Blair speaks of 'personal prosperity', he is able to summon up a set of images and ideas, not so much about secure employment and rising wages, as about each individual's 'human capital', property portfolio and 'business plan' for their life.

Slower growth and higher rates of inflation in the affluent First World countries in the 1970s was an opportunity for leading European economists, who had criticized Keynes's theoretical model since the 1930s, to come to the fore as influences on political leaders, especially in the USA, and later in the UK. In particular, two Austrian theorists, Friedrich von Hayek and Ludwig von Mises, had contributed the basic theoretical elements for the new model. They insisted that government actions to plan investment and redistribute income were responsible for policy failures, because the aggregates in which they dealt were irrelevant and misleading. Their interventions were distorting the operation of market forces, causing 'discrepancies between the distribution of demand among the different goods and services and the allocation of labour and other resources among the production of those outputs' (Hayek, 1978, p. 25).

Hayek and Mises (1966) argued that the only way to achieve both efficiency and equity in the long term was to return to the *individual* basis for theory and policy. Outcomes should, as far as possible, emerge from the choices of ordinary people pursuing their subjective preferences. They should be co-ordinated by the 'invisible hand' of the market, which allocated all resources, including human labour, to their optimum uses through the price mechanism, and not through government action. They recognized a limited case for 'public goods' and redistribution, but only for identifiable cases of 'market failure' (see pp. 30–1).

They were joined by the US economist Milton Friedman (1975) in blaming the long wave of inflation in the affluent countries, culminating in very rapid price rises in some of them in the 1970s, on these long-term distortions. In particular, Keynes's assumption that wages should not be allowed to fall in any part of the economy meant that governments must constantly create credit or expand the supply of money, to create demand for goods at unrealistic prices, and maintain unrealistic wages and levels of employment. In the long term, this meant that many industries had become inefficient and needed to be restructured. Some firms must close, some goods must be produced in fewer quantities, and some workers should retrain themselves and move elsewhere (Hayek, 1978, 1979).

An important part of the argument for the new model was therefore that decisions about the funding of business investments should be made by commercial banks, and not by governments. Money could only go to its most efficient uses if bankers were free to make loans to those they judged to have the best prospects of being profitable. All this should happen within an overall supply of money which increased only in line with the growth in production (Friedman, 1975); better still, government should get right out of the business of creating credit; money should be 'denationalized' (Hayek, 1976).

So the new model focused attention on individual choices (about spending, saving and planning for work and welfare) and the decisions of financial intermediaries (banks, insurance companies, trust funds). It insisted that these provided the basis for sustainable growth, and it relegated government to holding the ring for these processes. In the rest of this chapter, I shall show how the whole financial sector – from the IMF to local mortgage companies – set out to use this power, and how this transformed employment, income and personal welfare worldwide. This power rests on a dubious set of connections between personal freedom and moral sovereignty, markets in goods and services, government by consent, and the commercial supply of credit. We must first analyse these connections in more detail, before turning to how the financial sector used its power.

Money, property and production

The idea that each individual should be able to use their knowledge, skills and resources for their own purposes (moral sovereignty) is the core principle of political liberalism, first established in the late seventeenth century; the idea that each such individual should count as equal in political decisions is the basis for liberal democracy, which was not implemented in the UK and Europe until over two centuries later. Liberalism therefore defined freedom in negative terms; a morally sovereign individual could not be coerced by government and was not beholden to any system of authority.

The new model of economic and social policy which emerged in the 1970s regarded welfare states as having eroded the freedom and independence of individuals by encouraging them to look to the state for *collective* decisions about their well-being, and generalized provision for their needs, based on the manipulation of aggregates. It wanted to restore the primacy of individual liberty, markets and a form of government which saw the preservation of these as its first task (Hayek, 1960, 1982).

In choosing to use the term 'property-owning democracy' about the kind of society she wanted to create through her reforms, Margaret Thatcher was referring mainly to the sale of council houses and the privatization of public utilities. However, in the writings of Hayek in particular, the term 'property' referred to an individual's ownership of his or her life, personal rights and material resources (Hayek, 1960, pp. 54–62; 1982, vol. 1, p. 107).

Private ownership and the opportunity to start a productive enterprise are therefore the cornerstones of the economic independence which underpins the moral sovereignty of individuals in the new model. This extends to their choices over income in retirement, health-care insurance and education for their children. It implies that, where the state supplies a system of publicly funded pensions, hospitals or schools, it both allows scope for private alternatives and gives opportunities for choice about which facilities to use in the public sector (see chapters 5, 6 and 8).

In the neo-classical tradition, revived by Hayek, Friedman and their school, money is simply a neutral medium for signalling prices, the 'veil' for the goods and services which make up the real economy, and a technical device to facilitate transactions (Schumpeter, 1994 [1954], p. 277). As well as being a convenient medium of exchange and a unit of account which standardizes the values of very different commodities, it is also a store of value and a standard for deferred payments.

However, commercial banking makes its returns on creating credit for future production and consumption. Banks advance sums to companies and individuals, and are paid interest on these 'loans'. Of course, businesses also raise funds on the stock market by issuing shares, on which they pay dividends from their profits. But most of these shares are bought by banks, pension funds (on behalf of those individuals and companies who save for retirement through their schemes), insurance companies and investment funds (which use the savings of private individuals). So the financial sector has a controlling interest in the productive sector – it has the power to decide what is produced, where, and by whom.

This is not always made clear to the general public, whose savings ultimately supply the basis of this power. (Even the loans made by the Chinese authorities to the US government – see pp. 5–6 – are actually the savings of Chinese citizens.) For instance, the 'business news' on the radio and TV or in the press seems to be an account of how firms are performing in the 'real world' economy. However, almost all of it is mediated by the perceptions and assumptions of financial markets; it is how fundholders and banks consider their prospective profitability that determines share prices and credit ratings. Money is not the servant of business, but its master.

So the financial sector plays an active part in shaping business investments, the labour market and output, as well as credit and debt patterns among individuals, organizations and governments. Money is not a neutral medium of exchange, or even just a store of wealth; the interests of the financial sector predominate over all others, especially in the USA and the UK, traditionally the global centres of financial markets. Far from leading to 'the euthanasia of the rentier', welfare states ushered in a period when the world economy became more accountable to financial interests than ever before.

This hierarchy of power, from the IMF and the World Bank, through the financial sectors of the rich states, holds productive businesses and governments accountable for all decisions, ensuring that its return (in interest payments and dividends, or through speculative trading in stocks and currencies) is paramount. So the 'freedom' which individuals enjoy, their 'independence' and 'moral sovereignty' and their 'consent' in the institutions of government, all are directly conditional on the approval of these invisible and largely unaccountable authorities. The fact that individuals have a stake in this order through their savings, pensions, home ownership, share ownership and insurance policies does not, in reality, give them any control over the decisions made at any level of the system (see also chapter 14).

The version of human well-being which sees it as being maximized globally when as many individuals as possible are independent, property-owning and free to choose in markets refuses to recognize or analyse these power relations. The new model of the global economy treats the choice of a certain technology and factory organization to produce goods in Indonesia or China, and to close another site in Dundee, Dortmund or Detroit, as an instant flow of capital to a more efficient allocation. But those who mediate such decisions through financial markets are quite disconnected from the human activities involved. If the workers made redundant in the latter sites put their severance payments into unit trusts, they become the passive parties to other such decisions, affecting other workers on either side of the world. This is not 'freedom' or 'independence', and certainly not 'sovereignty'. It links the well-being of the global human community in covert and paradoxical ways.

Tying individual incomes to financial markets has also had serious consequences for vulnerable people throughout the world. The 'pensions industry' has failed to protect retired people, and those planning retirement, in the UK because of the decline in the stock market in the early years of the twenty-first century. Financial crises in Russia, East Asia and South America have wiped away the value of millions of people's savings. Individual holdings, for the sake of growth or income, are far less reliable than state benefits, though they can give substantial gains to the fortunate.

In the next section, I shall analyse why the patterns of employment now deployed throughout the world take the shape they do, and how these relate to financial markets, government lending and borrowing, and personal credit and debt.

The global division of labour

As we have seen (pp. 30–1), the starting point of the Washington Consensus (neo-liberal or neo-classical) model of the economy, the role of government, and social policy was that the three post-war decades of state intervention had distorted the allocation of resources and caused high inflation and low growth. Everyone would be better off if, instead of relying on the government to manage investment strategies, maintain high levels of employment, prevent wages from falling, protect the incomes of those outside the labour market, and provide public services for all, individuals made their own choices. If people were responsible for training themselves for work, improving their own earnings, planning their own savings for retirement, and choosing the services they needed, markets would co-ordinate all these decisions in more efficient ways.

Under the new leadership of the IMF and the World Bank, and of President Reagan in the USA and Prime Minister Thatcher in the UK, this model was urged or imposed upon countries in the developing world. These policies strongly reinforced the processes of transformation which were already taking place through the new global strategies of multinational corporations (see pp. 25–30). Whereas governments in Germany, France and the other continental states of the EU acted to try to keep a balance between their financial, industrial and service sectors, and especially to rescue ailing giants among their industrial firms, the Anglophone nations (including Australia, New Zealand and Canada) embraced 'restructuring'. They saw the loss of manufacturing sites as a necessary process of adaptation; they regarded bankruptcies and redundancies as aspects of 'creative destruction'; they facilitated the firing of workers and the weakening of trade unions; and they cut benefits and services to encourage unemployed people to be more mobile, motivated and self-reliant (see pp. 131–5).

As a result, patterns of employment changed more rapidly in the Anglophone countries than in the ones with Christian democratic or social democratic governments, or in Japan. The shift from employment in construction, mining and manufacturing (which had supplied almost 50 per cent of jobs in the UK and Germany in the early 1960s) to service work, and the growth of female employment, were more marked in the former (see table 3.1).

These changes were, of course, matched by the growth of industrial (and particularly manufacturing) employment in the newly industrializing countries (see table 2.1, p. 41). The proponents of the new model

Table 3.1   Changes in composition of workforces, 1961–2000

Country	Percentage of workforce in industry		Percentage of workforce female		Percentage of workforce in services	
	1961	2000	1975	2000	1965	2000
UK	48.8	25.6	36.7	44.1	51	72
W. Germany	49.4	36.1	36.3	42.3	42	62
Italy	38.2	33.3	27.8	38.5	34	62
France	38.1	25.5	35.2	45.1	42	73
USA	32.8	23.0	37.8	46.0	59	74
Japan	29.9	34.5	39.6	41.4	42	64

Sources: World Bank (1985, 2000, 2002); OECD (1970); ILO (1978).

could claim, with some justification, that this was welfare-enhancing for the world as a whole. First, the gains in jobs in countries such as South Korea, Taiwan and Hong Kong in the 1970s, and Malaysia, Thailand and Indonesia in the 1980s and early 1990s, were greater than the losses in the UK, Germany and France (the *absolute* numbers of industrial jobs were still growing in the USA and Japan, though their proportion of the workforce was falling). Second, wages and output grew much faster in those countries than they had been increasing in Europe and North America in the 1970s (see table 3.2 below). Third, even in those countries where benefits had been cut, First World workers had some entitlements to assistance, which gave them time to retrain and relocate. And fourth, they benefited, along with the rest of the populations of those countries, from the supply of goods imported from the newly industrialized countries, which produced them more cheaply than they could have been made in the affluent states.

In one important respect, these restructurings led to greater equality within countries as well as between them. In the USA, Australia and the UK, women joined the paid workforce in large numbers, and some gained well-paid positions, especially in the professions. As the real wages of male manual workers fell, especially in the USA and Australia (Pusey, 2003, appendix C), some partners' earnings were required simply to stay solvent; but other two-career households increased their incomes. At the same time, some of the least skilled

Table 3.2   Growth in GDP, manufacturing earnings and social security spending, 1970–97

	Annual rate of growth of GDP		Average growth in real annual earnings in manufacturing	Percentage expenditure on social security
	1973–9	1990–7	1970–92	1990–7
USA	2.4	2.5	0.009	14.5
UK	1.0	0.8	0.035	18.2
France	3.0	0.8	n/a	23.7
Germany	2.3	1.1	0.023	22.3
South Korea	11.6	6.6	0.080	3.0
Taiwan	n/a	7.1	0.081	2.2
Hong Kong	10.3	5.7	0.036	1.2
Malaysia	7.3	8.4	0.019	1.4
Thailand	6.9	8.2	n/a	0.7
Indonesia	7.0	7.6	0.009	1.1

Sources: World Bank (1985, table 2; 2000, table 11); Bowles (2000, fig. 6); Gough (2004, table 5.2).

members of the workforce – especially those in one-earner families and lone parents – lost ground relative to the mainstream. Members of minority ethnic groups were more polarized than the white majority; the poorest fell into destitution, while a successful middle class emerged, and some whole groups (such as Indians in the UK) were upwardly mobile, doing better than indigenous white populations.

Esping-Andersen (1990, 1999) has noted that 'welfare regimes' which switched from maintaining male industrial employment to accelerating the growth of private-service jobs (or public-service work in the case of the Scandinavian countries, especially Sweden) were able to achieve higher rates of economic growth in the 1980s and 1990s. This shift often resulted in higher rates of unemployment for men as well as more economic participation (mainly part-time) for women; in all but the Scandinavian countries it also led to more inequality of incomes (Iversen and Wren, 1998). The more conservative regimes of continental Europe, which modified their corporatist institutions only slowly, began to develop structural, long-term unemployment in the 1990s – a cumulative problem in Germany following its reunification after 1989.

The new model of the world economy redirected government's attention from 'aggregate demand' to the 'supply side' – deploying productive resources in such a way as to make them responsive to market opportunities. In labour markets, this meant that the education, training and adaptability of the workforce were more important targets of social policy than their wages, which should be allowed to find their own levels through competition (Reich, 1993). In the USA and the UK, the 'human capital' of the workforce became the focus of flagship government programmes under the Third Way administrations of Bill Clinton and Tony Blair (Waddan, 1997; Jordan, 1998, ch. 2). Policy aimed to improve skills, incentives, the work ethic and enterprise, seeing the workforce as the key to national prosperity.

The differences between welfare regimes in the First World countries were apparent in how they tackled unemployment. Starting from high rates following restructuring of labour markets under Reagan and Thatcher in the 1980s, the USA and the UK adopted active measures to reintegrate unemployed people into formal work in the 1990s. The Clinton and Blair governments justified 'welfare-to-work' programmes of training and counselling, combined with threats to curtail benefits for failure to take available opportunities (Reich, 1997; DSS, 1998). They insisted that entitlement to benefits (including those for lone parents and disabled people) implied responsibilities to work and earn if this was feasible, and that work was 'the most reliable route out of poverty'. They also consolidated tax credits as systems for supplementing the earnings of low-earning households, in order to improve incentives to take low-paid and part-time work (see pp. 77–80).

All this contrasted with continental European regimes, which were far more reluctant to accept the principles of the new model. For example, despite its continued success in world markets for high-tech products, the German economy has failed to generate enough jobs, especially in the private-service sector, to make up for the decline in industrial employment. Ever since the 1970s, the response of governments has been to expand state protection for redundant workers (through unemployment, early retirement or disability benefits), and their numbers have risen inexorably. This has been funded by increased social security contributions by employers and employees, which stood at 20 per cent of gross wages in 2000. As a result, the cost of employing a new worker at the minimum wage contains an extra 50 per cent of non-wage costs, taking account of all taxes and contributions (Scharpf, 1999; Manow and Seils, 2000). This contrasts with the effective subsidy paid to employers of wages at the (much lower) minimum wages in the USA and the UK through tax credits. The German government has, in 2005, finally begun the process of adapting to the new model's requirements by cutting unemployment benefits and subsidizing new job creation – but not before the number of its unemployed reached 5 million (BBC World Service, 2005a; Möhle, 2005).

The new model facilitates a global division of labour reflecting the strategies of multinational producers, but shaped by the interests of the financial sector. In First World countries, the main expansions of service jobs have been in that sector itself – in banking, mortgage companies, insurance and business services – and in low-paid, part-time employment, in retailing, catering, hospitality, leisure, cleaning and personal services (such as hairdressing and care of elderly people). The financial sector has seen an enormous rise in personal credit (i.e. debt) in the USA, Australia and the UK (in the EU, 75 per cent of credit card debt is owed by UK citizens). Financial products, advice and fund management now supply an employment market which scarcely existed in the early 1970s, and which pays relatively high salaries to its workers. But this sector has in turn funded a growth of small enterprises and self-employment in the lowest-paying end of the market for private services, employing mainly women, young people, members of minority ethnic groups, and others on the margins of the economy (see pp. 213–15).

The financial sector earns its income partly from transactions on global currency and stock markets, from investments in the newly industrializing countries, and from loans to individuals and households and to small businesses on its home territory. In the First World countries, it shapes a division of labour between those with a stake in its global operations (through pension funds, shareholdings or unit trusts) who become part-time rentiers, and those in its debt, many of whom serve its employees and stakeholders in menial roles (checking out their purchases in supermarkets, waiting table at restaurants, cleaning their houses, or looking after their children). Thus the global division of labour, in which most manufacturing takes place far away from where its products are consumed, creates societies with a fundamental division between those who draw incomes related to the creation of credit and the lending of money and those who pay interest on debt.

Conclusions

In this chapter, I have shown how the purposes of the international financial and trade organizations have been changed in response to the transformation of finance and industrial capital worldwide. The development of the South and East Asian economies which was analysed in the first section of the book was structured by these new principles and policies, which came to be known as the Washington Consensus because they were closely linked to the strategies of the US Treasury and US financial interests. The creation of new global division of labour, in which most manufacturing is now carried out in China, India, South Korea, Taiwan and increasingly also Indonesia and Brazil, is a product of this shift in the theoretical and organizational basis of the world's most powerful economic institutions.

Because post-war welfare states were forged from political settlements in First World industrialized societies between capital, labour and state organizations, this has meant that they themselves have had to be transformed in line with the shift in production towards the newly industrializing economies, the new global division of labour, and the new theoretical basis for institutional design. Because the economies of the affluent First World states have been restructured, so too have their public sectors and government agencies themselves, along with all the 'social partnership' arrangements through which social policy was negotiated and delivered. A detailed analysis of this transformation will be made in chapters 7 to 10.

But the Washington Consensus has itself been transformed at the start of the twenty-first century. Its failures, such as the case of Sri Lanka, set out in the previous chapter, and the South-East Asian financial crisis, have led to the emergence of a modified approach, especially within the World Bank. This gives more priority to engaging with the governments and civil societies of countries needing assistance, and to changing institutions from within by processes of negotiating, rather than simply imposing market solutions and government spending cuts (World Bank, 2001).

From the mid-1990s also, the neo-liberal social policies of Ronald Reagan and George Bush senior in the USA, and Margaret Thatcher and John Major in the UK (as well as their Labour equivalents in Australia and New Zealand), have been modified, in line with the new Third Way ideas of Bill Clinton and Tony Blair. The transformation of European social policy, which came later than in the Anglophone countries, has therefore incorporated many of these modifications. These too will be analysed in chapters 7 to 10.

In the next chapter, I shall focus on how the transition from the Washington Consensus to the new World Bank model for economic and human development, which occurred during the evolution of new societies in the former communist countries of the Soviet bloc, led to new relationships of credit, debt and power worldwide – and how these in turn shaped social policies.

4

Social Policy, Credit and Debt

In this chapter, I shall analyse how the scope for global redistributive policies is related to the new division of labour, credit and debt in an integrated world economy. Keynes's model, in which governments – both individually and in concert, through the IMF – acted to maintain employment and wages, and keep interest rates low, through the manipulation of aggregate demand, has been abandoned. There has been no 'euthanasia of the rentier'; financial markets determine the flow of funds for productive investment worldwide, and this in turn shapes patterns of employment and earnings.

The world has returned to a version of capitalism which was analysed and criticized in the later nineteenth and earlier twentieth century by Karl Marx, Thorstein Veblen and Joseph Schumpeter, among many others. What all three of these recognized was that money does not play a neutral role, as a means of exchange and a store of wealth, in the 'circular flow' of goods and services (Hutchinson et al., 2002). Development requires new combinations of capital and labour, producing new products or organizing production in new ways; it *interrupts* the circular flow, pushing resources in new directions. In a capitalist economy, it is the financial sector which, through the provision of credit (and the creation of debt), supplies the means of innovation and development by selecting certain projects for funding. As Schumpeter put it:

> the money market is always, as it were, the headquarters of the capitalist system, from which orders go out to individuals, and that which is debated and decided there is always in essence the settlement of plans for further develop-ment. . . . Thus the main function of the money or capital market is trading in credit for the purpose of financing development. Development creates and nourishes this market. In the course of development it is assigned still another,

that is a third function: it becomes the market for sources of incomes themselves. (Schumpeter, 1961 [1934], p. 127)

The big issue for the finance ministers of the affluent states is that their policy decisions directly affect *both* the incomes of workers in the world's poorest countries, producing food, minerals and clothes for global markets, *and* the incomes of their own citizens, either employed in their financial sectors or holding stakes in international investments through that sector. When Tony Blair declares that his government's priority is to promote the 'personal prosperity' of UK citizens, he is implicitly accepting the world order in which choices about credit and debt are entrusted to financial institutions through free markets in funds for development. Following the lead of the US Treasury and the IMF, the basis of the new model of the world economy is that financial markets will make the most efficient allocations for such investments, and that these will give the best returns to individuals in the affluent states, for their savings, shareholdings and pension funds. In all, 95 per cent of transactions on world markets are purely financial – trading money for money (Hutchinson et al., 2002, p. 5).

The scope for global redistribution within this model is limited because of the reliance of individuals and households on personal credit, mortgages and loans from the financial sector, and because the growth of the economies of these states stems largely from that sector. In the USA in 2001, the total indebtedness of private individuals stood at $28 trillion, 300 per cent of GDP (*The Guardian*, 2001). In the UK, the equivalent debt reached £1 trillion in 2004 (BBC Radio 4, 2004b), where the profits of the financial sector accounted for one-third of growth of GDP in 1996–7, and a half of that growth in 1999 (Hutchinson et al., 2002, p. 4). The US and UK governments are therefore very cautious about adopting policies which might be perceived as challenging the strategies of financial institutions, even when these involve lending to governments or farmers in very poor countries at high rates of interest.

Instead, these governments adopt social policies at home which favour the financial sector and enable its expansion. For example, President George W. Bush has promised to privatize part of the social security scheme in the USA during his second term, creating profitable opportunities for commercial banks, insurance companies and pension funds. In the UK, successive governments adopted policies in the 1990s which promoted the growth of private pension provision.

However, the links between national policies over 'personal prosperity' and world development policies, including those concerning poverty and debt, are well disguised. It is of the nature of capitalism that the role of the financial sector is veiled; its power is discreet and concealed. While Tony Blair makes speeches about the prosperity of UK citizens, his Chancellor of the Exchequer, Gordon Brown, visits schools in Tanzania, and promises to help fund secondary education in that poor country. The constraints on such decisions, from the reliance of the UK economy on the financial sector, are not made transparent. Nor does President Bush advertise his dependence on world financial markets for his war and reconstruction plans in Iraq.

In this chapter, I shall analyse how the new principles, purposes and policies of the IMF, the World Bank and later the WTO acted on governments and societies to restructure relationships both within and between them. In particular, I shall consider how this influenced countries in post-communist transitions – how the liberalization and privatization programmes imposed on them after 1989 created new patterns of ownership and power and new institutions for public administration. Social policy in these countries was shaped by financial liberalization and public-sector restructuring. But I shall also show how credit and debt influenced the restructuring of government agencies and the realignment of policies in developing countries, and how the treasuries (finance ministries) of the USA and the UK came to take over aspects of redistributive activity from welfare-state institutions.

Restructuring and debt

As a means of extending the Washington Consensus model of the global economy to all parts of the world, and integrating them into a single system, the IMF and the World Bank used their power to press for two further restructurings of the institutional order of the Keynesian period. They made their loans to governments conditional on ending barriers to the free movement of money and products worldwide – the liberalization of financial markets and trade. They also required governments to sell off some of the productive assets, resources and agencies which made up the public infrastructure – the privatization programme. For the twenty years after 1980, these were two principal features of the Washington Consensus for transforming the world economy. This meant that they were central to the transition from state socialism to markets in the Soviet bloc countries, after the collapse of their regimes in 1989. As Guy Standing (1996) and Bob Deacon (1997) show, this in turn shaped their labour markets and social policies in that transition.

The liberalization of trade has proceeded through a number of stages (the 'rounds' of the General Agreement on Tariffs and Trade). In these, lengthy negotiations have resulted in the lowering of barriers to free trade, but often in ways which favour the affluent countries and disadvantage the developing ones still further. For example, in the Uruguay Round (1994) the latter were persuaded to open up markets for information technology and financial services, but the affluent states refused to reciprocate in relation to maritime and construction services, where the poorer countries might have had a competitive edge (Stiglitz, 2002, p. 61). The unfairness of these trade negotiations have made them the targets of street protest from anti-capitalist and global justice campaigners, notably in Seattle in 1998. They have also been the focus of criticism from famine relief and aid charities and NGOs (Oxfam, 2002).

The liberalization of financial markets has had more dramatic effects. In the post-war era, governments kept control over movements of currency across national borders, restricting the flow of funds both into and out of their economies, and into particular sectors internally. European states did not open up their financial markets until the 1970s, and Sweden was among the last to do so, in the mid-1980s. However, the IMF and the World Bank argued that these reforms were essential to ensure that money flowed to its most productive and profitable uses, and imposed the rapid liberalization of financial markets on governments which applied for loans. This has caused a series of crises all over the world, as financial institutions bought and sold currencies and moved funds for investments in line with opportunities for short-term gains (Stiglitz, 2002, chs. 4 and 5).

Much more spectacularly, the financial crisis in East Asia which followed liberalization of capital markets there illustrated how this destabilized the delicate arrangements under which the government, the banking sector and industrial firms had built up their export-orientated manufacturing sectors. Starting in Thailand, where the currency collapsed after speculative selling, this crisis affected the much longer established economies of South Korea, Japan and (to a much lesser extent) Malaysia; it also led to the collapse of the regime in Indonesia (see pp. 37–8).

Liberalization has meant that all over the world, from Nigeria (1998) and Russia (1998) to Argentina (2001), money 'flows out of the country in a recession, precisely when the country needs it most, and flows in during a boom, exacerbating inflationary pressures' (Stiglitz, 2002, p. 100). It also leads to property price booms and slumps, as occurred in Thailand, and forces governments into spending less just when they ought to be spending more (ibid., pp. 106–8).

The IMF adopted the principle of privatization as an element in the restructuring requirements it imposed on applicant governments seeking loans. It insisted that they withdrew from many of their interventions in their economies, and opened them up for commercial firms to buy existing resources and supply services. They also demanded cuts in welfare programmes (Barrientos, 2004, p. 141), and that all this was done quickly, often leaving a lack of a provision for a service on which many other facilities in the infrastructure relied, especially in poor countries (Stiglitz, 2002, pp. 54–8).

The most spectacular examples of programmes for privatization having massive unintended consequences occurred in Russia and the other countries of the Soviet bloc after the collapse of those regimes in 1989. Under state socialism, all productive resources, including land, were owned by state 'enterprises', which also supplied most of the welfare services, among them kindergartens, clinics and even holidays, for their workers. The pressure from the IMF and the World Bank to privatize these enterprises, and other aspects of the public infrastructure, therefore had more drastic implications for the well-being of the whole population than in mixed economies in other regions of the world. When this was combined with the liberalization of financial markets, the results affected the whole political development of the former superpower, leading to a return of authoritarian leadership and a mistrust of democracy among citizens.

The problem in these countries was that privatization was pushed through by the IMF and the World Bank before adequate measures had been taken to secure private property rights, the rule of law, or adequate systems of corporate governance, under which the directors of firms are accountable to shareholders. Various methods of privatization were adopted, all of which turned out to be open to corruption and fraud, either in the original purchase of the assets or in the way they were subsequently bought up by particular individuals and companies.

In the case of Russia, the fraud involved the sham sales of huge assets to private banks and companies, largely made up of former managers of state enterprises or political insiders. This created the new class of 'oligarchs', who became instant billionaires (Stiglitz, 2002, pp. 138–40). By the end of the 1990s, Moscow had more of these per square mile than any other city in the world, but the rest of the country, where previously 'many were cold but few were frozen', was substantially poorer than it had been under the Soviet regime.

This made the whole Russian economy particularly vulnerable to crisis following financial liberalization. Russia relied excessively on exports of oil to the East Asian countries. When they experienced their sudden downturn in 1997, demand for oil fell. The following year, the Russian government was unable to meet interest payments on its loans from abroad, and speculation against the currency led to a collapse. Because so much of the country's wealth was now in the hands of the oligarchs, the latter were able to move their funds to banks in other countries. The cost (in unpaid wages, unemployment, homelessness and destitution) was met by ordinary citizens.

In this section, I shall turn to how all these transformations, which strengthened the power of international financial organizations and commercial financial interests worldwide, influenced the scope for and nature of social policy. The affluent countries where these interests were concentrated, the newly industrializing countries where most of the world's production took place, and the developing countries which relied on exporting raw materials each faced characteristic constraints on social policy. The post-communist states of the Soviet bloc experienced a combination of all these, and were also a kind of laboratory for the international financial organizations to experiment in social policy design; they will be analysed in the following section.

The developing countries of Africa, Asia and Latin America face notorious constraints on social policy arising from that indebtedness to the international financial system – to the World Bank and commercial banks in the affluent countries. This mountain of debt was built up through the post-colonial period, as each model of world economic development worked against their emergence from poverty.

In the first stage, up to the late 1970s, post-colonial governments tried to build up their capacities for industrial development, and for the export of foodstuffs and new materials in world markets, by establishing agencies to plan investment and production, to co-ordinate producers and negotiate with foreign interests. Not all such attempts were as successful as Sri Lanka's (see pp. 44–7); many post-colonial governments' interventions were inefficient and wasteful, and public spending was misused or misappropriated. This was hardly surprising, given the inexperience of many ministers and officials, the low salaries of agency staff, and (above all) the disadvantageous position of these economies in the global market. The former colonial powers had substantial holdings in their countries, and aimed primarily to secure low-cost raw materials and outlets for their products. When multinational corporations invested in these economies in the late 1960s and 1970s, it was to integrate the supplies of these materials into their new global systems of production and trade.

As a result, these governments entered the 1980s in a dependent and vulnerable situation. Their reliance on the IMF and the World Bank at points of downturn in the prices of commodities, or the world trade, made them targets for restructuring under the new model. As we saw from the case of Sri Lanka (pp. 44–7), even regimes which had been outstanding in their ability to promote human development were heavily criticized and made to adopt new market-orientated strategies which reversed all their previous priorities. Since the assumption behind the new model was that all politicians and officials acted to increase their budgets and power (see pp. 146–7), the new requirements for loans insisted on the closure of many interventions and agencies and on cuts in spending on schools and clinics, infrastructural projects and redistributive measures.

Zimbabwe represented a clear example of these policies. From 1963, when the white-dominated government of Ian Smith declared independence unilaterally, to 1980, when it handed over power to the black resistance which had been fighting a guerrilla war, Zimbabwe had experienced economic sanctions from the wider world, but covert support from the regime in South Africa. After 1980, Robert Mugabe's government was rather successful in its programmes for education, health and housing, adapting the good infrastructure of public services established for white citizens (many of whom emigrated in that decade) to the benefit of the whole population. But a number of misfortunes, including a drought in the early 1990s, forced his government to turn to the IMF for a loan. The conditions for this demanded cutbacks in education, health care, housing and welfare provision, and a switch from the gradual redistribution of land that was taking place. Most commentators would date Zimbabwe's slide into economic destitution, authoritarian rule and intercommunal conflict to that change in the direction of policy. As in Sri Lanka, the political balance between the ethnic groups in the country could not be sustained during the economic shock of market-orientated reforms and cuts in public spending.

Stiglitz's critique of the Washington Consensus contains many detailed examples of how the rigid application of the model to vulnerable economies caused political upheaval and institutional failure. It also added to the existing burden of debt; interest repayments acted as a strong constraint on the scope for policies for developing human capital, the precondition for a successful transition to the next stage of economic development.

We have seen that the newly industrializing countries of South and East Asia were able to make considerable space for improving human development within their version of the new model (chapter 1). However, the liberalization of trade, and especially of financial markets, left them more vulnerable to the movement of funds out of their countries during a temporary downturn, or on any evidence of fiscal problems. Speculation against the currency, and a flight of money held within the country, can set back social programmes. Gough's analysis of the East Asian financial crisis shows how this led to 'remorseless pressure' from international organizations to 'de-statise' economies and privatize services (Gough, 2004, pp. 199–200).

In South Korea, Taiwan, Malaysia and Thailand, rapid growth through export-orientated industrialization has not led to greater inequalities of income, despite the fact that, by international standards, they devote low proportions of public spending to benefits and pensions. Wages rose in line with gains in productivity, and land reforms contributed to a pattern of relatively equal earnings in the economy as a whole (following the example of Japan). Families provide the main basis for care of people with illnesses and disabilities, and in old age. But India, Indonesia and Brazil are very large countries, now in the forefront of industrialization worldwide, where rapid growth has not been accompanied by greater equality (World Bank, 2001, pp. 51–5). In China, too, inequality is growing along with national income and manufacturing output (see pp. 5–7).

New forms of income transfer in the USA

The scope for social policy programmes in the First World countries is also strongly constrained by financial markets, even though most Third World debt is held by banks and other institutions in these states. This is because of the domination of these economies by a combination of the financial and service sectors, and the division of populations into petty rentiers and service workers. This means that policies must be consistent with the interests of the financial sector and with commercial service providers. Especially in the USA and the UK the former make their income on their home territory through loans to individuals and households for the purchase of houses, cars and other large items, and through personal credit; the latter do so by developing supplies of low-wage, flexible labour power. So interest rates must be high enough to sustain the financial sector, and wages low enough to provide profits for service firms.

In the case of the US economy, the interest rate must also currently be high enough to attract loans from Japan and China (where savings rates of citizens are very high) to the US government in order to fund foreign policy activities – wars against 'failed states' and those who 'harbour terrorists' – and consumer spending, much of which goes on services. But successful redistributive measures must also be consistent with the second requirement of the economy – they must improve incentives to take work at the minimum wage, including irregular and part-time workers. The Reagan administration took office with the clear intention to cut both social security (contributory social insurance benefits) and Aid for Families with Dependent Children (AFDC). In 1981, it succeeded in removing some 500,000 households (mainly black lone parents) from the latter means-tested programme.

However, low-wage white workers were an important element in the electoral coalition mobilized by Reagan, especially in the Southern states (Pierson, 1994). His cuts and reforms did not touch Earned Income Tax Credits (EITCs). This was an innovation of the Nixon presidency in 1975, under which a 10 per cent tax credit on the first $4,000 earned and $400 minus 10 cents for every dollar earned between $4,000 and $8,000 was paid to *working* families with dependent children. Newman (2003) argues that this programme survived because it was a treasury and tax initiative, not a welfare benefit; because of political resistance and inertia; because the working poor were seen as deserving, and hence the measure as fair; and because of the strong institutional basis for its administration. However, its consistency with the interests of finance capital and service firms, because it provided a subsidy for flexible, low-wage work, seems more crucial. In effect, taxpayers were subsidizing firms who employed such workers.

For example, Wal-Mart is the largest company in the world, employing 1.5 million people, mainly low-paid women shop assistants in the USA. Wal-Mart does not allow its employees to join trade unions, but it gives them classes in how to apply for tax credits (BBC World Service, 2005b). A huge service corporation accepts a generous subsidy from the treasury on behalf of its shareholders.

This measure might be contrasted with the institutional system of the post-war era, in which social insurance systems complemented corporatism and industrial capitalism in two ways. Unemployment and industrial accident and sickness benefits sustained the human capital of the workforce (mainly male breadwinners) by giving them modest security of income during periods outside employment. They also ensured that unemployed people did not exert downward pressure on wage rates during recessions by competing for jobs at lower rates of pay (Solow, 1990). But neither of these features of social insurance systems fitted the new service economies of the USA and the UK. First in the former and then (since 1997) in the latter, tax credits have enabled women in particular to receive income support while doing 'non-standard contract' work.

Indeed, in the USA, while social assistance benefits were being remodelled by the Clinton administration in the 1990s, to make them more conditional and restrictive and to build in education and training for greater 'responsibility' (Waddan, 1997), EITC was expanded. By 1992 it included over 11 million families; in 1999 it cost $31 billion and assisted over 19 million. By then, the maximum payment per household was $3,756 and the range of earnings among claimants extended to $30,000 per year. It also embraced households without children. By the mid-1990s it redistributed twice as much as AFDC, and at much lower administrative costs.

Newman (2003) contends that this expansion of the scope for redistribution through EITC (and another scheme, Lifeline, for subsidized telephone services for low-income households) represents an example of Polanyi's (1944) 'double movement' in the dialectic between private property, market competition and free movement, on the one hand, and the protection of human values, groups and communities, on the other (see p. 2). In one sense this is an appropriate application of Polanyi's theory; during times when the political forces driving market liberalization were in the ascendant, as during the Washington Consensus worldwide, the 'second movement' had to find new ways of taking collective action to sustain social relationships and new institutional forms to utilize scope for social policies.

However, his characterization of these measures as 'stealth welfare' (the same term is used about the tax credit system in the UK) is slightly misleading. EITC and its New Labour equivalent are indeed Third Way instruments for accomplishing new versions of greater social justice and for protecting populations from poverty and exclusion. But they are not stealthy in the sense that they conceal the intentions of political leaderships. They use a new administrative device for the overt goal of promoting higher rates of participation in low-paid work and greater labour market flexibility (Standing, 1999, 2002). These programmes have been successful because they appeal to a key section of the electorate who want to avoid the stigma of claiming increasingly conditional, restricted and circumscribed social assistance benefits, and because they are highly compatible with the interests of the financial and service sectors.

The tax credit programme in the UK, introduced in 1997, has served the same purposes by the same means, and now has 5.1 million recipient households. It has ensured that all households with two children, earning up to an average salary, receive tax credits, and that those earning up to £21,200 pay no net tax (other than social insurance contributions). But it also means that all those in this group get only 30p per £ on additional earnings, as tax credits are withdrawn – see pp. 132–3 (Channel 4 TV, 2005a).

This can be contrasted with the political scope for redistributive measures in the continental European countries, and particularly

Germany. Because of the enduring institutions of 'social partnership' between federations of (mainly industrial) employers, trade unions and officials from the Department of Employment, the German institutional system has been slow to adapt to the new world order. It still gives priority to sustaining the (already high) wage levels of all workers, including those on the official minimum wage. It uses the social insurance scheme and labour market regulation to make rather generous transfers through benefits, and to try to police attempts to introduce 'informal flexibility'. It is only recently that, stung by criticisms of rigidities, and alarmed by rising unemployment, the government has both expanded schemes for recruiting 'flexible' supplies of workers from Central Europe (Vogel and Cyrus, 2003), and introduced programmes for the reintegration of those outside the workforce at lower costs to employers (Möhle, 2005).

Case study: social policy in Central Europe

After the collapse of the Soviet bloc in 1989, the post-communist countries of Central Europe (Poland, Hungary, the Czech Republic, Latvia, Lithuania, Estonia, Slovakia, and later the newly independent former Yugoslav state of Slovenia) embarked on their transitions to democracy and capitalism. They also applied to join the EU, a massive enlargement of the single market which eventually, in 2004, required major reforms of the latter's political and economic institutions. So the transformation of these countries' economies and societies was begun at a high point in the Washington Consensus, when privatization and rapid liberalization of trade and financial and labour markets were central features of the model for restructuring, and when cuts in food and fuel subsidies and other redistributive measures were integral to the reform strategy. Thus the transition took place at a moment in the history of social policy in which Polanyi's 'second movement' of resistance to market forces was very much on the defensive; many social and political forces in the post-communist countries, especially among young people, were also strongly favourable towards the principles of free movement, open societies and individual moral sovereignty.

However, as both Guy Standing (1996) and Bob Deacon (1997, ch. 4) show from their experiences of working in these countries during the transition, the balance of power between international organizations and economic interests at this time was delicate and complex. Because the post-communist states of Central Europe were applicants for membership of the EU, its official representatives had a good deal of influence on the processes of institutional transformation taking place. Through the protocols of the European Commission (EC), they were able to require the accession states to adopt many of the standards of the European Social Model, rather than moving straight to a more radical Washington Consensus version. The IMF was able to exert a more radical influence in Russia itself, with the consequences already noted (see pp. 74–6).

The clearest case of the influence of the European Social Model, obviously, was that of the former German Democratic Republic. Because reunification after the fall of the Berlin Wall made this state part of the Federal Republic, it immediately adopted the West German 'social partnership' institutions; its citizens were paid pensions and benefits on West German scales, and the slow process of retraining the workforce used the model from that country, in which high technical standards were inculcated, in preparation for industrial employment which no longer existed. Unemployment rates in the former GDR have consistently been double those of the former West Germany ever since, and the incorporation of the ailing economy of the communist state has been a factor in the Federal Republic's poor economic performance. It has been notable that new enterprises and new employment have been least evident in this area of Central Europe.

For the rest of the region, there were other factors which favoured the adoption of some aspects of the European Social Model. First, all these countries had been parts of the Austro-Hungarian empire, and there were traditions from the Hapsburg legacy which survived, at least in official cultures and some institutional structures. Second, it was in the interests of the existing EU member states to urge social insurance schemes as a kind of extension of their own. If the accession countries had no unemployment, industrial injury and sickness benefits, there could be 'social dumping' as their surplus workers offered themselves at lower wage rates, making their manufactures cheaper and attracting investment away from existing member states. Third, without adequate security, large numbers might choose to move to seek work in the existing Union, both irregularly before accession and later, when free movement was established. They might also turn back towards authoritarian politics. As the EC put it: 'Co-operation between the Union and the CEE countries on the social dimension of transition is essential to reduce the risk of the population rejecting democracy and the market economy because the social and human costs are too high' (European Commission, 1993, p. 70).

There was a third international actor in the struggle for influence over the transition process, the International Labour Organization

(ILO), a United Nations agency representing trade unionism and traditionally campaigning for employment security and social insurance benefits schemes. However, its representative in the region, Guy Standing, was convinced that the transition situation presented a unique opportunity for a new principle, citizens' or basic income. Instead of replacing guaranteed employment, food and housing subsidies by markets, underpinned by social security benefits, he argued that – following Van Parijs (1989) – a flexible, mobile and adaptable labour force would be more likely to emerge from restructuring if the old forms of income protection were rolled up into an unconditional guaranteed sum for all citizens, which would be there as security when they were in work or outside it. It would function as a kind of fusion of tax credits and social assistance benefits, and be withdrawn through the tax system (Standing, 1991, 1996). (The basic income principle is further discussed below – pp. 246–7 and 250–4.)

The tensions between these three different approaches to the redesign of social policy in Central Europe were played out slightly differently in each of the applicant countries (Deacon, 1997, ch. 4). In Poland, the largest in terms of population but not the most prosperous in terms of income per capita, the IMF model was adopted in relation to economic restructuring – 'shock therapy' in the adoption of financial markets, privatization and market reforms (the Balcerowicz Plan) – but the political reaction to this saw the return to power in 1995 of the former communists. In social policy, Poland introduced social insurance measures on the European model which, although they did not cover the whole population, protected many from the worst consequences of 'creative destruction'. However, by the early years of the new century, Poland had rates of unemployment (around 18 per cent) much higher than Germany's, as well as substantial numbers claiming social assistance (especially women, and families in rural areas and depressed regions). A similar pattern could be recognized in Slovakia, where market reforms were delayed under the populist President Mečiar, but softened by social insurance benefits when he was replaced by a more reformist coalition.

In social policy the lead-up to enlargement of the EU therefore produced some very messy compromises between the models recommended by the international organizations with a stake in the transition process. Reflecting on the outcomes in 2002, two World Bank economists compared the performance of these economies unfavourably with Russia's, focusing on the fact that the unemployment rate there was about half the average in the EU accession states. Russia's IMF-led emphasis on structural reforms has led to lower income tax and social contributions and hence, they argued, to a more employment-friendly enterprise environment and a more adaptable workforce. They also criticized the accession states for insufficient attention to 'activation' and conditionality of benefits (Aslund and Warner, 2002). These strictures rather overlooked the fact that the national incomes of Russia, Ukraine and most of the constituent republics of the former USSR were still below their 1989 level. And if the goal of policy was employment, even if citizens had to be coerced into low-wage work, how was this different from the Soviet system of compulsory labour contribution?

The case of the post-communist accession countries illustrates the fact that social policies have transnational implications. In the enlargement of the EU, the fifteen existing member states used their influence, through the Commission and its PHARE and TACIS programmes, to promote reforms which would prevent the new members' policies from undermining the European Social Model. Even so, the IMF and the World Bank had some success in making the outcome reflect a greater reliance on 'safety nets' (social assistance schemes) than in existing member states.

The UK, meanwhile, was seeking to cultivate a coalition of Southern European and post-communist states, both to promote a more market-orientated set of social policy reforms of the EU as a whole and in support of its backing for the USA over Iraq. Accordingly, at the point of enlargement in May 2004, the UK and Ireland were the only member states to allow virtually free movement of workers from the accession countries; Germany and Austria led the rest in postponing the implementation of this basic right, much to the resentment of the new member states. In Central Europe, as in the rest of the world, affluent countries are able to protect their citizens more effectively than poor ones. They have greater scope to delay the impact of global competition and to use the earnings from their financial sectors to bolster failing institutional systems until new ones can be implemented. But this has not prevented the issue of free trade in services becoming an important one in referenda over the post-enlargement EU constitution (see p. 188).

Conclusions

The pitfalls for governments of the affluent states of being the bases for the 'headquarters of capitalism' are varied. In the USA, citizens used the expansion of personal credit in the 1990s to buy stocks and shares; when Wall Street prices fell heavily in the early years of the century, this left millions worse off. In the UK, the financial sector has funded an enormous boom in house prices, as mortgage lending grew in response to the fall in share prices. Although the Bank of England appears in early 2005 to have slowed this inflation in the housing market by its interest rate policies, the number of first-time buyers able to afford homes reached a new low in 2004; prices were out of their range, in relation to average earnings, in over 90 per cent of districts in the UK (BBC Radio 4, 2005e).

The industrial sectors in the affluent countries rely on innovation, research and development for their profits. New technology and new uses fuel product replacements which constantly seek an edge over competitors, as DVDs replace VHS tapes, or iPods replace personal stereos. Money flows into companies which promise high returns through such breakthroughs, as it did into the whole information technology sector in the USA and the UK in the early 1990s; it equally quickly deserts them if they fail to deliver on their promises or are overtaken by rivals. Now that mass production has been relocated in the newly industrializing countries, this speeded-up version of the dynamics of creative destruction in the struggle for competitive advantage is built into this part of affluent states' economies.

The overall effect of the new division of labour, credit and debt in the world economy is to make individuals and households reliant more on their own resources and less on the direct policies and provision of governments. This was intended by the new model which informed the Washington Consensus. If the choices of individuals were co-ordinated by impersonal market forces, it was argued, resources would be more efficiently used and global welfare enhanced. However, because of the opaque role of financial intermediaries, individuals and households are often left to make decisions which determine their life chances, but without the knowledge or control necessary to do this rationally. For example, farmers in Sri Lanka or Indonesia, forced to borrow money at high interest rates to produce for competitive markets, cannot tell in advance whether the risks involved are worth taking.

Not all the affluent countries have generated cultures of personal debt, aspirations of property ownership or private markets in retirement incomes. For example, the private savings rate in Japan is far higher than that in the USA, the UK or Australia. But a decade of economic stagnation has left citizens vulnerable because of high expectations of material opulence, in personal consumption if not in housing. Since the financial crisis of 1997–8, the suicide rate in Japan has been over 30,000 a year, mainly men in financial trouble (BBC Radio 4, 2005f). In the continental European countries there is less home ownership and private pension and share purchase than in the

Anglophone countries. But young people take far longer to complete their education, are slower to get a foot on a career ladder, and have a shorter working life. The system of social insurance benefits, a source of stability and security hitherto, is now under criticism and faces restructuring.

Section 1C

Commercial Provision of Social Services

5

The Global Market in Services – Health Care

The previous section examined the constraints on redistributive social policies, both within and between states. In a global economy in which money flows freely between countries (speeded by electronic transfer facilities), financial institutions invest worldwide and firms have production sites in many states; governments are accountable to capital markets. In the affluent First World, governments are also accountable to electorates in which many work in the financial sector, or have incomes from stakes in it. In the developing world, governments must exercise prudence, demonstrating a viable 'business plan' to international organizations (IDA, 2001), aim to attract foreign investment, and produce what world markets demand.

This emphasis on the constraints on national governments, and especially on welfare states, has been characteristic of social policy analysis in the 1990s and beyond. Since the beginning of the Washington Consensus around 1980 and the collapse of state socialism, ideas of social citizenship, extending social rights, equality and justice, have waned because they seemed to presuppose the power of national governments to determine the allocation of resources of all kinds within their borders. Globalization empowered international financial intermediaries and multinational firms; it disempowered governments, so the argument goes (Scharpf and Schmidt, 2000a). They still had influence over less mobile factors of production (labour power and land), so they could make choices about how to develop and deploy human capital (Hemerijk, 2001) and territory. In a predominantly service economy, they could focus on any two of the three priorities of budgetary restraint, equality of incomes or employment growth, but not all three at once (Iversen and Wren, 1998).

All this has put social policy analysis, as an academic discipline, on the back foot, making its normative stance an essentially conservative one. As conveyed in Newman's (2003) analysis of 'stealth welfare' in the USA (pp. 78–9), it has made government action to offset inequalities and marginalizations among citizens part of Polanyi's (1944) 'second movement' in defence of communal organizations and values. The implication is that progressive policies for social justice are, at best, biding their time, waiting for a more propitious moment to reassert their claims on electorates and political parties.

In this chapter I shall investigate the claim that this analysis misrepresents the true picture. Influential Third Way thinkers such as Tony Giddens (1998) and Perri 6 (2003) support the arguments of Tony Blair (1998) that social justice is best served by going with the logic of global markets, and adopting national and international policies which *promote* the interests and strategies of multinational companies. Just as the US and UK governments now back the global plans of pharmaceutical and biotech firms, arguing that new drugs and GM crops will increase global welfare and improve the situation of the poorest, so also they support the involvement of private finance and private service corporations in public services. Starting with telecommunications and the public utilities, and extending into railways and air traffic systems, this approach now embraces education, health and social care systems. Where outright privatization is deemed inappropriate, 'partnership' with private financial intermediaries or providers is the preferred initiative.

I shall show that this is not simply a way of extending the scope for funding new hospitals, schools and care homes, or of making efficiency savings in how they are run. It is a far more concerted effort to tailor the long-term trajectory of domestic social policy to the strategies of those financial interests and service corporations on the world market. Because the General Agreement on Trade in Services (GATS) promises to open up all these for competition worldwide, the cultivation of resources and experience in these sectors within the domestic economy puts the leaders in this field (the USA and the UK) in favourable positions in the global market. The scope for social policy innovation at home is intended to be greatly enlarged by the earnings of these firms, taking over education, health and social care services abroad, and especially in the developing world. Those countries which establish a critical mass of such companies will become the predators of GATS competition; those that do not will become the prey (Jordan and Düvell, 2003, chs. 2 and 4).

In order to pursue these policies, Third Way governments in the USA and the UK have been required to redefine social justice and equality in new terms. This will be discussed in chapter 9. They have also restructured their services to enable citizens to express their individual preferences through the 'choice agenda' – see chapter 8. But in addition they have had to reconceptualize the goals of social policy in line with globalization. The scope for improving the welfare of their citizens is enhanced by linking it to the fortunes of service corporations abroad whose headquarters are in their territories. Just as citizens' incomes rely, in whole or part, on dividends from investments in the industrial sectors of the newly industrializing countries (see pp. 76–7), they will also be enlarged by the dividends from running formerly public services there and in the poorest states.

In the light of this whole strategic orientation to trade in services, it is possible to make sense of President George W. Bush's emphasis on 'freedom' in his inaugural speech of 3 February 2005. The goal of opening up statist and protectionist regimes in the Middle East, Africa and Latin America, while nominally concerned with democracy and good governance, is at least equally about promoting the GATS agenda, and with it opportunities for capitalist development of their public infrastructures. Indeed, the toppling of Saddam Hussein in Iraq was motivated at least partly by the goal of creating a model state in that region, which exemplifies the advantages of a fully open set of infrastructural services. Iraq was supposed to supply this opportunity, first by the post-war reconstruction process (contracted out almost exclusively to US-based companies), and then through the privatization of all the rest of its resources and services.

But there is a problematic relationship between the two elements in the strategy, democratization and privatization. If all the public infrastructure is provided by private firms, and some is funded by private finance, how does this affect the autonomy of national governments and the scope for social policy choices? What powers does it give to electorates in decisions about public services and redistribution? The Agreement gives nominal safeguards to governments over protecting the pace and reach of openness; but once competition is permitted the process is irreversible. Democratic elections cannot alter the decision to open a service, whatever the consequences (Gould and Joy, 2000).

I shall trace the origins of the GATS to show that – right from the start of the negotiations to bring it into being – governments acted in concert with big business and global finance. The original sponsors were not just the USA and the UK, but also the member states of the European Union. France, for example, considered that it had much to gain from bidding to provide the material infrastructures of other states; the EU as a whole reckoned that it was the largest exporter of services worldwide (Hatcher, 2002, p. 13; Bertrand and Kalafatides, 2002, p. 206). All the affluent First World countries recognized in the GATS an opportunity to link domestic social policy with the strategies of global corporate businesses, gaining advantage in new world markets. In this chapter I shall focus on health services, in the next on education.

This analysis therefore complements the explanations of the global dynamics of economic and human development in chapters 1 and 2. Services are central to human development, as we have seen (pp. 23–5). Redistributive policies are constrained by the requirement of good returns for highly mobile funds, which pay incomes mainly to citizens of the affluent states (pp. 75–7). The GATS links up the development of human capacities in the newly industrializing and developing countries with the global strategies of firms in the service sector. It also feeds into the strategies of educated and skilled professional staff of services in the Second and Third Worlds, because those corporations recruit extensively from their labour markets for employees in the affluent countries. Thus what were originally the social services integral to the welfare-state model of citizenship (national systems of sharing in a culture of democratic participation and membership) become instead the means for mobility between regions of the world for some skilled workers, and for profitable activity by international capitalist organizations.

The origins of the GATS

Although the GATS was not signed until 1994, and is still in the early stages of implementation, its origins can be traced to events in the late 1970s, when the new model of the global economy, based on neo-classical economic theory, was beginning to influence governments. Far from being an afterthought of the Washington Consensus programme, or a belated addition to the strategic repertoire of multinational corporations, it was part of the very long trajectory of plans for liberalization and privatization by the international financial community, and had been on its agenda from the start of its programme.

In 1979, the heads of American Express, Citicorp and AIG (the leading insurance group in the USA) started to campaign for the inclusion of services in the next round of negotiations for the General Agreement on Tariffs and Trade (GATT). These financial giants sought allies outside their sector, and found them throughout the commercial services. The Coalition of Service Industries (CSI) emphasized the growing importance of services in First World economies, their contribution to skills among the workforce, and their relevance for labour productivity in the economy as a whole (Bertrand and Kalafatides,

2002, p. 203). Reports from the CSI, the international chambers of commerce and the Organization for Economic Co-operation and Development (OECD) all emphasized the role of trade in services in growth and development; the US Treasury established a special agency, the Interagency Task Force on Services and Multilateral Trade Negotiations, stressing the new knowledge economy, information technology and the priority for services in multilateral agreements on the lowering of barriers to free movement (ibid., pp. 203–4).

These initiatives were rebuffed by India and Brazil, in particular, on behalf of the developing countries. By campaigning to isolate the leading radical nations in this group, including Egypt, Nicaragua, Cuba, Tanzania and Yugoslavia, the sponsor countries succeeded in getting trade included in the Uruguay Round of negotiations under the GATT. The CSI sought to introduce a 'commercial presence' into government activities and the public sector generally, so that multinational service corporations could win contracts as suppliers; the developing countries resisted, fearing their service industries and public infra-structures would remain underdeveloped and that they would never become exporters of services. In the bargaining process, the affluent states argued that developing economies could benefit from the recruit-ment of their workforces into transnational firms, and hence from the free movement of staff worldwide (Bertrand and Kalafatides, 2002, p. 209). In 1993, US and European chambers of commerce and con-federations of industry strongly backed the final negotiations; the GATT pressed through the new Agreement on Services, eventually signed on Marrakech on behalf of 124 countries, establishing both the World Trade Organization (WTO) and the GATS.

However, the compromises reflected in the Agreement did not satisfy the business lobby, and its representatives sought continuously to modify the terms in their interests. In particular, while offering assurances about governments' powers to protect sensitive parts of their political and social infrastructures, they used their influence to reduce this sphere to a minimum. Nowhere in the text of the Agreement did the expression 'public services' appear, not because these were outside its scope, but in order to deny the valid existence of such a category (Bertrand and Kalafatides, 2002, p. 214). The definition of those services excluded by its terms was that they were 'provided through the exercise of government power' and without participation of any other type of provider (Sinclair, 2000), giving the WTO substantial discretion in defining these, in addition to substantial disciplinary powers in relation to the services listed for lib-eralization. The EU agreed to include education at every level, profes-sional training, hospital services and social services, for 'progressive liberalization', with periodic renegotiations for effective access to markets, under the sanction of a right for commercial firms to sue for compensation if this was not granted (European Commission, 1994).

WTO documents argued that the health-care sector represented a brake on economic growth, and could contribute to expansion if commercial (and specifically international) firms were given access. They also discussed the potential for treating Asian Pacific patients in India, and moving Indian doctors to that region. Gains in efficiency and productivity became the driving logic of new initiatives in this sector; nurses and midwives trained in Jamaica were migrating in large numbers to the USA and Canada, but the WTO argued that they could be replaced by staff from Nigeria, Ghana and Burma. Private-sector provision expanded in the affluent countries, despite studies revealing that its costs were higher than those of the public sector (Woolhandler and Himmelstein, 1999; Fédération des Infirmières et Infirmiers du Quebec, 2000).

By the conclusion of the next round of negotiations in 2000, international companies had gained a substantial foothold in all these states. The GATS rules stipulated that, once a sector was included in the process of liberalization, these firms must be treated on the same basis as local private and public enterprises, and the numbers of providers and foreign staff must not be limited.

Issues are further complicated, in the case of health care, by the question of patents and intellectual property rights (Correa, 2002). The global pharmaceutical corporations use patents strategically to protect its profits on new drugs and to block or delay competition from the products of rival companies. Governments seek to identify new treatments which provide the least costly interventions; those of developing countries try to counter the restrictive strategies of the pharmaceutical giants. The WTO's Agreement on Trade-Related Aspects of Intellectual Property Rights (TRIPS) regulates this aspect of exchange and licensing. It is specially relevant for countries with a tradition of active clinical involvement by pharmacists outside the medical system, such as Korea (Kwon, 2002). These aspects will be analysed in the later sections of the chapter.

Throughout the world, the globalization and commercialization of health care were therefore promoted by a coalition of transnational financial and service interests, under the auspices of the WTO and World Bank. As I shall show in this section, the consequences were highly profitable for these banks and corporations, but contributed substantially to debt among governments in the developing countries and among individuals everywhere. Given the crucial importance of health and education to human development and well-being (see pp. 23–5), and the substantial progress made by government policies and public services in many poor states, how were such programmes justified, and why have they been accepted with relatively little resistance by electorates worldwide?

The transformation of health care: extreme measures

In this section, I shall show how the public health-care system was liberalized and 'reformed' in two countries, China and Argentina, which give contrasting case studies, but both illustrate the extremes of these processes. In the case of China, this transformation was initiated by the state authorities and involved mainly internal reforms of its system. In that of Argentina, the changes were triggered by the financial and fiscal crisis of the state, which in turn was a consequence of the restructuring required by the IMF and the World Bank; they were responses to external forces, acting on the Argentinian economy. What they have in common is that both followed market principles and both involved citizens in having to contribute much more to the costs of their care.

As we saw in the introduction (pp. 23–4), the Chinese communist government of Mao Tse-tung achieved considerable success in improving the life-expectancy and general health of the population in the 1950s and 1960s. This was an example of 'support-led' human development (Sen, 1999) which was not accompanied by rapid economic growth. Mao's successors, in turning to a growth-led strategy based on export-orientated manufacturing (pp. 5–7), also chose to switch from basic, labour-intensive approaches (barefoot doctors), supplied through local co-operative systems, to one based on payments by patients. State spending on health-care provision as a proportion of GDP fell from 0.11 per cent in 1978 to 0.04 per cent in 1993 (Zhu, 2000, p. 45). Only 14 per cent of total medical expenditure in hospitals comes from the public purse; the rest is paid by patients (Xing, 2002, p. 248).

Although the shift towards fee-charging and commercial provision was urged by the World Bank from the early 1980s, we have seen that the Chinese authorities would have been able to resist such pressures had they chosen to do so (pp. 34–5). Their adoption of the model must therefore be seen in the context of the authorities' strategy for dividing Chinese society between a largely state-socialist rural sector and a capitalist, industrialized, urban coastal fringe (see pp. 5–6), but without the support-led infrastructure of the Maoist period. The end of the rural communal system coincided with the dissolution of health-care collectives, doing mainly preventive work, and state responsibility for funding treatment. Obviously, the adverse effects have been felt most strongly in poor rural provinces, and in the countryside generally.

Under the new, divided system, about 80 per cent of doctors live in the cities, but a similar percentage of patients live in the countryside (Xing, 2002, p. 250). As the state has withdrawn from health-care provision in the rural areas, more than 700,000 former collectively funded clinics have become privately owned (UNDP, 1999, p. 17). Whereas 85 per cent of the rural population was covered by the old system of health-care finance, only 10 per cent are now. The same report found that 83.5 per cent of villages with 88.4 per cent of the population had to pay for health care out of their own pockets (ibid., p. 37, table 3.8). Even the official party newspaper acknowledged that 'Over 37 per cent of Chinese rural people could not afford to go to see doctors, with another 65 per cent of sick farmers not having access to hospitals, a 1998 official investigation revealed' (*People's Daily*, 2001).

These inequitable impacts were further exacerbated by the rising use and cost of drugs; the cost of these and diagnostic tests increased by 11 per cent a year in real terms from 1986 to 1993 (Xing, 2002, p. 250). The pharmaceutical industry has expanded rapidly to become the fifth largest in China in terms of output and profits, and there has been foreign investment of over $1 billion in this sector (about 1,500 enterprises) (Saywell, 1999, p. 46). A far higher proportion of total health-care spending – over 50 per cent – went on drugs, compared with 14 to 40 per cent in other developing economies (Tomlinson, 1997, p. 835). The interests of the industry are served by this skewed pattern of spending.

Because there are so few doctors in rural areas, and there is also a tradition of self-medication, an unregulated market has resulted in ill-informed use of these products among poor people. Adverse side-effects and inappropriate treatments have been reported, as well as unnecessary expenditures (Zhan et al., 1997). Expensive Western medical equipment has also been purchased by hospitals (Lipson and Pemble, 1992) and used both to diagnose and treat rich patients and to raise revenue for hospitals through fees.

In the case of China, cutting back public provision for health care and promoting the pharmaceutical sector were parts of an overall programme for private-sector expansion and foreign investment-led growth. The authorities were proactive in transforming the institutions of the health-care system in order to reinforce (rather than offset) liberalization and privatization. In the case of Argentina, a more developed economy with a manufacturing sector and a long tradition of exporting food to world markets, the process of transformation has been quite different, and the outcomes even more extreme.

The whole government sector in Argentina was restructured under the conditions of an IMF loan in 1987. Unemployment and sickness benefits were cut and the social insurance pension scheme transformed into a commercial system. The new structures gave priority to the interests of finance capital, encouraged foreign investment, and sought to attract multinational companies into sectors previously controlled by the government (Iriart et al., 2002, p. 246). As part of these reforms, multinationals penetrated the health-care service, as they did in many other Latin American countries (Stocker et al., 1999), ending the right to such provision for all citizens, introducing market principles, and focusing government support on the very poor. The rest were increasingly expected to pay for their own treatment.

After the second fiscal and financial crisis in 1998 (p. 73), the PAMI – a scheme for social-insurance-funded health care for retired citizens – was unable to fund any further treatments. In the country as a whole (with over 25 per cent unemployment rates) many lost access to care of any kind because they could not afford insurance. Even among the insured, co-payment fees made more expensive treatments beyond the range of accessible interventions. As a result, Argentina experienced epidemics of illnesses such as cholera, leptospirosis, dengue, hanta virus and typhus, which had been eradicated. Measles led to increased rates of infant mortality (Iriart et al., 2002, pp. 245–6).

New commercial provision involved increased returns to investors and managers; these, plus promotional costs, made up 20 per cent of health expenditures. Co-payments amounted to 41 per cent of all outlays on care (Iriart et al., 2001). The total context of the Argentinian economy since the crisis has been a collapse of all institutions, including government and the currency (doctors are paid – if at all – in bonds issued by provincial governments). The underlying vicious circle is that foreign debt, which caused the original crisis in the 1980s, has grown rather than diminished since then. Reliance on foreign companies merely worsens the problem. Rising interest rates and borrowing mean that repayments take up 17.5 per cent of current government spending. Giving priority to meeting these payments has meant higher taxes (21 per cent on all sales), lower salaries and cuts in services. Each rescheduling of the debt has increased the overall burden and involved greater sacrifices by citizens (Husson, 2002).

Argentina illustrates the extreme case of how the Washington Consensus model and the interests of finance capital have destroyed a system of health care (and all other welfare-state institutions). Although government corruption has increased the suffering of the population, this has often involved the collusion of financial intermediaries, as in the case of the debt rescheduling organized by the president of the First Boston Bank (Husson, 2002). The strategies of multinational health-care corporations have taken advantage of the opportunities of these catastrophes and profited from them. The introduction of co-payments from citizens – or, more commonly, of a fee-based private care system – was not the result of an equitable division of the costs between those giving social and those providing private benefit (see pp. 113–16). They simply followed the logic of profit and competitive advantage among service producers.

Health service restructuring and world poverty

The Washington Consensus model and its modified successor, the World Bank Development Programme, are clear about the links in the process of restructuring and reform, leading from increased market competition, through greater efficiency, to growth of incomes and improved health. Higher national income will produce better health services, but not through greater government involvement. On the contrary, more participation by commercial investors and service providers will remove barriers to overall economic expansion, as well as improving performance in the health-care system. Poor populations benefit, both because of the general rise in incomes per head, and because resources for health provision can be focused on those who are most vulnerable.

For this model to work in the ways claimed for it, international financial organizations should co-operate with governments, both over the reforms necessary to attract investment for overall growth and in regulating the health-care sector so as to combine commercial initiatives most effectively with state programmes. The outcomes of this co-ordination should be reflected in overall statistics, such as life-expectancy rates, infant mortality figures, and access by poor people to services. Under the World Bank's Development Programme, a set of institutions now provide the framework for co-ordination and measurements of this kind. First, developing countries' governments seeking loans from the World Bank are required to submit Poverty Reduction Strategy Papers, in which they demonstrate that their plans for restructuring and growth are combined with fiscal prudence, good governance, resilient revenue sources, and social policies which favour their poor citizens (IDA, 2001). These papers usually contain general statements on health policy, normally from their ministries of finance rather than from health ministries themselves (Dodd, 2002, pp. 344–5).

In addition to these mechanisms, there is an International Finance Corporation (IFC), which is part of the World Bank Group, promoting private-sector development through financing projects in developing countries and helping private companies in these countries to access finance in international markets. One part of its work specifically addresses health care (IFC, 2002). The performance of these countries is then monitored by organizations such as the United Nations Children's Fund (UNICEF), the United Nations Administrative Committee on Co-operation – Subcommittee on Nutrition (ACC/SCN), and the World Health Organization (WHO).

The reports of all these agencies allow a picture of the consequences of the model to be drawn. In this section, I shall look at how the involvement of private finance and service companies has influenced the restructuring of services in some of the poorest countries, and how governments in turn have responded to the promptings of the World Bank and the activities of the commercial sector. This should answer the question of whether the combined strategies of governments and the private health sector have indeed improved the health of poor people as part of the World Bank's overall plan.

In a review of ten Poverty Reduction Strategy Papers (PRSPs), from Bolivia, Burkina Faso, Mauritania, Mozambique, Nicaragua, Tanzania, Uganda, Ghana, Cambodia and Vietnam, the WHO found that their health components (with the exception of that from Bolivia) were not drawn up in collaboration with parliamentarians, local governments or civil society groups and had limited participation by health officials. They presented analyses of the health problems of their poorest citizens, but not of the impact of co-payment systems, costs of travelling to clinics, or the economic impact of illness on earnings. Although they reported planned increases in government spending (from very low baselines), they did not analyse how these would overcome existing biases against poor patients in the provision of services or contribute to the development of co-ordinated pro-poor national health policies. They failed to tackle the issues of how health care could reduce poverty by improving the capabilities of their most disadvantaged citizens; they did not analyse how this aspect of a human development strategy could contribute to their strategy for economic growth, or how aspects of the latter which damaged the health of the poor could be mitigated. Indeed, this largely reflected the model of the World Bank's Development Plan, by seeing improved health as a by-product of growth rather than an integral part of such a strategic approach. Health was treated as a cost and a limit on productive potential, rather than a way of enhancing performance (Dodd, 2002).

Some of the reasons for this shortcoming in the PRSPs' analyses become clear from the reports of the IFC's Health Care Policy Committee on the development of markets and the private health-care sector in the developing countries. These recognize that the main problems faced in the poorest of them are an increase in infectious diseases (some of which had disappeared), HIV/AIDS, a rise in the elderly population and escalating costs. But, as a part of the World Bank, the IFC sees its main role as being to finance commercial initiatives which protect the middle class against health risks. Accordingly, the IFC focuses on private insurance schemes, along with private management of public services and private provision. Its own investments during the 1990s were mainly in larger hospitals and pharmaceuticals. In Africa, these were limited, chiefly to new or extended hospitals and individual practitioners; in Latin America, investments were far more extensive, and included whole managed care systems, often in the face of the collapse of public provision (see pp. 96–8). In Asia, investments are mainly of high-tech and hospital care projects, and health-care companies (Lethbridge, 2002, pp. 350–1).

These patterns of funding reveal the economic logic behind the World Bank Plan in relation to health. The IFC expects a reliable return of about 5 per cent on its investments, comparable with those to US companies in their domestic markets. African countries are too poor and insecure to supply many such prospects; there are more opportunities in Latin America. The strong bias towards high technology, including pharmaceutical companies, does not address the main health problems acknowledged to exist in the developing world. Instead, the IFC offers finance capital in affluent countries opportunities for profits and middle-class citizens in poor countries more choice and scope for improved private facilities. The assumption is that this leaves governments with more resources to co-ordinate overall health policy and to focus its provision on the most vulnerable groups. But there is no evidence that this is happening, or that private health providers are effective in meeting the most pressing needs. Nor does it address issues such as the funding of traditional practitioner services (Lethbridge, 2002).

The consequences of the lack of co-operation between the strategies of commercial interests and those of government ministries are reflected in the worsening health status of the majority of citizens in many of the poorest countries, especially those of sub-Saharan Africa (Sanders, 2002). The background to these statistics is one of economic decline and civil strife. In twenty-eight of the forty-eight countries in that region, the average per capita income was less than $1 per day in 2000. This compares with nineteen of thirty-six countries (because of border changes) in 1981. Along with civil wars, the HIV/AIDS pandemic has been a major factor in this worsening of the plight of the poorest countries. Africans form 70 per cent of the infected world population, about 28 million people. Overall, the population in seven of the forty-eight countries had a lower life-expectancy than in 1970, and in seventeen it was lower than in 1981 (UNICEF, 2000). Infant mortality rates decreased less in sub-Saharan Africa than the rest of the world, and young child malnutrition worsened significantly in the region (ACC/SCN, 2000). Access to immunization improved in the 1980s, but declined in the 1990s (UNICEF, 2000). There was a resurgence of communicable diseases, such as cholera, tuberculosis, malaria, yellow fever and trypanosomiasis (Sanders, 2000).

The structural adjustment programmes of the World Bank throughout this period have forced governments to give priority to liberalization and enterprise at the expense of health care, seen as a drain on resources for potential growth. Debt repayments have taken precedence over social services, and especially health care. In retrospect, these programmes have damaged human development and well-being: 'The majority of studies in Africa, whether theoretical or empirical, are negative towards structural adjustment and its effects on health outcomes' (Breman and Shelton, 2001).

One area of progress has been that of the purchase of drugs, especially those for HIV/AIDS treatments. Under the leadership of Nelson Mandela, in 1997 the developing countries made arrangements for importing these at lower prices than the pharmaceutical companies were seeking to charge. At the Doha meeting of the WTO in 2001, these arrangements were ratified as legal under the terms of TRIPS, despite attempts by the US government to pressure the South African government to rescind its commitments. This sequence of events showed that the developing countries could, if they acted together, achieve better terms in their relations with health-related corporations. It also demonstrated that the US administration backed the strategies of financial and business interests in the developing world, regardless of their impact on the most vulnerable populations.

Assessing the impact of all these forces on health in sub-Saharan Africa, Sanders (2002, p. 258) detects a general decline, especially among the poor. For example, full vaccination of one-year-old children rose dramatically in the 1980s worldwide, more slowly in sub-Saharan Africa; it declined slightly in the world as a whole in the 1990s (from 75 to 72 per cent), but in that region from 58 to 51 per cent (UNICEF, 2000). The priority given to new technologies and hospital care, rather than to services reaching broader populations, is a product of the neo-liberal model, which has had a very adverse effect on Africa in particular.

Conclusions

These negative consequences of the penetration of commercial interests into public health provision may exaggerate the dangers of GATS and privatization. The examples given in this chapter dwell on the opening up of markets in direct health-care services, or insurance systems in which better-off individuals are enabled to leave public schemes. But an alternative is to reform existing systems, especially those – as in the continental European tradition – in which health care is covered as part of social insurance, for which all employees pay out of contributions made jointly with employers and governments, as deductions from salaries. These schemes reflect the post-war welfare-state approach to the collectivization of risks and costs, which would otherwise fall most heavily on those least able to pay.

In an unregulated market in health insurance, companies will offer high-premium policies to those who can be ascertained to be high-risk customers and low-premium policies to those who are apparently low-risk (Rothschild and Stiglitz, 1976). This 'cream-skimming' is the phenomenon which in the USA has led to a publicly financed scheme for the poorest and left a sizeable proportion of the population without any cover, because they (or their employers) cannot afford private plans.

The solution to this problem adopted in countries such as Germany and Switzerland has been state regulation of health insurance schemes, which requires all of them that form part of the social-insurance-funded system to offer uniform premiums and take members from a full spread of ascertainable risks. Although the aim is to achieve equity through risk pooling, this is not always attained. For example, a healthy young low-wage worker may be subsidizing an unhealthy but rich older entrepreneur or manager who makes frequent use of services. Furthermore, there are few incentives or opportunities for schemes to improve efficiency (for instance, by offering members reductions in premiums if they take steps to improve their health).

An alternative approach to 'managed competition' between health insurers (Enthoven, 1986) would be to allow schemes to offer differential premiums on the basis of perceived risks, but then to compensate members (especially those who become ill and need treatment) if they cannot afford to pay these premiums (Van de Ven and Ellis, 2000;

Zweifel and Breuer, forthcoming). This would improve efficiency in a number of ways. It would allow companies to develop specialized schemes for particular risks; it would give customers incentives to seek out the schemes which offered the best terms for their risks or conditions; and it would enable companies to offer incentives for preventive or ameliorative actions by members. Thus a means-tested transfer system which subsidized health insurance premiums to the extent that they exceeded a certain proportion of household income (but not so much as to remove the incentive to seek the best option) is recommended for optimum efficiency (Zweifel and Breuer, forthcoming).

The issue of fairness is more complex. An unsubsidized high-risk customer on a modest income would have to pay higher premiums by virtue of an unfavourable health endowment. But, conversely, a rich high-risk customer is, as already noted, subsidized under current schemes. Hence the advocates of this approach regard it as no less equitable than existing systems, and capable of delivering more efficient health care at the same cost. But they do acknowledge that it might still be necessary to have a state-funded residual insurance scheme for very high risks (Herring and Pauly, 2001).

This in turn raises the question of how public and commercial systems can be combined in the best ways. In the examples from the developing world given in this chapter, they had not been, because privatization led better-off people to leave public health systems (and hence reduced political pressure to improve provision), while commercial companies supplied services which did not benefit those most in need of preventive and low-tech interventions (hospital treatments rather than public hygiene and health-promotion activities). In the next chapter, I shall consider whether there are any general principles which can distinguish the proper roles of the state as a regulator, funder and provider of these services, with special reference to education.

6

The Business Agenda in Education

In this chapter, I shall analyse the wider motives of business corporations in becoming involved in education policy. I shall also examine the theoretical basis for 'co-payments' by citizens for education and other services, and how governments might seek to balance the public and private benefits of the acquisition of knowledge and skills.

The education system was central to the success of the East Asian 'productivist' economies which achieved fast growth of per capita incomes and of human development indicators in the 1980s and 1990s. It was also an important factor in the 'supply-side' emphasis of those who recommended that adaptable and flexible labour forces were more important than the management of 'aggregate demand' in labour market policies. Under the Washington Consensus, improved education was therefore a legitimate priority for governments, and this was even more strongly emphasized in Third Way models of the 'social investment state' (Giddens, 1998). Commercial interests have a direct stake in the sphere of education. Schools, colleges and universities provide much of the human capital that employees bring to the companies which hire them. Business has sought to influence what is taught and the balance between the different elements in the curriculum; it has also aimed to shift the culture of education away from citizenship and social relations, towards enterprise, technology and the 'hard sciences'. All this is in addition to the multinational corporate involvement identified in the above analysis of the health sector.

In education, too, the fact that private sectors existed in all countries gave the GATS scope for including this sector in its liberalization programme. WTO papers presented the 'knowledge market' as in urgent need of modernization and reform. US corporations such as Cantor, Edison, School Inc., Jones International and Sylvan International Universities set out to capture a dominant share of what was claimed to be the $2,000 billion world budget, 5 per cent of global GDP (Edinvest, 2000); for the 2000 WTO negotiations, they combined to form the National Committee for International Trade in Education (NCITE). These initiatives coincided with national policy measures, urged by the World Bank, to make students and their families bear a bigger share of the costs of higher education (Edinvest, 1999).

Having required governments of the developing countries in the 1980s to cut their spending on education, they now argued that they should expand this sector, but involve international companies. This applied especially in India, Latin America and Africa, where its agency, Edinvest, was sponsored by the Alliance for Global Learning, an e-education organization comprising J. P. Morgan, Goldman Sachs, Ernst and Young and Sun Microsystem, among others (Martin and Schumann, 2000). All this prompted Bertrand and Kalafatides to ask whether the WTO was becoming the planetary ministry of education (2002, pp. 241–4).

In Europe and the UK, governments have adopted many of the principles of the business agenda in their 'modernization' of schools and universities. The language of the 'knowledge economy', the 'higher education market' and the 'social investment state' (Giddens, 1998) is now adopted. Information technology has provided a commercial opportunity and an entrée for corporations into education systems (Bertrand and Kalafatides, 2002, pp. 238–9). A sectoral lobby group, the European Round Table, headed by the president of the Anglo-Dutch company Reed-Elsevier, and with a former president of GATT as its chairman of the working group on exterior economic relations, has campaigned for a leading role for industry in education and training (ibid.): 'A profound reform of education systems in Europe is needed. . . . Greater emphasis must be placed on *entrepreneurship at all levels of education*' (ERT, 1998, p. 18; emphasis in original).

At the same time, a similar set of priorities and programmes was being set out by Asia-Pacific Economic Co-operation (APEC), the organization of eighteen Pacific Rim countries, including the USA, Japan and China. In a paper prepared for the APEC meeting of 1997, the Ministry of Labour of the South Korean government argued that education was far too important for economic purposes to be left to 'intellectual elites'. Business interests should form partnerships with schools which allow them to 'take part in curriculum development pertinent to their industry to make the curriculum realistic to the needs of industry'. The schools culture should equip students for the work environment, develop a work ethic suitable for their employment careers, and give them a skills-based achievement record, to help employers select

and recruit suitable workers. There should be more emphasis on voca-
tion and technical subjects and colleges (Kuehn, 1997).

Clearly both business leaderships and governments recognize that
there is global competition of several kinds involved in these issues.
Both the European Commission (1996) and APEC argue that an
enterprise-orientated and skills-based system will confer key advantages on its national economy, because of the knowledge and technical
component in productivity in advanced affluent countries. It will facilitate the rapid restructuring of the economy, and hence its adaptability
in the face of change. Competition between business corporations for
partnerships with schools and local government departments is good
for business, and for the country's economic performance. And the corporate sector can gain important experience and critical mass to
prepare firms for global competition in world markets for education
under GATS. Overall, the business agenda running schools and colleges *as* businesses, *with* businesses, *for* employment in businesses will
confer advantages on a state and its citizens in the global economy.

The same themes have been taken up by the Organization for
Economic Co-operation and Development (OECD), urging the affluent states to be more 'performance orientated' in these services (OECD,
1995) and arguing through its education branch, the Centre for
Educational Research and Innovation (CERI), that there should be
'substantial involvement of transnational as well as national companies in schools' (CERI, 2000, p. 556). Driven forward by the Global
Services Network and European Services Forum (see pp. 93–4), the
business agenda pushes liberalization as part of the creation of a world
education market (Eduventures.com, 2001); EU policy now aims to
enable corporations to compete with US rivals, following the priorities
of business, and specifically the information technology industry in
relation to e-learning.

> It is doubtful if our continent will keep hold of the industrial place which it has
> achieved in this new market of multimedia if our system of education and train-
> ing does not rapidly keep pace. The development of these technologies, in the
> context of strong international competition, requires that the effects of scale
> play their full role. If the world of education and training does not use them,
> the European market will become a mass market too late. The transformation
> of education and training will then be shaped by other players. (European
> Commission, 1996, pp. 62–3, para. 156)

This allusion to the 'predator or prey' choice is exactly the perspective
on the transformation of the education sector in the First World countries (and eventually the whole world) presented by the commercial
services through their lobby organizations. The goal is to make that

sector function much more like a market, giving parents choice over schools and students choice over training and higher education. This would, in the World Bank model, lead quickly to a far more efficient allocation of resources and development of both the 'knowledge economy' and the formation of human capital. The European Round Table argues that governments should turn towards private investment in education and better management of education budgets: 'From their own experience in restructuring for greater competitiveness, industry believes that it is better to spend available funds more effectively than to spend more' (ERT, 1998, p. 14).

Despite the apparent unanimity among so many international and regional organizations (World Bank, IMF, APEC, OECD, EU) on the desirability of the business agenda for national prosperity and global welfare, governments face many political constraints in attempting to adopt this model. The most obvious of these is the trade unions and professional associations representing teachers and other educational staff, most of which have resisted the transformation process. Local governments and university departments involved in professional training have also resisted, as have a broader coalition of interests representing the older values and goals of education for citizenship, cultural inclusion, creativity, or even for its own sake. In the continental European Union member states, these groups and their organizations have been able to slow down the implementation of the business agenda, if not to halt it.

However, in the UK, the New Labour government of Tony Blair has actively espoused this agenda, and under its programme for transformation the process of change has been far faster. Below I shall use the UK as a case study of a government strategy which sees privatization, competition and a global corporate reach as an opportunity rather than a constraint, aiming to harness business to the policy goals of 'modernization' and the 'export of services'.

Private and social benefits

In the economic theory on which supply-side programmes were based, health and education provision has two distinct elements, public and private. In terms of the benefits from their contribution to the development of human capabilities (or 'capital'), they both increase the potential productivity (and hence earnings) of the recipient of the service, and confer advantages on the community as a whole, because a healthy, well-educated workforce attracts more investment in the global flows of capital, and (over a long period) therefore has higher levels of national income, from which all benefit (Buchanan, 1994). So – other things being equal – there is a 'social' or public benefit for all living in a country with a healthy and well-educated population because there is more to share among all citizens, and more to invest in a good public infrastructure (Barr, 1994). But those who get the best health care (the most high-tech scans and treatments) and the most sophisticated education (university degrees, doctorates, professional training) get the greatest personal benefit, and are advantaged over the rest.

So from the perspective of the economy as a whole these services are regarded, within the theory, both as collective or 'public' goods (because part of their benefit cannot be captured by individuals, but goes to all members of society) and as 'private' goods (because they give advantages in the labour market which accrue to individuals). But these elements cannot easily be separated from each other in the actual provision of the service. For example, perhaps half the benefits of a university degree may go to the community, through higher overall standards in the most productive sectors, such as research and innovation, media and culture; but this cannot be packaged and supplied separately from the part which gives benefits, in higher lifetime pay, to the student.

The proposed solution to the problem has been to get individuals to make a contribution (known as a 'co-payment') to a public service which roughly corresponds to their private benefit. The clearest example of this is higher education; the student can be charged tuition fees which correspond to the long-term market value (salary increment) of the degree, and which also pay part of the cost of the course. Because this is based on future earnings, most students will have to borrow to meet this bill, but the interest payments on their debt can be included in the calculation of what it is fair to expect them to pay for their career advantage.

The obvious difficulty of this solution, of course, is that such charges fall far more heavily on poor people than rich ones. Tony Blair's son was not alone in having parents who could buy a flat for him (or even a whole student house) for his period of study, leaving him with a housing asset, rather than a debt. Many parents also pay their offspring's tuition fees. Schemes which exempt students from low-income families from the latter charges seldom cover living costs during study. Poorer prospective students are more likely to be put off long courses or professional qualifications because of the prospect of years paying back loans.

In the case of health care, the problem of separating out social and private benefit is much more complicated. Measures which give the greatest benefit to the whole community at the lowest cost concern public health, sanitation, vaccination and immunization, and health-promotion activities. Income redistribution, public safety, childcare provision and attention to the work environment contribute more than curative medicine. The most expensive health-care measures are those given in hospitals and specialized clinics. They focus on people near the end of their lives, either elderly or suffering from acute conditions. Most of these are not in a position to pay for their individual gain from these treatments, and many do not live long enough to pay by instalments.

So any system for co-payments in health care runs the risk of falling on people who cannot afford to pay the large and unpredictable costs involved in major treatments, or of further disadvantaging people who have a chronic condition, less expensive to treat, but damaging for their capacities to earn. Yet other conditions, such as disabilities, require care, support and enablement rather than medical treatment, but are costly over a long period, perhaps a whole lifetime. Insurance schemes may be able to cover some of these risks, but not the latter ones; and those who most need health-care insurance (poor people, who have more illnesses and accidents) can least afford the premiums.

In the model for global development sponsored by the World Bank and the IMF, primary education, and especially education for *girls* (Sen, 1999), is seen as fundamental for the public benefits of overall human development. Without the literacy and access to the public sphere (the economy and civil society) that basic education supplies, individuals cannot realize their economic and social potential, and the whole community is disadvantaged (World Bank, 2001, pp. 52–3). Certain measures of public health, infant care, immunization and health promotion are regarded in a similar light (ibid., pp. 55–6). But secondary and higher education, and more advanced forms of hospital care, are seen as appropriate targets for co-payment measures, so that individuals contribute to meeting the costs of these improvements to their capabilities and well-being.

It is not obvious how the liberalization of education and health care enable greater efficiency and equity in making these distinctions. Especially in health care, beyond the most basic level of public provision, the incidence of need is inversely related to ability to pay, and schemes targeted on the poorest leave large proportions of the population vulnerable, even in affluent countries such as the USA. In the following sections, I shall give examples from a number of contrasting newly industrializing and developing countries to show how the interactions between the strategies of service corporations and the policies of governments have impacted on individuals and households.

Case study: education reform in the UK

The Blair government has built on the programmes of privatization and business-style public management of the Thatcher and Major administrations, and extended their principles far more radically. It seeks to introduce new managerial principles at every level of the public sector, from schools to national government; to contract out large parts of the service to private companies; to enter into partnerships with national and international corporations for new and existing facilities; to set targets and quality controls relating to skills outcomes; and to offer choices to parents and students. But, right from the start of this programme of 'modernization', UK ministers linked it with the drive to export services. Peter Mandelson, then Secretary of State for Trade and Industry, said in 1998 that the UK had a vital interest in the liberalization of trade in services because it was the second largest exporter of these after the USA. In 1997, its exports of services were worth £53 billion, equivalent to 8 per cent of GDP (People and Planet, 2000, p. 7).

In his analysis entitled *The Business of Education: How Business Agendas Drive Labour Policies for Schools* (2002), Richard Hatcher has charted the extent of influence of the model developed by the ERT and disseminated in the UK by the Confederation of British Industries (CBI). That demanded autonomy for schools to manage themselves and allot their resources, including staffing arrangements, under the leadership of business-minded heads, with accountability of teachers to deliver outcomes. The role of government was to set national standards and tests of skills, to evaluate and publish statistics on schools' performance, to make schools compete for pupils, and to link resources to results (CBI, 2000). All this accepts that the goal of education is to maximize work-related skills, and the means for technical rationality (Ball, 2001). Although there is disagreement, even in the business community itself, about the best content for a curriculum and culture to serve these goals (Jones and Buckingham, 2000, p. 10), the principles of a business-friendly environment and the goals of developing human resources for commercial use are strongly endorsed by the government. The Chancellor of the Exchequer, Gordon Brown, called for every young person to be taught about business and enterprise in school, and for 'every teacher to be able to communicate the virtues and potential of enterprise' (*Times Educational Supplement*, 29 June 2001).

Hatcher outlines the main policies adopted to serve these goals, including the increase in commercial activities (contracts to companies for providing services, and selling goods to pupils and parents, for profit) and creating a business culture in the school environment. At the time of his book's publication (2002), the UK led the rest of Europe in implementing the ERT/CBI agenda, having succeeded in nine of its ten performance indicators, well ahead of the other EU member states (Hatcher, 2002, p. 3). The main components of the government programme, set out in a report from the Department of the Environment, Transport and the Regions (2001) and a White Paper from the Department for Education and Skills (2001), were as follows:

(a) *Commercial sponsorship*: Large corporations, such as the supermarket Tesco, sponsor particular activities and goods, for instance by distributing vouchers for their educational products.
(b) *Privatization of national government education services*: Companies have taken over schools inspections, professional development for teachers and the administration of performance-related pay schemes.
(c) *The Private Finance Initiative (PFI) to finance and operate schools*: Under contracts with leading firms, which borrow on financial markets, schools are built and run, and the government contracts to pay back the loans over twenty-five to thirty years. Each project involves the creation of a special company with construction, management and financial components. The largest project, in Glasgow, cost £1.2 billion.
(d) *Franchising out local education authority services*: Some of those local authority support services heavily criticized in the reports of education inspectors (mostly in deprived areas) have been handed over to private companies such as Cambridge Education Associates and Serco, an international corporation with a turnover of nearly £1 billion in 2001.
(e) *Running schools*: Local education authorities have contracted with companies to run state schools deemed to be 'failing' by the inspectors. The practice was pioneered in Surrey, but has been adopted as a model in the White Paper *Schools: Achieving Success* (DfES, 2001, p. 49, para. 4.23). It also involves franchising out 'city academies' to replace 'failing schools', on condition of paying 20 per cent of the capital costs but getting the land and existing buildings free. Companies can also bid to manage schools as 'partners' (paras. 6.23–4), with the decision of who should be awarded the contract for a 'failing' establishment to be made by the Secretary of State (paras. 5.24–6). The private sector, which provides 7 per cent of all education, has organized to bid for contracts. Companies are planning chains of branded state schools.

(f) *Information technology*: The government has established a partnership with the commercial sector to supply the infrastructure for internet access and other information technology in schools. E-learning provides opportunities for profit, and for the gradual transformation of teaching practices for further involvement of these systems. Entrepreneurial heads have put courses on line to generate revenue for their schools. (Hatcher, 2002, pp. 8–12)

Hatcher shows that in the early years of the decade, when share prices were falling, those of educational companies in the UK rose sharply, and specifically in reponse to the government White Paper in 2001 (2002, p. 16). Capital Strategies, financial advisers to the education industry, reckoned the UK market to be worth £2.5 billion a year at that time, and £5 billion in 2006. Stocks had risen at a rate well above the FTSE index since 1996 (Capital Strategies, 2001, p. 23). Companies from other sectors have entered this market because of its prospects for profit: 'The business of education is booming with 30 takeovers worth £1 billion in a 16-month period between 1999–2000. Britain is providing a model for the World Bank's Edinvest service which facilitates private investment in education in developing centuries and the global education market' (Whitfield, 2001, p. 83).

All these innovations have provoked opposition and resistance among teachers, governors and parents, for example in Pimlico and Haringey against PFI schemes for building schools, and in Leeds, Waltham Forest and Haringey against contracting out of LEA services (Hatcher, 2002). Of these, only the one in Pimlico, concerning a single school, was successful – perhaps mainly because it focused opposition in one locality, and it was therefore easier to mobilize parents and the local community.

The UK government aims to make its schools modern, efficient and accountable; its chief education adviser described the reforms as leading to 'a world class education service' (Barber, 2001, p. 39). The consequences of the attempt to give parents choice of schools for their children will be analysed in the next chapter.

In addition to this transformation of the school system, the UK government has also introduced co-payments into higher education. Not only do students have to pay for their living costs; universities can now charge up to £3,000 a year in tuition fees. This is intended to reflect the private benefit of degrees, and to allow a competitive market between universities. For students from lower income backgrounds, bursaries are available for the fee element as well as loans for living expenses.

The creation of a 'market in higher education' is also related to international competition. Universities in the affluent countries compete for students, researchers and staff in an integrated world system. In the UK, they can charge higher fees for students from outside the EU, and also for postgraduates. While the elite establishments seek to attract the top-flight recruits from the world as a whole, and to lead the world in research, other universities compete for lucrative services, such as Chinese students. The interests of equity among citizens soon become low in priority as all pursue strategies for maximizing their incomes.

The UK government has adopted most of the business agenda in its education policies while keeping the state system as its major provider of schools. Within the overall framework of comprehensive education, a system designed in the 1960s and 1970s to encourage equality and a culture of inclusive citizenship, it has aimed to create far more diversity in educational styles. Its promotion of specialist and faith schools, as well as the involvement of commercial suppliers, has tried to increase efficiency and effectiveness and to enlarge parental choice. But it has always had at least half an eye on the global market in education and on preparing UK firms to capture as much of this as possible. Just as private finance and management is embraced to broaden the resources for modernization, so the export of education services is intended to boost national income and supply further scope for reform and development. The logic of global capitalist transformation becomes part of the dynamic for expanding social policy programmes.

Public and private value

The example of education illustrates how both the goals and the means of social policy development have changed since the era of welfare states. In those days, schools were seen as providing opportunities to train future citizens for democratic membership, co-operation and mutual respect as much as preparation for labour-market roles. The cultures in which education took place were regarded as seriously as the curriculum and pedagogic methods. Political goals informed the restructuring of education systems, and political ideology (for equality and social justice) motivated the teaching profession. The business agenda seeks to substitute enterprise and employment-related skills for these elements, and to focus all the levels of management and service-delivery on the goals of producing workers with relevant human capital.

This agenda has been persuasive in countries where governments have gone with the flow of global economic integration, and sought to make their labour markets adaptable, flexible and competitive. Within the model of the World Bank and the WTO, the 'social investment state' is urged to improve its citizens' stock of innovative potential and productive capabilities, and to nurture firms which can earn good profits in the global market for services. Opening up its own infrastructure for investment and management opportunities, and some direct commercial provision, is seen as achieving all these ends. The UK has followed this model with enthusiasm.

Among the continental member states of the EU, the reluctance to abandon the political goals of the welfare-state era is linked to a continued commitment to regulated labour markets and extensive social protection. Minimum wages are higher than in the UK, as are social insurance contributions and benefits – hence new enterprises are harder to start, and firms face disincentives to hire new workers (see pp. 66–7). Education policy fits this model. The state retains more control over schools and fosters a more traditional curriculum. Although the government in Germany, for example, spends a far higher proportion of GDP on systems of apprenticeship and retraining for unemployed people than does that of the UK, the nature (mainly craft training for industrial work) and conditions of these courses fit into the structures of labour markets and earnings rather than seeking to transform them.

How can social policy analysis clarify the issues and options at stake in the field of education? As we saw on pp. 107–10, the value and cost of education and training is *public or social* as well as private or individual. Society as a whole gains from having a membership which is well informed, aware, capable of analysing and adapting, and with certain key skills. Even a market-minded theorist such as Buchanan (1994) recognizes the social benefit of this human capital, made up of the capacities of its individual citizens. But – in a market economy – each such individual also has incentives to improve their education, and gains from doing so. The role of government is to follow policies and choose programmes which create the optimum balance between these public and private benefits.

However, in a global economy run as an integrated market, this balance is complex. The amount of money which can flow into education in any country relates to international financial movements and corporate investments, as well as the co-payments which citizens are willing and able to make. The GATS programme assumes that funding and physical capital will flow to wherever the *private marginal return* on investment is higher than the *private marginal cost*. As in any market, the commercial sector will continue to increase supply of schools and colleges until marginal revenue equals marginal cost. But this takes no account of public or social benefit, except in so far as that country's citizens provide the workforce (well or badly educated) for these enterprises, and are more or less able to pay for them.

Governments must therefore try to calculate how much the net private gains from the global business agenda (efficiency gains at home, and earnings from contracts of home companies abroad owing to experience and expertise in home markets), plus increased revenues from taxation, compensate for any net public losses (such as increases in inequality, damage to the morale of teachers, and the costs of parents moving to be near successful schools). They should add to the opportunities for business involvement in the education sector only if gains in private value are greater than losses in public or social value, and if they can successfully compensate the losers from public deterioration in viable ways (Mishan, 1967, pp. 53–73).

But the calculation on which this balance is made looks very different in the UK than it does in Germany. The Blair administrations have been very optimistic about the prospects of large corporate profits for the British education sector from financial deals and con tracts in the developing world. So they anticipate a big gain in private value from GATS, which will feed into tax revenues and into income for shareholders in the UK. In addition, because the UK economy now relies so much on small enterprises in the service sector, and on self-employment, it counts much of the gain in entrepreneurialism and risk-tolerance inculcated by the business agenda for education as a *public* benefit. So the balance in favour of partnership with companies, and business influence on the curriculum, is tilted both by hopes of service exports and by the social value of education within a culture of commercialism in schools.

The same is not true in Germany. There both in the home economy and the export market the country's high reputation for technological development, engineering excellence and production quality is still the basis for success – *Vorsprung durch Technik*. The dominance of industrial capital and trade unions have led to a priority for education and training which consolidates the public value of Germany's reputation in these fields. Schooling, along with labour-market regulation, social security and health care, reinforces stability rather than innovation. So the business agenda is seen to confer less private value than in the UK, and to have greater potential to damage public value, by eroding the culture of an integrated industrial economy. Even if the government wants to shift the balance in the direction of the agendas set by the large service companies, this tends to be resisted by industrial employers and trade unions, as well as teachers and parents.

Conclusions

In this chapter, I have analysed the ways in which the model for improvements in global welfare through the participation of transnational and local firms in the education sector has influenced policy programmes in this field. In the previous section, I concluded that governments' calculations of the optimum role of business in education balanced private with social benefit, so that the last dollar spent on this service should give equal value of both kinds. But this equation will be quite different in countries where export potential for education services is perceived as high, and, because of a large and important small business and self-employment sector, the public value of entrepreneurialism is high also.

This might lead to the optimistic conclusion that the business agenda for education will be implemented to the extent to which it contributes to the improvement of the welfare of the citizens of the country, because governments can take account of both these elements of value and compensate for any distributive inequalities in other ways. There are two difficulties about this view.

First, the calculation of public and private value for citizens takes no account of possible consequences for foreigners. Under GATS, the goal of transformation is to open public services such as education to market competition, including corporations from abroad. If a transnational firm wins such a contract, profits are mostly distributed in the affluent country in which it has its headquarters. Dividends go to shareholders (rentiers) in the First World, not to citizens of the poorer countries. It is only by making themselves more productive, in industries financed and managed by industrial companies from the First World, that those citizens can gain higher incomes (and hence improved welfare) from the whole process. Furthermore, their government has to deal with the inequalities caused by privatization. For instance, if there are substantial co-payments for secondary and higher education, and this favours higher-income students, it is the governments of poor countries which must find ways of subsidizing low-income students, as well as paying for the education service itself.

The second issue concerns the political culture of education. We have seen that in post-war welfare states this was aimed at preparing pupils for equal citizenship, co-operation and a democratic form of membership. In that period, the public value of education was political as well as economic. It socialized children and young people for their roles as citizens and made them loyal to the institutions of the country – to trade unions and political parties of labour, as well as to government and the market economy. Any government included this political value in its calculation of the balance between social and private benefit.

In the new model of education urged by the World Bank, the WTO and the large education companies, this culture is seen as a cost, not a benefit. Countries which spend public money maintaining education systems for solidarity and redistribution are creating rigidities and hindering enterprise. They are subtracting private value, because they produce school leavers and graduates who are ill-equipped to compete, especially as entrepreneurs. Hence welfare-state protectionist governments are inflicting double damage (public and private) on their citizens.

This way of thinking takes no account of the possible effects of the business agenda on democracy itself, or the possible costs of a culture of unrestrained rivalry between citizens. Commercialization and the 'choice of agenda' in education encourage parents and students to seek private value without regard for the consequences to other citizens, or for the institutions of which they are members. They give incentives for 'exit' strategies – moving to a school with better exam results – rather than 'voice' ones – participating to try to improve the school (Hirschman, 1970). They erode loyalty and interdependence, encouraging autonomy and competition rather than sharing. This may damage the very public culture on which democracy and citizenship rely.

As we shall see in part II of the book, the US and UK governments have encouraged this approach to education by their citizens. In the UK, the Blair government has published league tables of schools' performances, enabling parents to choose those with better outcomes. The flight of more resourceful residents from less successful schools and colleges, often in poor areas, has contributed to polarization of life chances. The social cost of areas of concentrated poverty and disadvantage has been paid in high rates of crime, mental illness, truancy and homelessness (Jordan, 1996; Jordan and Jordan, 2000).

The GATS agenda has been sold to governments of developing countries as a programme which will give their better-educated citizens access to employment by international companies, and hence to work in the First World. It is true that, as in health, the global market in education has encouraged both students and teachers from poorer countries to study and work in affluent ones. It is not clear that this confers a net public benefit. If citizens are encouraged to pursue private advantage through work and residence in richer countries, there may be a 'brain drain' problem for poorer ones. Loyalty to the country of origin, and the sense of membership and belonging, may also be eroded, at a cost to democratic citizenship.

Even the affluent First World states are becoming aware of these issues. In the UK, for example, public-service professionals are a good deal less well paid than their counterparts in the private sector. As a result, there are recruitment and retention problems for employers, including those in education. In the UK, public-service professionals make up the largest group of foreign recruits entering the country on work permits (Salt and Clarke, 2001). This may not be a problem if private value alone is counted; but the erosion of a culture of public service among citizens is a public cost of the business agenda, in education and health care.

Finally, as we shall see in part III, there are questions about whether autonomy and choice for the sake of private advantage can be the basis of a public culture, and especially of democratic citizenship. These doubts are now expressed by neo-conservatives such as President George W. Bush, as well as by those on the political left. 'Values voters', who rejected choice in favour of religious tradition and moral bonds, were decisive in the presidential election of November 2004. The business agenda for education discounts membership and belonging and promotes the 'rational egoism' of microeconomic models. This cannot address issues such as 'community cohesion' which have troubled the UK government (Home Office, 2002a; Blunkett, 2004); nor can it promote 'civil renewal' and democratic participation (Blunkett, 2003). We shall return to these themes in chapters 7 and 8.

Part II

Human Well-Being: Autonomy and Membership

7

The Basis for Individualism and Choice

In the first part of the book, I analysed the strategies of organizations – financial institutions, business corporations and governments – and human development programmes, mainly in the newly industrializing and developing countries. In this part, I shall focus on how individuals and households have responded to the transformation of collective life which globalization has entailed.

Here I shall rely mainly on examples from affluent First World states, where economic restructuring has penetrated every aspect of social relations. I shall show how ordinary people have modified their strategies and life plans to this new environment, and how this in turn has affected their identities and commitments. Governments have redirected social policy, both to take account of this cultural transformation and to try to shape and steer it.

In a sense, both individuals and governments are struggling with forces beyond their control and agendas they have not set. Programmes for 'structural adjustment' were, as we saw in chapters 3 and 4, imposed by international organizations, in the interests of finance and industrial capital. But both have internalized this struggle, and largely adopted the model of societies constructed out of the market-orientated choices of rational maximizers of utility. This part of the book will explore the ramifications of this model for social relations and human well-being.

In this chapter, I shall show how the processes begun by Margaret Thatcher, Bob Hawke, David Lange and Ronald Reagan were amplified and made far more subtly pervasive by Bill Clinton and Tony Blair; they are now percolating through to all other First World societies, not least through the World Bank and WTO programmes analysed in the previous section. My aim is to show how ways of thinking and behaviour patterns which were adopted by individuals and households in the

1980s, in response to new structures, risks and insecurities and to new market opportunities as well as reduced state protections, have been developed into Third Way ideologies, rhetorics and programmes. Played back to citizens in the form of political speeches, recycled as press releases and guidance notes from new agencies, and finally implemented by front-line service practitioners, these have in turn been incorporated (often in modified form) as the everyday repertoires of ordinary people. What started as unconscious or apologetic strategies for sustaining status and living standards (Jordan et al., 1994) have now become the elements in an interlocking culture of mutually reinforcing norms shared by governments and mainstream publics (Jordan, 2004). I shall explore why these ideas carried conviction, especially in the Anglophone countries.

My analysis in this chapter focuses on the transformations in the USA, the UK and Australia, as the leading nations in which these processes have been furthest developed; New Zealand is an even more spectacular case (Kelsey, 1995), partly because of its previously statist institutions, but is a smaller and less industrialized country. I aim to show how the shift from collective mutual security to individual self-reliance was achieved as much by the persuasive propaganda of commercial organizations, and the habits bred by participation in markets, as by reform policies. I shall also show how governments reinforced these patterns in their new interpretations of citizens' responsibilities, and how they in turn encouraged strategies through which their more resourceful members could seek advantage within public systems. The outcome has been a new cultural basis for the relationship between mainstream populations and state officials in these countries.

The outcome has also been the emergence of large groups of citizens and immigrants who are not part of this mainstream. They are identifiable by not owning property and not having savings or other personal assets. They are often claiming benefits on account of long-term illnesses or disabilities, lone parenthood or unemployment. Many of them are involved in the informal economy of undocumented activities, some in drug dealing or other crime. They often live in concentrations of squalid housing, with disorder and violence, poverty, and an inadequate infrastructure of services (both commercial and public). Their plight will be analysed in chapter 9.

For the mainstream (the broad middle class, including skilled workers and households with two or more adults in regular employment) the new model is ambiguous. As has been regularly recognized, economic reforms have led to higher returns for banks and business corporations and lower real wages and salaries (Pusey, 2003, pp. 5–7; Luttwak, 1999, ch. 7). Citizens had to pay more for their own pensions, for health and social care, and for their children's education, and their jobs were less secure. They had to work longer hours and retrain more often. But all this was partly compensated by property incomes of various kinds. In the USA, this took the form of share ownership; under Ronald Reagan and his successors, 'popular capitalism' led to millions of new stock-market investors with small holdings. In the UK, it was the housing market which gave about two-thirds of households a stake in the new order, because it supplied a basis for expanded personal credit, as house prices continually rose much faster than those for other commodities.

Political leaders, both neo-liberal and Third Way, were able to weave these compensatory benefits of economic reform and public-service transformation into their new discourses of autonomy and responsibility. They could produce statistics to show that mainstream households were better off as a result of all the changes around them, and that this was through their own efforts. But the evidence on well-being is far more ambiguous. Mainstream individuals did not *feel* better; self-assessments of happiness, taking in all aspects of their lives, showed no gains, and some declines (Lane, 2000; Frey and Stutzer, 2000; Eckersley, 1998; Layard, 2005). In this part of the book, I shall examine the reasons for 'stalled well-being' in the affluent states, and how social policy measures can address this new phenomenon.

Rival conceptions of property, justice and equality

We have already seen in chapter 3 that the transformations of the 1980s and 1990s reflected a shift in the whole theoretical basis for economic analysis. The model developed by Keynes in the 1930s and 1940s (pp. 55–60), and implemented through welfare states under systems of national management, was replaced by a neo-classical model which took the whole world as its unit of account and individual choices within markets as its fundamental principle. Given that the USA, the UK and Australia, along with New Zealand and Canada, are all democracies with parties broadly representative of labour interests, how was the *political* conversion achieved (especially in Australia and New Zealand, where the governments which launched economic reform were both from the Labour Parties)?

After the Second World War, governments in all these countries (which had been active combatants against fascism, in alliance with the Soviet Union) sought legitimacy and loyalty from their citizens through programmes for *shared* prosperity, in which the gains from planned growth and restrained competition were distributed among the whole population by agencies which enabled co-operation and minimized class conflict. The technical basis for this approach (demand management, wage regulation, income transfers) was justified by an ideology of democratic social citizenship, in which the state acted on behalf of all – unlike the state socialist regimes, which persecuted capitalists, bourgeois dissenters and idlers. The Cold War focused the minds of democratic parties on the task of improving the living standards of whole populations; as women and black people drew attention to their exclusion from these processes, they were gradually accommodated, through programmes such as President Kennedy's New Frontier, President Johnson's Great Society, and the Equal Opportunities legislation in the UK (see chapter 9).

It is important to recognize that these years saw transformations of pre-war social structures in these societies through employment and wages more than through benefits systems or the redistributive effects of public-service delivery. This was especially so in the USA and Australia, where transfers through social security, and public spending on health care, were low by international First World standards; much the same was true for Japan (Castles, 1985). Because of the prolonged boom in industrial production, full employment, and government policies based on the principle that no group should suffer falling incomes in a buoyant economy (see pp. 39–40), men working in the private sector and the public utilities had steady increases in earnings, above the overall rate of inflation. Furthermore, especially in the UK and New Zealand, the new institutions of the welfare state provided opportunities for a whole new class of professional staff (social workers, planners, environment and public-health officers, etc.) to arise, including women as well as men. These contributed a new social and economic force in society, the product of processes of 'managed crowding' (Hirsch, 1977), under which governments created upward mobility for the best-educated children of pre-war working-class families. As secondary and higher education expanded (themselves creating many new jobs in the public sector), this process transformed class structures, formerly dominated by male manual industrial workers.

All these changes were strongly reinforced by widening home ownership, especially in the USA and the UK (it had long been the norm in Australia, Canada and New Zealand). Finance capital in these countries found profitable ways of making loans to households, with good returns on mortgages related to durable assets. The foundations for the new model were laid by the transition from working-class households living in houses rented from private landlords or local authorities to home-owning ones whose children aspired to professional and technical jobs and university education (Saunders, 1993).

Although the USA remained a society in which final incomes were very unequally distributed, mainly because of a small group of very wealthy individuals with massive property incomes and a large group of very poor black and Hispanic people, other states in this group were much more successful in achieving equality of incomes. In particular, Australia – a country with plentiful supplies of land, rich mineral resources, and a propitious climate on its coastal strip – became one of the most equal societies of the world (for all except the Aboriginal population) through growth in workers' *wages and salaries*, not a redistributive tax–benefit system (Bolton, 1990; ABS, 1990).

The very success of the Keynesian economic programme and its welfare-state institutions made it vulnerable to political disillusion once rates of growth slowed in these countries in the 1970s. Aspiring workers, who had improved their living standards and changed their lifestyles, did not attribute these successes to the government or its officials; they saw them as the consequences of their own efforts. Already deriving their long-term economic security as much from home ownership and company pensions schemes as from the welfare state, they could readily be persuaded that it was the rigidities of regulation and the greed of bureaucrats, trade unionists and public-sector workers which were to blame for stagnation and escalating social conflicts in the 1970s.

Perhaps decisive in the political shift which gave rise to the new model was the unsustainability of the growth of employment and salaries in the social services and the public sector generally. After the mid-1970s, in all these countries, the new middle class saw the financial sector and private services as supplying the best opportunities for careers for their children. Whereas the most common employment for new graduates in the UK in the early 1970s was as teachers, by the 1980s it was as accountants. This reflected the new expansion of the financial sector, fuelled by incomes from currency dealing and overseas investments, and from the massive increase in personal credit for individuals and households (Schor, 1998). In Australia, rates of personal borrowing were even higher. In the 1990s, Australian citizens were the most indebted in the world, and the volume of total personal borrowing doubled again between 1995 and 2002 (Pusey, 2003, p. 81).

Because the mainstream citizens of these countries were already turning to individual and household strategies, to markets and to credit organizations, and away from collective action, public services and state benefits, it was not too difficult for Margaret Thatcher, Ronald Reagan and Bob Hawke to persuade them of the merits of the new model. They already saw that Keynesianism and welfare states were faltering, and they used the advantages they had gained under those regimes as launching pads for their new action plans. Banks and businesses were already promoting products, such as private pensions and health insurance, which enabled this shift.

However, the more challenging task was to persuade these mainstream groups, with their history of working-class childhoods, trade union membership and collective solidarity, that these new strategies were advantageous for society as a whole. Here political leaders appealed to old traditions, analyses and values. Above all, they cast their arguments in terms of the theory upon which global capitalism and liberal democracy were ultimately founded. This was the idea that very unequal distributions of wealth benefited the poorest members of society, because the rich invest, raising the productivity of workers, and hence the incomes of all.

This foundational argument of liberalism, taken from the work of John Locke (Jordan, 2004), was recast in neo-liberal rhetoric. It told mainstream citizens of Anglophone countries that they were entitled to accumulate private resources, to own houses, and buy shares, insurances and pensions. Citizens were equal under the laws of the market and as democratic electors, rather than equal as interdependent members of a Keynesian body politic.

The formula for the order of choice

To understand developments in social policy under Bill Clinton, Tony Blair and Paul Keating in the 1990s, it is necessary to trace some of the reasons why these arguments were so persuasive in the Anglophone countries. These were, after all, the ones in which liberal democratic systems had survived the high tide of fascism and communism in the 1930s and 1940s. Whereas virtually all of Europe, Central and East Asia, and much of Latin America had succumbed to totalitarianism, these countries and their colonies had retained civil and political rights throughout the Depression and the Second World War, and defeated fascism in military combat (with a lot of help from the communists). Continuity of political institutions and traditions, originating in liberal principles, was therefore a strong feature of the Anglophone countries. Welfare states were reconciled with these principles by the ingenious arguments of politicians such as President F. D. Roosevelt and intellectuals such as Sir William Beveridge (1942, 1944). But they never overrode the liberal individualism of their older traditions.

The new model revived a formula for human well-being which was invented by a number of European thinkers during the Enlightenment period. According to this formula, well-being is most reliably sustained and improved by the actions of ordinary individuals, because these are co-ordinated by processes beyond the imaginative scope or political control of governments. In other words, *well-being relies on the unintended collective consequences of individual choices.* Although the Enlightenment has given us a heritage of rationalism and scientific experiment (Lyotard, 1983), it was this idea of co-ordination by forces beyond rational organization or planning which has been perhaps its most enduring legacy. It is also important to understand this, because new psychological evidence on well-being, and new developments in social policy, now cast doubts on the validity of the formula, especially in affluent societies (see chapter 10).

The formula has been identified and set out by three social theorists, Robert Merton (1949, pp. 475–90), Jon Elster (1985, pp. 28–9) and Mary Douglas (1987, ch. 3), as follows:

1 A pattern of behaviour, or social outcome (such as property ownership and commercial markets), is produced by an institution, or set of institutions (money, banking and credit),
2 This pattern or outcome is beneficial for all the individual members of a community (in this case, because it raises the productivity of labour, and hence wages),
3 This pattern or outcome was not intended by the individuals who initiated or participate in the institution (i.e. bankers, financial dealers),
4 The fact that their actions produced the pattern or outcome is not recognized by the individual members of the community (the masses, who adopt money for exchange and to store wealth),
5 The institution (money) sustains the pattern or outcome through a 'feedback loop' passing through individual members (the masses) by their interactions (buying and selling).

Merton, Elster and Douglas separately identified this formula as the one which encodes a successful *functionalist* explanation of social phenomena. In fact, as I have argued more fully elsewhere (Jordan, 2004, chs. 1–3; 2005), this form of argument is part of our legacy from the Enlightenment. Those socialized in the Anglophone tradition seem almost predisposed to accept arguments cast in this way.

In order to be able to present the model as a credible basis for a viable social order, for justice between citizens, and for human well-being, political leaders have contended that such choices create stable institutions for better government as well as efficient allocations of productive resources. Adam Smith's refined version of the formula as the idea of an invisible hand, guiding transactions between self-interested agents in free markets to produce the optimum distributions among all participants, was also applied to the transformation of political institutions in the same processes. For a stable social order to arise through individual choice, these philosophers had to show how institutions such as sexual morality, marriage, parenthood and family were sustained without authoritarian threats of legal punishment or divine retribution.

But this order, relying on choices rather than moral rules and obligations, requires particular kinds of cultural conditions for its flourishing. Individuals must be encouraged to be self-developmental and self-improving – to seek personal realization, in relationships, in work, and in property ownership. They can then form the required members of a new kind of polity, first made explicit in the social policies of Bill Clinton and Tony Blair.

As the following chapters in this section of the book will show, the culture of individualism has important implications for social and political relations also. Social theorists have developed accounts of the transformation of identities and intimate relationships in these societies, from conceptions of fixed roles and traditional obligations to ones of negotiated equality and reciprocity (Giddens 1991, 1992; Beck and Beck-Gernsheim, 1995, 2002). They have also theorized a link between this transformation and the change from post-war welfare states to new kinds of polity (Giddens, 1994, 1998; Beck, 1992, 1994). Other theorists, in the tradition of Michel Foucault (1988), have made connections between these new conceptions of the self and close relationships and new forms of governance pioneered in the USA (Rose, 1996).

Under the Third Way governments of the later 1990s, these elements have been brought together in a new approach to social policy, which combines the individual autonomy and mobility of market relations with elements of a socially conservative view of the family and civil society – the 'responsible community' (Lister, 2000; Jordan and Jordan, 2000). This combination, as I shall show, has been influential in continental Europe, where it allowed aspects of the Christian democratic tradition to be combined with neo-liberalism and the supply-side approach to labour market restructuring (Bleses and Seeleib-Kaiser, 2004; Seeleib-Kaiser et al., 2005; Fitzpatrick, 2003). This new 'liberal-communitarian' model is now the dominant orthodoxy in the affluent countries; the features of its social policy regimes will be analysed in chapters 8 to 10.

However, the sophisticated social-theoretical analyses of these new social relations and their political outworkings have not penetrated to the deeper layers of assumptions and institutions underlying this new order. The plausibility and persuasiveness of Third Way politics and its new model of social policy lie in a formula linking individual liberty, market choice, private property and consensual government, first developed in the Enlightenment period (Jordan, 2004, chs. 1–4). The fundamental mechanisms achieving these links are the unintended consequences of millions of decisions by 'free' individuals seeking their own well-being, and in the process creating institutions which benefit them all.

Self, society and social policy

The new model of the world economy during the Washington Consensus assumed that individuals would maximize their utility within a set of institutions (families, markets, polities) inherited from earlier generations and constantly renewed in their interactions. But it also sought to erode, transform or abolish the collectivist legacy of the Keynesian and state-socialist periods. So individuals had to become more self-reliant than they had been in the welfare-state era. Instead of expecting collective solutions to issues of the life cycle, the economic cycle, change and crisis, they were required to develop personal resources and material property to cope with all eventualities.

In the Anglophone countries, as we have seen (pp. 61–3), financial and business organizations were already developing new strategies and products to assist this process. From the perspective of the neo-liberal governments of the 1980s, it was much better for people to borrow from banks than to pay taxes and receive benefits, because personal debt was chosen by the individual, whereas the tax–benefit system was imposed by the collective authority. Similarly, it was much better to pay interest on a mortgage than to pay rent to a local authority, and to start a business than to look for secure employment in the public sector. The new order fostered and facilitated all these priorities. Without necessarily subscribing to the ideology of neo-liberal regimes, mainstream citizens of the Anglophone countries began to participate in these new institutions and adopt new life strategies for greater autonomy and enterprise (Jordan et al., 1994; Pusey, 2003).

Social theorists in the 1980s started to recognize that the shift towards self-reliance was transforming governance itself. The new regimes were nurturing a kind of self-government among their citizens, in which they ruled over themselves with many of the disciplinary powers which had formerly been exercised over them. Michel Foucault, the leading theorist of the self as subject and the use of knowledge in political relations, recognized very late in his life that this was a new phase in the evolution of authority and scientific govern-ance. It involved the adoption of new 'technologies of the self', in which individuals developed new attitudes to their responsibilities for self-management and self-realization, as well as specific skills. They were expected to keep re-evaluating their performance, and how well it matched their potential, in every aspect of their lives. In this stage of self-governance, they should (perhaps after receiving counselling and training) be able to use these technologies 'to effect by their own means or with the help of others a certain number of operations on their own bodies and souls, thoughts, conduct and way of being' (Foucault, 1988, p. 18).

The most subtle aspect of this new culture was its basis in personal development and relationships. Mainstream citizens were already gradually committing themselves to 'projects of self' which concerned the realization of their full potential, in all aspects of their lives. Theorists of 'intimacy' and 'individualization' described a change from traditional bonds of obligation, based on moral rules and kinship ties, to ones in which

> The self is seen as a reflexive project for which the individual is responsi-ble . . . . We are, not what we are, but what we make of ourselves . . . . [W]hat the individual becomes is dependent on the reconstructive endeavours in which she or he engages . . . . The moral thread of self-actualization is one of *authenticity* . . . based on 'being true to oneself'. . . . The morality of authen-ticity skirts any universal moral criteria, and includes references to other people only within the sphere of intimate relationships. . . . In contrast to close personal ties in traditional contexts, the pure relationship is not anchored in external conditions of social or economic life – it is, as it were, free-floating. . . . [S]elf-identity is negotiated through linked processes of self-exploration and the development of intimacy with the other. (Giddens, 1991, pp. 75, 78–9, 89, 97)

The challenge for Third Way social policy was to spread these cultural standards to the population as a whole, so that the main targets of their programmes to engage marginal and 'dependent' groups in the labour market, and in every aspect of self-governance – 'welfare mothers', unemployed and disabled claimants, even truants, homeless people, drug misusers and offenders – would come to use 'technolo-gies of the self' in these ways. In the USA, researchers of projects to motivate and activate such claimants identified self-esteem and self-worth as the key elements in the success of these programmes. During Bill Clinton's presidency, the whole momentum of welfare reform was sustained by ideas of 'inclusion' and 'empowerment' which drew on this approach (Cruikshank, 1994, 1996).

As the background to these programmes, the Third Way redefinition of social justice insisted that rights must always be balanced by responsibilities (see pp. 132–4 below) – there should be no public provision for income support without a commitment by citizens to help themselves be more autonomous, enterprising and self-developmental.

In the UK, the Blair administration launched a set of policies for increasing the participation of poor people in the labour market, using very similar principles and vocabularies. These deploy 'technologies of the self', through which participants are transformed from within – acting upon themselves, under the guidance of official documents and personal advisers. In Cruikshank's formulation, the aim is to target a particular group: those who fail to link their 'personal fulfilment to social reform are lumped together as social problems, are diagnosed as "lacking self-esteem" and are charged with "antisocial behaviour"' (Cruikshank, 1996, p. 334).

All this points to the fact that the social order based on individual choice is fragile when it is applied to those with little education, few skills, and no stake in property or mainstream associations. It is a model in which self-motivation and self-improvement are built into the dynamic as assumptions; when it addresses the choices of poor and marginal members of society, it requires buttressing with various kinds of advice, counselling and sanctions, such as the threat of removal of benefits.

The new contract (or new covenant)

Under Third Way governments in the 1990s, the requirement for 'self-responsibility' and 'independence' was made explicit. In the Anglophone countries, citizens were expected to develop marketable skills, and accumulated property rights (including pension entitlements) sufficient to sustain them and their families through the life cycle. The onus on them was to demonstrate that they had attempted and were attempting to do this, and that they were prevented from achieving it by forces beyond their control, such as illness, disability, or the lack of available employment of any kind.

In the UK, all this was spelled out in the government White Paper *A New Contract for Welfare* (DSS, 1998), which helpfully presented a welfare contract chart listing the respective responsibilities of individuals and the government.

Duty of government	*Duty of individual*
• Provide people with the assistance they need to find work	• Seek training or work where able to do so
• Make work pay	• Take up the opportunity to be independent if able to do so
• Assist parents with the costs of raising their children	• Give support, financial or otherwise, to their children and other family members
• Regulate effectively so that people can be confident that private pensions and insurance products are secure	• Save for retirement where possible
• Relieve poverty in old age where savings are inadequate	• Not to defraud the taxpayer
• Devise a system that is transparent and open and gets money to those in need	

Duty of us all

• To help all individuals and families to realize their full potential and live a dignified life, by promoting economic independence through work, by relieving poverty where it cannot be prevented and by building a strong and cohesive society where rights are matched by responsibilities. (DSS, 1998, p. 80)

The difficulty with this contract is that it provides no mechanisms and principles to ensure that any overall increase in the nation's income and wealth is shared out fairly among the population. Markets in money, goods and labour power may well, as the new model claims, produce the highest overall outputs of private commodities from finite material resources, but they cannot guarantee 'independence' to any specific proportion of the population, either globally or nationally. In principle, there is nothing in the model to prevent an enormous concentration of wealth and income falling into the hands of (say) the top 10 per cent of owners and earners. The commitment of the government to sustain the rest of its citizens at a level of subsistence (through tax credits and means-tested benefits) is a double-edged sword, because it implies that these will be held on or just above the poverty line. If claimants' earnings rise slightly above this, a very high proportion of the extra income – far higher than the rate of tax paid by the rich – will be taxed back, or deducted from tax credits and benefits (see chapter 14, pp. 249–54).

In other words, all the government is committing itself to in this contract is supplying private enterprises of various kinds with labour power. If the minimum wage is low, and security of employment is tenuous (as in the Anglophone countries), a large proportion of the workforce may need to be subsidized in work and supported by means-tested benefits in retirement. Not only will the authorities refuse to pay any public money to anyone unwilling to take low-paid, casual, unpleasant and exploitative work; they will also hold an ever-growing proportion of the population in a 'poverty trap', so that their incomes are effectively tied to the level which the state deems necessary for subsistence. Clearly this system favours employers such as Wal-Mart (see p. 78), the largest of its kind in the world, which systematically pays most of its staff less than a living wage but coaches them in how to claim tax credits.

In the new model of rights and responsibilities, the 'independence' of citizens is therefore precarious. Even skilled, flexible and adaptable people are at the mercy of market forces; the 'safety nets' provided by the government are heavily stigmatized, with constant surveillance and checks by officials (see pp. 179–80). The commitment to 'make work pay' is valuable for high earners, because tax rates are low, but less so for low earners, because it refers to the fact that tax credits are more generous than means tested benefits – a small incentive to take work which may well be unpleasant and demeaning. Studies of life on the minimum wage in the USA (Ehrenreich, 2002) and the UK (Abrams, 2002) suggest that it is physically debilitating, emotionally stressful and very insecure.

Of course, many individuals and households have gained from the implementation of the new model and the social policies associated with it. These have mainly been people who rely on holdings of property assets (investments, private pensions, etc.), who are mobile, and who can therefore take advantage of differential opportunities and costs. By contrast, those without such assets and incomes, who are bound to their relationships with kin and others by ties of mutuality, and who therefore cannot shift and switch, are disadvantaged and often lose out.

Those with assets, who can move and choose, are able to act strategically within state-funded as well as commercial systems. In a study of retired North European citizens moving within the EU, Dwyer and his associates (Dwyer, 2000; Ackers and Dwyer, 2002) found that they chose to bring their higher private and public pensions to countries where the costs of living were lower. A French man living in Corfu said he could live twice as well there as in his home country; a Swedish woman living in France said that she paid 20 per cent less tax; a British pensioner obtained NHS care on the basis of being resident in the UK, but was actually living most of the year in Greece; a German citizen living in Greece declared that he was officially resident with his children in Germany and received medical treatment there – he had been doing this for thirteen years (Dwyer, 2004, pp. 144–5). As Dwyer points out:

> while, to some extent, these migrants are operating in the 'shadows' of the law, the divide between benefit shopping/welfare tourism and 'reflexive'/'active' citizenship of the kind envisaged by Giddens (1994) would seem to be finely drawn. . . . Why then, if we are all dependent upon public welfare and we are all in a variety of ways actively trying to get the best deal for ourselves, are only certain types of welfare dependency and risk management considered to be irresponsible? (Dwyer, 2004, p. 146)

These strategies are not confined to citizens of rich countries. Under 'managed migration' systems, all First World governments now allow firms in their territory to recruit substantial numbers of professional, managerial, high-skilled and entrepreneurial individuals from abroad, and to transfer staff between branches of their companies (Salt, 1988). The research studies which I conducted (with Franck Düvell) found that young work-permit holders who came from Poland and India to the UK to be employed as financial experts, information technology analysts, academics, researchers, managers and nurses relied mainly on the companies which recruited them for the supply of infrastructural facilities and supports. However, their choices of destinations, lengths of stay, contracts, accommodation and even leisure facilities reflected strategies for getting the most advantage, in terms of both short-term lifestyles and long-term career development (and asset accumulation).

Successful 'projects of self' of resourceful individuals therefore combine a trajectory of self-realization and self-improvement with the strategic accumulation of property assets and stakes in corporate wealth.

In the USA from the 1970s onwards, increased mobility and suburban sprawl meant that those fleeing the inner city 'sorted themselves into more and more finely distinguished "lifestyle enclaves", segregated by race, class, education, life stage and so on' (Putnam, 2000, p. 209). In the UK, these processes have polarized the population. On the one hand, there is increasing residential segregation of income groups and an accelerated tendency for districts to display homogeneity of residents by class, education, age and ethnicity (Dorling and Thomas, 2003).

This is graphically illustrated in survey evidence, comparing the life experiences of three generations of UK citizens, collated by a research team from the London University Institute of Education. Among 3,713 male respondents born in 1946 and surveyed aged twenty-six, 43 per cent were members of trade unions; of these, 37 per cent of respondents in social class V (unskilled manual workers) were members. But of 5,762 born in 1970 and surveyed aged thirty, only 17 per cent were members of trade unions, and of those in class V only 6 per cent. Conversely, among the class V respondents born in 1958 (the figures for 1946 were not available), 13 per cent had at some point been arrested by the police; among the same group born in 1970 it was 47 per cent (Bynner and Parsons, 2003, table 10.1a, p. 266, fig. 10.1b, p. 267, and fig. 10.9, p. 290). In other words, among the poorest men reaching adulthood in the welfare-state era, trade union membership was nearly three times as prevalent as the experience of arrest; among those reaching adulthood in the neo-liberal era of economic restructuring, arrest was almost eight times as likely as trade union membership.

All this suggests that social policies aimed at maximizing economic growth and 'personal prosperity' have distributed life chances as unequally as income. The transformation of economic, social and public organizations under neo-liberal and Third Way programmes has greatly advantaged those whose 'projects of self' are based on material asset holdings and disadvantaged those who have no such resources. The concepts of autonomy, choice, responsibility and independence must be interpreted in the light of these findings. Individuals cannot be self-responsible in a market system without assets of these kinds.

In the next section, I shall give an example of a previously egalitarian society with its own distinctive version of social justice, and how it has been transformed by economic restructuring.

Case study: 'middle Australia'

This case study is based on the research project *The Experience of Middle Australia: The Dark Side of Economic Reform*, by Michael Pusey (2003). He conducted a survey of 403 Australian citizens, resident in Sydney, Brisbane, Adelaide, Melbourne and Canberra, all with household incomes below the top 10 per cent and above the bottom 20 per cent (i.e. between $57,541 and $36,483 per year in 2000). He also held focus groups in which participants on like incomes discussed issues of economic, social and political change affecting their lives. (The book says almost nothing about the impact of reform on Aboriginal Australians.)

As Pusey points out, Australia was distinctive among the Anglophone countries for the fact that its pattern of income distribution was one of the most egalitarian of all the affluent First World countries, including even the Scandinavian welfare states, in the period between 1945 and 1980. Furthermore this was achieved not by government transfer schemes, but through the labour market; Australia was a 'wage earners' welfare state', with very low spending on its (means-tested) social security system. Wages and salaries were high relative to profits and property incomes, and this had been accomplished by a well-established centralized system (the 'wage-fixing and arbitration' scheme) which tackled issues of distributive justice at source, by negotiations between employers, trade unions and government officials (Castles, 1985).

Australia's post-war growth therefore directly benefited the mass of the population, creating a 'Lucky Country'; most of its industries were protected by import tariffs until the early 1960s, but by the 1980s it was an open economy, with a very mobile workforce. The OECD conceded that Australia had been 'on average among the more flexible of the OECD countries . . . [and] Australia's labour force has been extremely mobile by international standards, both between industries and regions, and turnover rates are high' (OECD, 1988, pp. 70, 74). In fact, it had a floating currency, an open trade policy, and a small public sector, along with low rates of public expenditure and overall taxation (Pusey, 2003, p. 169). It was its wage-fixing and arbitration system which offended the purists of the Washington Consensus, and which was deemed to require reform, when its exceptionally high rate of growth (around 5 per cent throughout the 1950s and 1960s) slowed in the late 1970s.

Under the programmes initiated by the Labor governments of Bob Hawke and Paul Keating, and continued by the Conservative coalition of John Howard, Australia has moved to being among the three most unequal countries, in terms of income distribution, in the First World (see table 7.1). (The Gini coefficient equals 0 when income is perfectly equally distributed; it equals 1 when all income is concentrated at the top of the income distribution pattern.)

Calculating incomes by census collection districts (rather than by individual households), the researcher Bob Gregory found that 'for the bottom 70 per cent of collection districts average household income

Table 7.1   Household income inequality, relative to national median income (per cent of national median)

Country	Year	Ratio of 90th to 10th percentile	Gini coefficient
USA	1991	5.78	0.343
UK	1991	4.67	0.335
Australia	1989	4.30	0.308
Japan	1992	4.17	0.315
Spain	1990	3.73	0.290
France	1984	3.48	0.294
West Germany	1989	3.21	0.261
Italy	1991	3.14	0.255
Denmark	1992	2.86	0.239
Sweden	1992	2.78	0.229

Source: Mishel et al (2000)

has fallen in absolute terms and is lower in 1991 than in 1976'; the income gap between the top and bottom 5 per cent of districts had widened by 92 per cent in the same period (Gregory, 1996, p. 5). The total per capita increase for the twenty-year period after 1976 was the equivalent of the average three-year increase during the 1950s and 1960s (Gregory, 1998, p. 7). But these figures disguise the real *falls* in male earnings during this period, when men aged twenty-five to thirty-four earned 75 per cent less than they had in 1976, and younger men's decline in wages was even greater. Men over fifty-five also experienced declines in real wages of 50 per cent (between the ages of fifty-five and sixty) and 70 per cent (over sixty) during these twenty years. That household incomes rose slightly was owing to small gains by men aged thirty-five to fifty-four, and a large increase in female labour market participation (Gregory, 1998).

Pusey's research charts the reactions of 'middle Australians' to this 'hollowing out' of the earnings of the main components of the labour market, and to the other phenomena of economic reform – the second highest proportion of part-time and casual employment among First World countries, the highest rate of personal and household indebtedness in the world, and rising housing costs (Pusey, 2003, p. 81). His analysis of both the statistical and qualitative evidence is highly relevant to the themes developed in this chapter. Middle Australians continued to mourn the passing of the 'fair go' system which prevailed in the post-war period, and blamed both large corporations (the gainers) and the government, as well as the greed of rich individuals, for their plight. They did not accept these reforms as either inevitable or beneficial for the mainstream, and considered that the incursions of market forces into every aspect of social life were corrosive of family, community and civic values. The main differences between the respondents lay in their educational and occupational backgrounds, and in the extent to which they were reconciled with the changes which had taken place in Australian society.

Among those who had been the losers, in terms of household incomes, during the previous twenty years, one group of blue-collar, technical and service workers were 'survivors' who had largely internalized the requirements of the new, market-driven order; another were 'battlers' who railed against almost every aspect of it. Among those who had gained or remained on an even keel, the 'North Shore people', usually with direct links to the key institutions of the new order (such as banks and large businesses) and to global organizations, were accepting of the transformation, while the 'improvers' (professionals and managers, many in the public sector, and people with university degrees) were highly critical of the social and political consequences. The unreconciled, angry and critical made up the bulk of the sample (Pusey, 2003, pp. 58–61).

For example, when all 403 respondents were asked which of five different distributional patterns most closely corresponded to the current Australian situation, over three-quarters identified a pyramid structure, with the largest part of the population at the bottom. But they also identified Australia forty years earlier as a much more equal and open society, with the bulk of the population in the middle range of incomes; and they wanted it to return to that pattern (Pusey, 2003, pp. 122–6).

The respondents were highly critical of the effects of economic restructuring on civic behaviour (including their own), on solidarity and mutual support, and on family life. They considered greater equality between men and women to have been one of the few gains from the process; but they strongly asserted that women should have a choice whether to work or stay at home with their children, and not be compelled to earn by economic necessity (Pusey, 2003, pp. 84–8). Pusey identifies

> an emerging norm that the man and the woman should be able to decide on all questions concerning work and the family on equal terms and that the necessary institutional support, directly from the state, from employers – or indirectly through a more firmly regulated market? – should provide them with the legal and economic resources to do so. (Ibid., p. 89)

However, his study reveals that university graduates in his 'North Shore' and 'improver' categories were far more able to handle this version of 'negotiated intimacy' and 'democratic, reflexive household relations' than were the 'battlers' or 'survivors'. This was both because they were trained and experienced in the kinds of skills ('symbolic analysis', therapeutic discourse and personal development) required in such relations and because they were under less economic stress. The losers from economic restructuring were trying to learn to negotiate and co-ordinate their 'projects of self' against a background of insecure work, informal childcare and mounting debt.

Finally, although middle Australians wanted a return to a 'fair do' society, they were not for the most part nostalgic about a 'golden age' of traditional community values. Rather they looked back to a period of civic engagement, when government was proactive in shaping social relations. When asked whether they would join more associations if they had less compulsion to work, and more time, the largest group (47 per cent) said they would choose to pursue activities described by Pusey as 'self-improvement', such as forms of personal development, education and training (2003, p. 119). This suggests once more that middle Australians have, for all their rejection of the ethical basis for and social consequences of economic restructuring, actually internalized much of the culture of self-realization and individualism which that programme promotes.

Furthermore, for all the angry criticism of the business agenda and globalization, of greedy individuals and exploitative multinational corporations, they did, after all, re-elect the Howard government in 2001. Although this could be rationalized as an expression of their view that there was little difference between the basic philosophies of the two major parties (Pusey, 2003, pp. 159–63), the Howard coalition was clearly the alternative most committed to further and deeper reform and privatization, having already accelerated the transformation process begun by its Labor predecessors. This suggests that – as individuals and households – middle Australians were locked into strategies which went with the flow of market forces, such as share and home ownership, even as they still bemoaned the loss of an older, more civic type of society.

This is really the paradox of the transformation of social policy and social relations under neo-liberal and Third Way regimes – that government programmes reinforce strategic behaviour already promoted by new forms of capitalist institutions and innovations, while eroding the social structures through which balancing civic organizations and practices were sustained. Middle Australians seemed to understand and resent these processes, but to act in line with their requirements, and to identify with the collective consciousness which informed them.

Conclusions

As we have seen in this chapter, the new ideology of individualism and self-development has both reflected new strategies and trajectories of resourceful individuals and households, and been turned into an instrument of governance by Third Way regimes. As Niklas Rose puts it:

> [T]he self-government of the autonomous individual can be connected up with the imperatives of good government. Etho-politics seeks to act upon conduct by acting upon the forces thought to shape the values, beliefs, moralities that themselves are thought to determine the everyday mundane choices that human beings make as to how they lead their lives. (Rose, 1999, pp. 477–8)

However, the main targets for such attempted influence are not the mainstream population, who are perceived as having internalized the collective culture of autonomy, choice and responsibility. Instead, the homilies of Third Way governments are directed mainly at poor people, benefits claimants and other marginal groups.

Market-dominated societies create a kind of parody of choice, in which people are driven into a frenzy of consumption while remaining more than half aware that it is not conducive to their well-being. In Pusey's study, many Australians railed against consumerism, 'Americanization' and corporate values. But they admitted that they themselves often behaved in just the ways they criticized. A bizarre example of this culture occurred on the night of 9–10 February 2005 in Edmonton, London, where IKEA (a household goods and furniture store) was offering special discounts at the opening of a new store (at midnight). In all, twenty-two would-be shoppers (some of whom had been queuing all day) were crushed or suffered heat exhaustion, and one was stabbed, in a riot; the store was closed by police as emergency services arrived to assist the victims (BBC Radio 4, 2005d). This is what collective solidarity has finally come to in the new model.

In the next chapter, I shall examine more closely the theory of collective goods and public policy which has shaped social policy in the Anglophone countries, and which underpins the model promoted by international financial institutions, especially the WTO.

8

The Transformation of Collective Provision

In the era of welfare states, services such as health care, education, domiciliary assistance, day care and residential provision were allocated to citizens by professionals and other public officials. They were also organized and staffed mainly by employees of the state. As we have seen, the world trade in services has started to change all this (chapters 5 and 6). In the latest phase of the integration of a global market economy, multinational service corporations are competing for contracts to supply these facilities and international financial interests are investing in such ventures.

We have also seen how these new programmes for privatization and 'partnership' have been justified in terms of the individual and social benefits of services which develop the capabilities and functioning of citizens. In this chapter, I shall analyse the other perspectives on this transformation – governments' desire to give more scope for individuals to choose among a range of alternative amenities and providers; and citizens' strategies for finding the most advantageous facilities. As I shall show, both of these have been promoted in the new global model for the transformation of welfare states and public services, under a set of theoretical principles (public choice, club theory and fiscal federalism) which is highly compatible with the World Bank Development Plan (Jordan and Düvell, 2003, ch. 2; Jordan, 2004, chs. 5 and 6).

The first aspect of this transformation concerns the ability of citizens to express their preferences for 'collective goods' such as health and social care, and to organize themselves into sustainable groupings which share the costs of these services, and also share in their use. These analyses suggest that people are able to agree around issues of fees and quality of provision if they are free to choose between such organizations, and to switch between them easily (see also pp. 133–5). In an extension of the argument that individual liberty and property rights create the possibility of consensual governance (see pp. 147–8), this model promotes the private supply of 'collective goods' as the best way to improve both efficiency and equity among members of a polity (Wicksell, 1958 [1896]; Foldvary, 1994).

The second aspect of the transformation deals in the role of national and local governments. It argues that these should regulate competition, fund certain services for certain groups of citizens, and compensate for 'externalities' (gains or losses to individuals as a result of others' actions, for which they are neither rewarded nor charged). However, on this analysis governments should not be involved in direct provision of services except in clear cases of 'market failure' (no private supplier of a suitable quality is available at the rates which can be afforded by the service clientele). In practice, although no country has carried these principles to their logical conclusions, they have been very influential on social policy throughout the world.

This is partly because they are highly compatible with the ideal of a liberal, individualist social order based on the free choices of morally sovereign, autonomous beings. Governments have promoted the 'choice agenda' in public services (for instance, Blair, 2001) as the social policy counterpart of 'projects of self' and 'personal prosperity', arguing that citizens want to be able to choose the supplier and quality of service which suits them, and taking markets as their paradigm (DSS, 1998, p. 27).

This in turn has enabled a transformation in citizenship, briefly discussed in the previous chapter (see pp. 128–30) and fully analysed in chapter 9. As part of the 'new contract' or 'new covenant', citizens who are required to be independent and self-responsible are given new opportunities to seek personal advantage in their selection of these facilities. The public infrastructure is redesigned so as to promote choice, giving citizens information (for instance, in the form of league tables) about the performance of hospitals, schools and care homes, so that they can switch to the best amenities (6, 2003). This is also the main way in which governments seek to raise standards in public services.

Interviewed on the BBC Radio 4 *Today* programme on 12 February 2005, the co-ordinator of the New Labour government's campaign for re-election that year was asked why choice in public services was so important, and whether this could really be described as a 'transformation'. He replied:

> Yes, it is a transformation. . . . We live in a highly individualised consumer society; people want to know what's in it for *them*. . . . [We must] open up the public services for more choice. We live in a world where people exercise

choices all the time. It is impossible to insulate the public services from these processes. (Milburn, 2005)

As we have already seen (pp. 130–5), the new model presupposes that individuals are highly mobile, both geographically and in terms of their ability to acquire information, compare advantages, and switch between providers. It also assumes that the new self-managed units (hospital trusts, school centres, care groups, etc.) will be 'membership organizations', with rights to decide who will be admitted to their facilities and to exclude those who do not confirm to their requirements (Jordan, 1996; 2004, ch. 5). The benefits – in terms of efficiency, at least – to be gained from the choice-based model stem from these groupings of self-selected members and the power to exclude those who cannot afford or accept their terms for belonging.

The obvious problem about this approach, as we have already noted, is that it gives great advantages to those with the resources to move and switch. On the one hand, it means that they can purloin the best amenities, in effect turning them into closed 'clubs'. Because membership is exclusive, the costs of these forms of self-selection are borne by the least mobile and least well informed. This applies to public as well as private facilities; notoriously, in the USA, the UK and Australia, the best state schools are found in market towns, leafy suburbs or the wealthy districts of large cities, and much the same applies to health- and social-care facilities.

Conversely, poor and immobile people find themselves living in concentrations of others with similar disadvantages, and this in turn generates social problems, as groups compete within informal systems (of economic activity, street-level territoriality, or inter-ethnic rivalry). They get the worst education, health care and social services, because more resourceful people have moved away, refusing to share facilities with them (Cullis and Jones, 1994, pp. 300–1). Thrown back on informal and mutual systems of all kinds, they then subvert government programmes of surveillance, containment and 'reintegration', causing resentment among the taxpaying mainstream, and still further oppressive programmes (Jordan, 1996, ch. 5). Examples of this from Northern Ireland and France will be given in chapters 9 and 10.

The other troublesome aspect of this approach to the reform of public services is that it encourages an instrumental and strategic approach to citizenship itself. In calling service users 'consumers', Alan Milburn (p. 142) was encouraging the perception of choice between suppliers as akin to market decisions. Markets promote *exit* (changing to another product or provider) rather than *voice* (taking action with others to improve a commodity or service) and loyalty

(Hirschman, 1970). When this is carried over into decisions about the public infrastructure and the shared quality of life of communities, it impoverishes democratic culture itself (Hirschman, 1981, p. 252).

Mobility, boundaries and welfare

The new model of society, citizenship and social policy is derived from a microeconomic analysis which in turn can be traced to the Enlightenment account of the (unintended) links between individual liberty, money, markets, property and good governance (see chapter 7). But all these links are made through the mobility of money, technology, goods and people, including movement across borders. In the World Bank model of economic and human development, free trade is fundamental. By the end of the twentieth century, a quarter of the world's output of goods and services was traded across borders (World Bank, 1999, p. 229).

At a fundamental level, markets can be claimed to achieve efficient allocations of resources because they all *move*. The basic language of economics is one of shifts and movements. In the simplest microeconomic models, with perfect information, no legal barriers and zero transaction costs, everything responds to the laws of supply and demand. Capital and labour flow to whichever industry and territory can show a marginal product which exceeds its marginal cost; they behave exactly like the other commodities which are traded in markets. More complex models then analyse how other features – such as transport costs, imperfect competition or market failure – influence those decisions and flows. Policy analysis shows what governments can do to optimize the supply of public goods and the final distribution of income.

But there is a theoretical problem at the heart of any analysis of welfare which is derived from this account of individual freedom and economic dynamism. 'Welfare economics' (or 'public economics') refers to issues of distribution between members of a finite population of citizens. Political theories of justice, too, consider what such members owe each other, and the principles under which they can live well together. The starting point for the economics of social policy is how to reconcile efficiency with justice in nation states; governments, acting in the name of the common interests of all citizens, aim to redistribute income, wealth and power, to sustain freedom and work incentives, to support adequate living standards, and to maintain social integration (Barr, 2004, pp. 4–12).

Microeconomics, on the other hand, studies how markets allocate productive resources and goods for consumption in a world economy without such borders and boundaries. These two apparently incompatible sets of assumptions are reconciled by the adoption of a convention over 'political associations' (states) which is also borrowed from the Enlightenment tradition. In this, individuals come together to make a 'social contract', specifying the general rules under which they will voluntarily submit themselves to common laws and institutions. It is especially familiar in the work of the pre-eminent modern liberal theorist John Rawls (1971). His analysis is both individualist and contractarian in this tradition; embryonic citizens, as yet unaware of their endowments of talents and resources, agree principles (equal liberty for all, and equal distribution of opportunity, income, wealth and self-respect, unless an unequal distribution of any or all of these values is to everyone's advantage). Although there are other alternatives – such as the Marxist and libertarian ones, which lead to very different distributions of property – Rawls's is generally taken as the one which best captured the post-war settlements on which welfare-state institutions were founded, especially in the Anglophone countries.

But two contradictions immediately occur, both concerning mobility. Once the constitutional and institutional arrangements of the polity are in place, the theory assumes that something like a Pareto principle applies to all subsequent choices. Citizens will agree to decisions by governments which are 'allocatively efficient' – they distribute in such a way that no one can be made better off without making someone else worse off (Buchanan, 1967; Musgrave, 1959). But this assumption of unanimous consensus is only valid when citizens have the option of leaving the polity if Pareto efficiency is not achieved (Wicksell, 1958 [1896]). In Rawls's theory, no such rule applies; as he made clear at the end of his life, in his analysis of justice among members, although free movement *within* the state is one of the 'primary social goods' to be distributed equally among all citizens (Rawls, 1996, p. 181), the freedom to move between states is not. Membership of society is fixed, and members cannot leave it (ibid., pp. 136, 277). Migration controls are strongly endorsed as necessary for responsible governance (Rawls, 1999, pp. 38–9). In other words, the assumptions behind a reconciliation between markets and welfare economics are contradictory; the notion of consensus around constitutional principles *plus* the Pareto optimum is inconsistent with the notion of a finite membership with strong immigration restrictions under the 'original contract'.

Second, and more important for the new model of the 'choice agenda', there is the problem of exclusive groups controlling distributions of resources within society. Hobbes recognized that this was an important issue; how could the sovereign government claim to act for the common good if such 'systems' (as he called any organized collective action, whether a business or a voluntary body) could purloin resources and divide them up among members to the exclusion of the rest of the body politic (Hobbes, 1966 [1651], pp. 214–15)? In the same way, if each hospital, school, care home, local authority, utilities company, gated community, pension fund and charitable trust can accumulate capital and select its own membership, how can governments claim to be achieving justice among citizens?

This was not such a problem in the post-war era of welfare states. In the nineteenth century, to the horror of individualists such as Herbert Spencer (1969 [1860]), the state had (both nationally and locally) intervened more and more in issues such as the supply of clean water and sewers, public health and factory inspection, postal services, mental-health care and provision for orphans. In the twentieth century, governments had funded the expensive infrastructures for telephone networks, electricity supply grids and airports; they had eventually taken ownership of railways and mines, shipyards and parks. The collectivization of decisions about the welfare of citizens seemed to be a gradual but progressive tendency (Swaan, 1988); welfare economics could safely assume that distributive issues were in the hands of elected bodies, qualified officials or corporate institutions with responsibility for the common good of the whole population.

It was exactly these processes of collectivization that individualists, neo-classical economists and libertarians opposed. They sought to subvert the collectivist basis for welfare economics and restore the individual foundations of decision-making. They argued that the transfer of choices to government was not only inefficient, but also based on a phoney consensus, which reflected the selfish interests of politicians, bureaucrats and professionals (Niskanen, 1975).

But all collective organizations have the power to put boundaries around their resources, and to reserve the benefits of ownership, sharing, co-operation and membership to those *they* choose to admit. The rules for entry and participation may take many forms – purely economic, faith-based, ethnic, ideological or idiosyncratic – but the principle is universal. Insiders control distributions for their advantage, and may make outsiders bear some of the costs of their association (i.e. 'externalities' – see p. 142). For members, their interests take precedence over those of non-members (Cornes and Sandler, 1986, ch. 11).

Governments can, of course, regulate all such organizations, and make them compensate non-members who are harmed by them or who have to pay part of their costs. Governments can also make rules about access to membership; for example, it can outlaw associations which exclude black and Asian people, or discriminate against disabled people. Governments can even require organizations to include a diversity of membership by using powers to fund or subsidize such bodies as health insurance schemes or private schools. Or they can subsidize disadvantaged individuals, to give them the resources they require to choose the organization or scheme which best meets their needs (Zweifel and Breuer, forthcoming – see pp. 102–3). All these policies redistribute the benefits generated by these organizations, and might be seen as steps towards equity (Mueller, 1989; Starrett, 1988).

In the next section, I shall look at what economists of this school ('public choice' and 'fiscal federalism') have to say about mobility, membership and the boundaries of organizations, including jurisdictions. These are the analyses which have set the terms of the 'choice agenda' and the GATS.

Individual decisions, collective goods

These theorists set out to explain collective action (how groups formed, co-operated and maintained cohesion) and collective goods (those shared among the members of such groups) in terms of the decisions of their individual components. They were looking for an analysis of the strategies of such organizations as trade unions, cartels, political parties and lobby groups, and ultimately of governments themselves. Behind the search for such models was a scepticism (or even hostility) towards political debate and government intervention as a way of providing goods and services, and of political authority as the arbiter of justice and welfare. Coming from the Enlightenment traditions of individual liberty, and institutions constructed out of the unintended consequences of individual choices in markets (see pp. 127–8), these theorists mistrusted the post-war order of welfare states and criticized the assumptions behind the state's enlarged supply of public services.

Their first task was to challenge the longstanding analysis (going back to Adam Smith) of 'market failure' over the supply of certain 'public goods', without which the economy functioned at below its optimum potential output. Although Smith's list of such goods was short (concerned mainly with law and order and defence, with some poor relief), the scope for intervention on these grounds had grown for two centuries. As we saw (p. 124), a whole range of infrastructural facilities, and services for building and maintaining human capital, had been provided through the state on the grounds *either* that commercial firms would undersupply them, because they could not make everyone who used them pay (the 'free rider problem', which applied most obviously to criminal justice and defence); *or* that individuals would buy fewer of them than they really needed, because they could not afford them out of weekly income (which applied most obviously to health care, education and pensions).

These theorists developed two main types of analysis to challenge these orthodoxies. The first was to show that, under certain assumptions, people would sort themselves into groups and organize their own infrastructures and services if the government did not intervene and do this on their behalf. The second was to show that, in certain circumstances, a political authority with power to tax and spend would *oversupply* these facilities and services, to the detriment of economic efficiency, because the politicians, bureaucrats and professionals who controlled the public sector had perverse incentives to increase their budgets, staff and provision beyond the point where the whole population benefited. Both these strands of analysis converged around the methodology of individualism and the critique of the 'Leviathan power' of the state (Oates, 1985). By reducing political authority to a microeconomc formulation, they could demystify the collective logic of welfare states and expose fallacies at the heart of its legitimations of public-sector governance (Buchanan, 1980; Peacock, 1979).

One of the most influential early contributions to this new school of thought was a paper in 1956 by Charles Tiebout, in which he set out to show that – left to their own devices – populations could sort themselves into efficient distributions, among an infinite number of 'jurisdictions' (modelled as small cities), each with a full range of infrastructural facilities, with its own local taxes to pay for these. The model made a set of unrealistic assumptions – that perfectly informed households could move costlessly between these jurisdictions, which could all exclude non-contributors from the 'congestible' technologies for producing their collective goods (i.e. there was an optimum population to share facilities, and use could be controlled). They could also reproduce each other's most attractive features, without externalities (costs borne by each other). On these assumptions, for every 'collective good' in the infrastructure (i.e. roads, drains, parks, libraries, theatres, social services) there was a technically efficient population size that minimized the average cost per household of providing that service (Inman and Rubinfeld, 1997, p. 81).

This model revived a tradition in economic theory (Wicksell, 1958 [1896]) of explaining groups and sharing through chosen exclusive communities that govern themselves by agreement. It has been enormously influential, appearing in the programmes for devolution of decision-making over hospitals, schools and care homes. Its claims of greater efficiency rest on two mechanisms. First, if people can choose the quality of collective goods they wish to pay for, they will cluster together round facilities which maximize the advantages of cost-sharing, by supplying all those with particular needs and preferences in common. Second, entrepreneurs (whether in the public sector – i.e. council leaderships – or commercial developers building private communities) will supply exactly those collective goods which are required, at the lowest possible cost. So the model combines the virtues of the market (because of competition between jurisdictions, and exit rights for consumer households) and of democracy (because, by 'voting with their feet', households express their choices more clearly than they ever could in the ballot box).

We have already seen examples of governments adopting this model. The Blair administration in the UK has explicitly done so in relation to the 'choice agenda' for schools, hospitals and other public services (pp. 90–1), publishing 'league tables' to help households move in search of better value for their local taxes. Strictly speaking, there is an independent case to be made for 'local and particular' provision of collective goods, so that for each good the sum of members'/residents' marginal benefits equals marginal cost (Oates, 1999, p. 1122). These arguments for *devolution* merge with the Tiebout model for geographical mobility and 'voting with the feet'. We also saw that the Chinese municipal authorities have contracted with property developers to supply all infrastructural goods, including the full range of cultural facilities, in their construction of the new megacities of their Special Economic Zones (p. 5).

Reinforcing this analysis of self-selected clustering round infrastructural collective goods came the model of groups, membership and sharing through exclusive ownership. Buchanan (1965) showed that 'club goods' – those managed on behalf of fee-paying members for their common benefit – required technological means to exclude non-subscribers in order to be efficiently provided. To illustrate these aspects of such collectives, he chose the example of a swimming pool, which would become congested if it were open to all comers, and which would not be well maintained if some users did not pay towards the costs of maintenance. At the same time, Olson (1965) was developing a 'theory of groups' in which collective action required specific rewards for individual members, gained at the expense of non-members. In Olson's analysis, organizations such as cartels and trade unions were able to achieve sustainable solidarity because their co-operation gained their constituents advantages over unorganized firms and individual workers. Their rules outlawed competition among members, under various sanctions, and in this way ensured that 'economic rents' – the higher returns gained from monopoly power or special market position, over and above the return which could be gained in a competitive market (Tullock, 1980, p. 17) – were produced, sustained and distributed among 'insiders'.

The theory of 'club goods' was extended into the analysis of many kinds of human association, from the management of commons and water resources (Ostrom, 1990), to cultural and recreational facilities and social services (Cornes and Sandler, 1986). It drew attention to the potential for devolving the provision of amenities and services to firms or voluntary associations which could manage them on behalf of memberships. If governments funded their public-sector assets through such bodies, they could make rules about how memberships were to be selected, or even insist that whole local populations were to be eligible. This might be seen as a way to increase citizen participation in the running of public services, as in foundation hospitals and city technology colleges in the UK (Blears, 2003).

Fiscal federalism and political reform

This model had far-reaching implications for the way in which social policies were framed, agencies were organized, and services were delivered. It implied a regulatory and supervisory role for central government, autonomous, arm's-length agencies to manage the services (or contract them out to commercial providers), and staff who were far more cost-conscious, prioritizing their work according to evidence on risks, effectiveness and outcomes. But it also had more fundamental implications for the whole system of nation states, and their relationship to the supply of social services in an integrated world economy.

First, there may be good economic reasons why 'clubs' for supplying collective goods to members can be most efficiently organized on a transnational basis. Just as some telephone networks and pay-TV channels recruit subscribers from several countries, so health-care and education provision might bring together patients and students without regard for national borders. Other club goods might be supplied by regional or city-level organizations. In other words, if collective provision is to follow the prescriptions of this model, each membership system supplying these goods (either through a public authority or contracted out to a commercial company) will set different geographical and social boundaries, and there will be overlaps between them (Casella and Frey, 1992). Each might in principle be funded from a different stream of revenue, collected from a different constituency. Depending on whether a global, regional, national or local perspective is adopted, the optimum recruitment population and membership characteristics will vary (Jordan and Düvell, 2003, pp. 54–5), but the idea of 'fiscal federalism' implies that both clubs and jurisdictions overlap with citizens/subscribers/members having multiple affiliations and rights to switch between providers (Oates, 1972, 1999).

If these principles are adopted, which collective goods (if any) should the state supply to citizens rather than devolve to larger or smaller units of population? Some goods have been identified by researchers as vulnerable to undersupply, especially where firms and jurisdictions are competing to recruit subscribers/residents and to provide them with value for their payments. Among these are environmental protection and poverty alleviation, both of which can be victims of a 'race to the bottom', as local or regional authorities cut taxation to try to attract wealthy residents and corporate investment (Ackerman et al., 1974; Oates and Schwab, 1990, pp. 275–305; Brueckner, 2000). Along with the overall regulation of mobility and access, the state therefore becomes mainly a provider of income transfers and environmental measures, along with attempting to foster such intangible 'goods' as 'social capital', 'community cohesion' and the work ethic (see pp. 194–6 below).

But this model, derived from choices of individuals in search of utility, switching among suppliers of collective goods, and looking for others with whom they can most advantageously share benefits and costs, leaves the whole nature of politics ambiguous and contested. After all, it has only been in modern times – since the middle of the seventeenth century (Spruyt, 1994) – that nation states established their hegemony as *the* units of political authority in sovereign territories. Before that, empires, city states and city leagues competed with nation states (often successfully), and populations owed allegiance to more than one form of authority. The idea of 'fiscal federalism' revives the possibility of such multiple affiliations and memberships, as does the emergence of supranational authorities such as the European Union. Why should nations continue to have a single form of sovereignty over their territory? This question is perceived as threatening by social policy analysts who retain the welfare-state paradigm for their model of citizenship and social justice.

The idea of devolving responsibility for collective provision to the small unit or local jurisdiction ('subsidiarity', as it is known in the European tradition) coincides with Tiebout's model of small cities competing for residents, with mobile populations shifting between them.

Political membership in this version might promote active engagement, since this was the size of polity recommended by civic republicans such as Plato, Aristotle, Rousseau and Montesquieu, because groups can bargain and reach effective agreements in units of this size (Inman and Rubinfeld, 1997). Membership in that tradition is derived from self-rule and commitment to participation in debates and mobilizations about the common good; it promotes the identification of common interests, and more involvement of groups with divergent interests in dialogue with each other – 'bridging' social capital (Putnam, 2000, pp. 22–4).

However, greater mobility, more switching between residential districts and suppliers of collective goods, and more homogeneity between members of groups sharing lifestyles (see pp. 180–1) has been shown to *reduce* participation and engagement, not increase it (Oliver, 1999, p. 205). Cities designed for security and insulation from poor and disorderly segments encourage private retreatism and material consumption, not active citizenship (Davis, 1990). As we shall see in the next chapter, they also lead to resistance activity and rebellion among those excluded from the mainstream.

This is hardly surprising, given that the public choice model promotes an instrumental approach to membership of organizations of all kinds, based on calculations of individual utility available. The aim of these theorists was precisely to restore the approach of the Enlightenment philosophers in relation to choices of institutions and constitutions as well as specific collective goods. As Buchanan and Tullock put it in their foundational text of this new orthodoxy,

> all collective action may be converted to an economic dimension for the purposes of our model. Once this step is taken, we may extend the underlying economic conception of individual rationality to collective as well as market choices. Specifically this involves a working hypothesis that the choosing individual can rank the alternatives of collective as well as market choice and that this ranking will be transitive. (Buchanan and Tullock, 1962, pp. 33–4)

For the purposes of social policy, this means that individuals will rank suppliers of health-care, education and welfare services according to the utility they anticipate they will gain from choosing them. Although this will include a calculation of the costs and benefits of sharing with other members, they are unlikely to reckon this in a way which takes account of the good of non-members, still less of possible adverse effects on others further afield. And this approach does not promote 'voice' or 'loyalty', where members seek to improve the quality of what is shared with others – instead it encourages 'exit' options, moving to another supplier or jurisdiction (Hirschman, 1970, 1981).

In the next chapter, I shall turn to an example of the attempt to promote choice among 'consumers' of public services in the UK. I shall show how the reform of systems for funding and supplying social care have influenced patterns of provision and the actions of citizens.

Conclusions

In this chapter, we have seen how the principles of individual liberty, autonomy and mobility, derived from Enlightenment theory of a society constructed out of the choices of ordinary people, have been translated into reformed institutions of social-services organization, and finally into service delivery. This complements the picture of the new model for trade in services presented in chapters 5 and 6. In addition to opening up public sectors for competition by firms, including transnational corporations, the neo-liberal and Third Way programmes have sought to reshape these services through the expressed preferences of individuals and households. Whether 'voting with their feet' to move into districts with better amenities or transferring their allegiance to alternative suppliers, these 'consumers' have been encouraged to transform the public sector by their choices.

At the same time, government budgets have been devolved to the units which provide direct service, and managers have been made to compete with other jurisdictions and suppliers for the service users whose choices create revenue streams. The goal has been greater efficiency, partly through specialization – districts or facilities catering for particular needs and tastes – and partly through saving costs by allowing those with similar preferences to share facilities.

This has intentionally turned schools, hospitals and care homes into 'clubs' in the economic sense (see pp. 148–50) – exclusive units, seeking to recruit members who gain advantages in relation to non-members by sharing costs and benefits, and externalizing their 'waste products' (often in the all-too-human form of 'disruptive' or 'demanding' pupils, patients and residents) (Jordan and Jordan, 2000, ch. 5).

But the negative effects of these policies are not confined to the neediest (and hence most expensive) individuals. They are also felt in social division, polarization and conflict. These will be the topics of the next chapter. By reducing collective action to its individual components, by enlarging the scope for 'exit' options and reducing that for 'voice' ones, and by impoverishing the public sphere and political participation, these programmes have had hidden costs of their own.

9

The Transformation of Citizenship

In the era of post-war welfare states, the concept of citizenship was regarded as fundamental for the analysis of social policy. 'Social citizenship' was seen as the extension of the democratic principle (that each member of society is of equal moral worth, and their votes should count equally in constructing political authority) into ensuring equal *social* worth (Marshall, 1981). The justification for social rights of citizenship was that they allowed disadvantaged members to enter the mainstream and countered marginalization processes. The public services equalized the life chances of more and less fortunate citizens on many dimensions (Marshall, 1963, p. 107); state support was not related to economic value and contribution, and social justice replaced market reward as the basis for distributive shares (ibid., p. 100).

This was always an 'ideal type' of social citizenship. In reality, welfare states varied in the extent to which they redistributed resources and achieved greater equality. For example, in continental European states, where Christian democratic principles deeply influenced post-war reconstructions, the institutional order was aimed more at achieving social stability and enforcing the responsibilities of all parties to a 'social contract' (mutual insurance against unemployment and poverty) than at equality (Van Kersbergen, 1995). Redistribution was more across the life cycle, and within social status groupings, rather than between members of society as a whole; and family and community responsibility, especially the male breadwinner's primary role in household earnings, was reinforced (Esping-Andersen, 1990; Lewis, 1992).

The other aspect of the post-war development of citizenship was that the creation of extensive public services led to a new kind of social environment for relationships between members to be played out. It was the intention of those who designed the institutions of the welfare state to make a space for more democratic exchanges among citizens

(Cole, 1945; Macadam, 1945); public services were supposed to reflect a new ethos, to encourage participation and the sense of 'ownership' by those who used them. In the 1960s and 1970s, new movements of women, minority ethnic communities, and gay and lesbian people criticized the assumptions behind policy and practice in the social services and changed much of this through collective action (Williams, 1989).

The new model outlined in chapters 4, 5 and 8 aimed to change all this, by cutting back the role of the state as central arbiter in issues of distribution and making individual choice, rather than collective action, the decisive influence shaping collective provision. The transformation of public systems of social rights has been described as 'the end of citizenship' (Eriksen and Weigård, 2000) and the 'subversion of the public role of citizens through markets' (Freedland, 2001, p. 91). In this chapter, I shall examine how citizenship has been transformed and look at the strategies pursued by individuals and households within the new systems. I shall focus particularly on services for 'the family' – mainly women and young children – in the affluent countries.

As we saw in chapter 7, citizenship was indeed the target of transformation under the Third Way regimes of Bill Clinton and Tony Blair in the 1990s (pp. 128–30). Their 'new covenant' and 'new contract' aimed to redefine the roles of government and citizens, by placing new emphasis on responsibilities as well as rights; but they also sought to transform public officials, especially those in charge of benefits administration. In the UK, New Labour aimed to break the mould of the old, passive benefits system and to bring about 'a change of culture among claimants, employers and public servants' (DSS, 1998, p. 24). The philosophical basis for this shift was derived from communitarianism, and especially the version of this argued by the US author Amitai Etzioni (1988, 1993, 1999). This aimed to balance the constant innovation necessary for market economic success ('creative destruction') with a socially conservative set of family and communal relations, which acted as a glue or cement for society (Williams, 1998, p. 12). In Tony Blair's vision,

> no country can ever prosper economically or socially unless all its people prosper, unless we use the talent and energies of all the people rather than just the few, unless we live up to the ambition to create a society where the community works for the good of the individual, and every individual works for the good of the community. (Blair, 1996, p. 5)

There was clearly some tension between the two parts of this version of citizenship – the economic rationality of the individual in search of utility in markets and the responsible family member, active in the community. But, in Third Way rhetoric, the role of the government is to provide education, socialization and (in the last resort) compulsion – for instance, in the conditions surrounding benefits – to inculcate the work ethic, family values and reciprocity in social relationships. Although the constantly shifting order constructed by market choice seems fluid and ephemeral, while that of traditional community values appears stable and archaic, Third Way philosophy sees no contradiction. Both sets of institutions evolved from actions by individual agents (chapter 7), and hence from freedom and moral sovereignty. Responsibility in relationships means sticking to commitments and standing by the consequences of choices – not burdening others, or expecting the government to rescue situations. As Etzioni put it:

> First, people have a moral responsibility to take care of themselves. . . . the second line of responsibility lies with those closest to the person, including kin, friends, neighbours and other community members. . . . As a rule any community ought to be expected to do the best it can to take care of its own. (Etzioni, 1993, pp. 145–6)

This approach appeared to hark back to a nineteenth-century view of civil society and a version of well-being located in small associations and tight-knit residential districts. Such an idea seemed, of course, inconsistent with the kind of mobile, switching, utility-maximizing citizen produced by the economic agenda, or even with the self-realizing, self-developmental, self-improving individuals, cultivating their 'projects of self' (see pp. 130–1). But it related to specific aspects of social relations, notably the raising of children and young people, and to social order and discipline. It dealt in the hinterland of lifestyles, where individuals' choices, consumerist tastes and self-fulfilment projects might collide with each other, causing conflict and mutual resentment. Above all it touched on issues of crime and disorder – the violent, disrespectful, dishonest and inconsiderate actions which rampant individualism might spawn without the counterweight of these elements (Boutellier, 2004).

One way of looking at this mixture of neo-liberal and traditional communal elements in Third Way policy agendas is to see communities as 'economic clubs' in relation to family values, socialization and local order. At the same time as pursuing their interests in markets, and switching among collective units which supply welfare goods and services, families are encouraged to subscribe to groups of like-minded fellow residents, to form associations such as Neighbourhood Watch units, to join a church, and to support sports and leisure activities for children. In this way, they build up 'social capital' as well as property rights.

Although these features were most explicit in the Anglophone countries, there is growing evidence of their influence on European societies also. On the one hand, focus on the supply side of labour markets, the activation of unemployed people, the work ethic and conditionality of benefits all became features of the administration of countries such as Denmark and the Netherlands (Cox, 1998, 1999), as welfare-to-work measures sought to transform systems 'from safety nets to trampolines'. On the other hand, research also suggests that the combination of neo-liberal and communitarian approaches was the main characteristic of new regimes in other continental states. This seemed to apply whether Christian democratic or social democratic parties were the major components of government coalitions in any particular period (Bleses and Seeleib-Kaiser, 2004; Seeleib-Kaiser et al., 2005). Although Germany was the last (because of its Nazi history) to introduce tough conditionality into benefits for its unemployed people (Cox, 2001), its fusion of neo-liberal and traditional Christian democrat (socially conservative) themes is now in line with those of the rest.

In this chapter, I shall focus on how this transformation affects policies towards families. It is through women's roles, as paid workers, family caregivers and community activists, that the new model tries to reconcile these different elements, and that the tension between them is revealed.

Women and citizenship

The analysis of citizenship by Marshall and other theorists of the welfare state was criticized by feminists for its conception of an abstract legal status, giving rise to rights, and to a version of justice as impartial and impersonal (Squires, 2000). But its focus on the public sphere and denial of the relevance of domestic issues of power and exclusion was seen as disguising male domination in a cloak of equality. Although there were many strands to feminist theory – libertarian, liberal, socialist, welfare and black variants (Williams, 1989, ch. 3) – they had in common the demand that politics and social policy should take better account of women's real situation in the polity. This was directed especially at their roles in childcare and the care of elderly and disabled people (Wilson, 1977; Chowdorow, 1978; Eisenstein, 1984; Land, 1978; Lewis, 1982; Bryan et al., 1985).

Within these traditions, there have been many claims that women are denied full citizenship because of lack of access either to the labour market and to social rights (Nelson, 1984; Lister, 1997), or to the kind of political participation in which they could pursue their interests (Phillips, 1993; Voet, 1998). Some have seen in more communitarian accounts of citizenship a potential corrective to the legalistic contractarianism of Rawls (see p. 145) and other liberals, arguing for a politics of interdependence and the common good (Elshtain, 1981, 1998; Ruddick, 1983) – but with the community specifically seen as made by women. This approach advocates relationships of emotional attachment, the ethic of caring, and the recognition of difference, based on the experience of childcare by mothers (Elshtain, 1998, p. 375).

Others, however, see this appeal to traditional female values as potentially oppressive (Young, 1990, esp. p. 72). They argue for a modified version of liberal citizenship, with new attention to how women can pursue their agendas with 'a richer and more equal democracy' (Phillips, 1993, p. 114) and a deeper understanding of equality (Nash, 1998, p. 146). Some feminists seek a radical shift towards a civic republican version of political participation (Mouffe, 1993); others emphasize the need to balance the universalism of the liberal tradition with particularism, diversity and difference (Young, 1990; Lister, 1997).

One aspect of this dialogue is the simultaneous claim by feminists to equality in the public sphere (and especially the labour market) and greater recognition for the activity of care and the role of caregiver. As women have entered the labour market in ever greater numbers since the 1970s, the work–life balance has emerged as a significant issue for social policy. In the Third Way politics of the late 1990s, political leaders wooed women voters with claims that they addressed equal citizenship as an issue of social justice, and the provision of childcare as the means of achieving this.

In the Scandinavian countries, some such settlement had already been achieved, because women had never been outside the labour market. They made the transition from being active in a predominantly rural economy of family farms to the urban and industrial post-war economy as service workers, and the expansion of health and community services in the 1960s and 1970s saw them employed in the public sector as professional and para-professional staff (Esping-Andersen, 1990). In the 1990s, the shift in policy in these countries was towards including fathers in parenting (by giving paternity leave, for example) and constructing the care of children as a defining element in gender equality (Leira, 2002). However, women still work predominantly part-time, and do not either divide their time in the same way as men or earn at the same rates (ibid.).

In the Anglophone countries, the lack of a tradition of public child-care has meant that new policies have had to be developed, both to regulate and subsidize the commercial provision of childminding, crèches and nursery education, and to address the issues of early years socialization of children in deprived areas (see the next section). Childcare was traditionally a low-paid job, with little or no training and professional content (Lewis, 2001), so government has been required to intervene to try to improve the standard of supply as well as the quality (DoH, 1998). However, by giving tax credits to low-paid households, the US and UK governments subsidize the employment of women in unskilled, low-status work, including childcare itself. This consolidates inequalities between high-skilled and low-skilled women as well as between women and men.

At a fundamental level, the Third Way model of women's citizenship created a number of tensions and ambiguities, and it is questionable whether most women have been able to use these to their advantage (Williams, 2005). First, along with men, women were seen primarily as workers, with responsibility to earn, save and accumulate, so as to be 'independent' (see pp. 131–2); women, like men, must have 'projects of self', to realize their potential. In the new covenant and new contract, they become full citizens by demonstrating these forms of autonomy and competence. But this is in obvious tension with the values of care and interdependence which are intrinsic to family, kinship and community (Sevenhuijsen, 2002; Williams, 2001). The tension is especially clear in relation to women who care for disabled children or parents.

> An overarching emphasis on the obligation to engage in paid work obscures the extent to which citizenship rights may be reciprocated in other ways, such as care giving or providing insights into the experience of managing age and impairment which most of us face at some time in our lives. An appreciation that we act in response to our responsibilities towards others within the context of given relationships, rather than in response to ascribed obligations, highlights the injustice of making caregivers' rights to support conditional upon individualistic obligations to continue caring. Only care policy based on the precepts of relational autonomy might enable citizens to manage the ethical dilemmas they face in balancing responsibilities to self and others and/or provide the practical means by which people are afforded the time and space to combine paid work with care giving or receiving. (Ellis, 2004, p. 44)

Second, the Third Way model emphasizes the responsibilities of parenthood (Thompson, 1996; Dean, 1995), as in Bill Clinton's Personal

Responsibility Act (1996). Since women have become more engaged in paid work, expectations of parents have increased, not diminished, as a theme of social policy rhetoric. Children are constructed as extensions of 'projects of self', and the realization of their potential a duty of parents (DfES, 2004). Research shows that parents recognize that – as partnerships dissolve more frequently and earlier – relationships with children may be more enduring than those between adults (Smart et al., 2001). But government is quicker to criticize women, especially lone parents, for their performance than to offer support for parenting.

Third, although the child is the focus for welfare concern, and the interests of the child are paramount in disputes between parents, there is no clear framework for children's progress from dependence to maturity and membership of a democratic polity. Children are seen as vulnerable and in need of protection (Parton, 2006), and parents as potential threats to their well-being and development. Education prepares children for autonomy and competence in a competitive economy. It is unclear what particular links all the children in whom the state invests through schooling and training have in common, or how they will share membership in ways which respect diversity (Williams, 2005).

In the Anglophone countries, the pattern has emerged of families and communities sustained by women who work part-time in demanding jobs, and are pulled between the rival claims of earning and caring (Lewis, 2001, pp. 62–5). Although there are more opportunities for women in the labour market, those who have been able to take advantage of them, and pursue full-time careers, 'have come disproportionately from the more privileged backgrounds' (Woods et al., 2003, p. 104). Their reliance on childcare by women from less advantaged situations has added to the exploitation of those workers (Jordan et al., 1994, ch. 2). Women on lower incomes are also heavily involved in networks of unpaid care, supporting each other's earning activities.

These 'do-it-all' women are driven more by anxiety about their children's prospects than by ambition for upward social mobility. They recognize that the new model demands adaptability and skill, and see such things as home computers and mobile telephones as essential accessories of the lifestyle which youth demands in order to be part of the culture of self-realization. In the Third Way version of citizenship, women provide the glue of responsibility and commitment which links socialization to future autonomy and projects of self. That they do so through 'choices' over work and welfare is one of the conjuring tricks of the new model. The main way in which young adults deal with these pressures is to postpone having children or to decide not to have them at all (Pusey, 2003, pp. 99–105). Birth rates have declined in all the affluent and post-communist (Central European) countries, and couples are having children later; this is especially marked in the Southern European countries of Spain and Italy, which have moved from being among the highest to the lowest in terms of birth rates (Esping-Andersen, 1996). The new model imposes requirements on women in particular which – although accepted as part of the framework for their self-development, and for negotiations with partners – are difficult and stressful. The terms for these struggles are determined by outside economic forces, especially those who set wages.

> Given that reform is not a consensual process, the experience of dealing with its externalities, even in this most private realm of the family, means coming to terms with the power of others. As reform has broken up traditional cultural restraints and unsettled explanations of 'how things work', angry people try to make sense of their own experiences with various attributions of agency and blame. (Pusey, 2003, p. 101)

For women in poor households, government interventions are aimed at inducing this ethic of work and family responsibility, seeing it as having been eroded by the 'passive' welfare provision of the previous era. The goal is to convince mothers in particular that they have a crucial contribution to make in the future of their children by setting an example of autonomous, active competence, and by guiding them towards achievement in education. Support offered through tax credits is accompanied by services focused especially on pre-school children and their parents, and targeted services to address truancy, delinquency, drug use and teenage pregnancy.

In the UK, one of the flagship programmes of the second New Labour government (2001–5) was the Sure Start initiative, aimed at improving child development and family functioning in deprived areas. Behind this policy strategy has been a set of beliefs about the social relations of such communities, and the ways to change them. The local programme projects aimed to engage mothers in an active way in pre-school education and socialization to try to influence their relationships with their children and with each other – strengthening communal as well as family bonds (NESS, 2004).

Case study: social care in the UK

An example of the tensions between the two elements of Third Way citizenship – individual autonomy and choice versus family responsibility – is the field of social care. The expansion of women's employment opportunities and the construction of service users as 'consumers' are not easy to reconcile with an ethic of care in family and community.

As part of the restructuring of the public services by the Thatcher government, local authority social services were criticized as inefficient because they were standardized and inflexible, reflecting the interests of politicians and staff rather than service users (Audit Commission, 1986). Research studies had shown that older people could be supported in their own homes – which they preferred – for longer periods if a wider range of more flexible domiciliary services were available (Challis and Davies, 1986). Both people with disabilities (Oliver, 1990) and family carers, mainly women (Ungerson, 1987), criticized the shortage of services for 'independent living' and respite care. Ethnic minority groups received fewer services and were critical of the quality of those they did get (Harding, 1992, pp. 27–9). Among the declared goals of reform was therefore to promote choice by making services more responsive to the needs and preferences of those who required day-to-day assistance with looking after themselves, and to provide a more accountable relationship with a greater variety of service providers (Langan and Clarke, 1994).

However, another (perhaps decisive) force driving reform was the rising cost of state-funded residential care, mainly for elderly people. In the 1980s, the cost of this aspect of public spending rose from £10 million to £1.2 billion (Oldman, 1991, pp. 4–5). The vast bulk of this took the form of *social assistance* payments to *private homes*; those who qualified for means-tested income support could opt to enter such care, and their fees would automatically be paid by the Department of Social Security. In other words, the poorest elderly people did have a choice, but only between living at home on standard rations of home-help assistance, meals on wheels, and some home nursing support, or entering a residential home. This was officially described as a 'perverse incentive' for an expensive form of care (Griffiths, 1988), which research had shown not all such residents strictly needed (Wright, 1985). The impetus for reform was therefore largely the search for 'value for taxpayers' money' – that public funds should be targeted towards the most cost-effective services according to evidence of need (not incremental additions to budgets). The management of social services departments was criticized as lacking strategic vision (Kelly, 1991, p. 180).

Accordingly, as part of the reform of the National Health Service in 1991, the local authority social services departments were given responsibility for funding social care, but under regulations and guidance which were aimed at promoting a 'mixed economy', and which would stimulate domiciliary and day care as well as residential provision. The task of 'purchasing packages of care' for each person in need of support was to be carried out by 'care managers', who would assess means and needs and then allocate appropriate services. It was clear that the new arrangements were intended to broaden the range of commercial and voluntary agency provision, but not obvious how the reforms increased 'consumer choice'. People who previously had been able to enter residential care at state expense lost that option; instead, care managers decided what they needed, and bought it on their behalf. Care managers were also subject to strong managerial control and accountable in terms of standards of value for money (Audit Commission, 1992, p. 22). Devolved budgets were supposed to promote this process and encourage both individualized assessments and needs-led, flexible provision (ibid., p. 27); but many councils placed 'block contracts' for a number of units of domiciliary, day or residential care with large-scale providers, and then simply filled these places as applications for support were received – an approach as standardized as that of the old regime (Flynn, 1996, p. 45; Common and Flynn, 1992, p. 35).

Although the rhetoric of the reforms included ideas of 'partnership' with service users and carers, critics have found little evidence of this influencing policy or practice (Oliver, 1992; Jones, 1992); care managers assess and prioritize 'needs', but those claiming services have no entitlements. From a feminist perspective, the model promoted by the new services did little to recognize, value or promote an 'ethic of care' (Tronto, 1994). Because it aimed to prolong the 'independence' of the individual service user, rather than strengthen relations of interdependence and mutuality, it did not assist care managers in negotiating issues of power, responsibility and dependence between family carers (mostly women) and those they cared for.

When New Labour came to power in 1997, it immediately set out to achieve further reforms, but if anything hardened the principles of the Conservatives' system. In its White Paper *Modernising Social Services* (DoH, 1998), it outlined its 'third way' between commercialization of care and public-sector monopoly. This emphasized the 'independence' of the person needing care and the individualization of assessment (para. 1.8), and announced a switch from focusing 'packages of care' on the most dependent people to more generalized programmes of support (ch. 2), achieving good value for taxpayers by better targeting and risk assessment (para. 2.12). Still emphasizing choice, they introduced a set of top-down initiatives to ensure government monitoring of standards in assessment and contracting.

Nothing in this initiative met the criticisms levelled at the earlier reforms, and other parts of New Labour's programme reinforced that critique (Davis et al., 1997). Despite the rhetoric of 'empowerment' and 'inclusion', the main thrust of the Third Way notion of autonomy – independence through employment, earning and property – tended to devalue both those who needed care (who were therefore by definition 'dependent') and those who looked after them without pay (who qualified for benefits as carers, but only if they withdrew from full participation in the labour market). The liberal individualism of a political philosophy built upon the choices of free-standing property owners relegated care to the shadows, and supported it with reluctance and stigma (Sevenhuijsen, 2000; Williams, 2001). In this approach, responsibility was primarily towards the self, for realizing potential through work and ownership, and only very secondarily towards mutuality in family and kinship groups (Ellis, 2004).

Research confirmed that those who carried out social-care assessments subscribed to the Third Way code of individual independence and self-responsibility. Although they had a wider view of mutuality and need than members of the general public, social workers saw self-reliance and autonomy as the standard to be sought. They were also ambivalent about the idea of rights for those who needed care, because it represented a threat to their professional discretion in decisions about care (Ellis and Rogers, 2004). Furthermore, studies of service users found that they experienced little choice over allocations (Wigley et al., 1998; Hardy et al., 1999).

In view of all these problems in reconciling the purchasing of social care for elderly and disabled people with informal care and choice, it is understandable that the UK government simultaneously turned to another approach. In the Netherlands and Germany in the 1990s, new programmes had been introduced, under which elderly people became entitled to long-term care provision through their social insurance contributions. These benefits could take the form of services in kind (domiciliary, day or residential) *or* direct payments to claimants to organize and fund their own care (for instance, combining care by relatives with care by members of a local co-operative of domiciliary workers). Although the UK government still retained the means-tested basis for such services, it began to encourage local authorities to make direct payments to those who needed these forms of care.

Direct payment schemes have proved popular with service users (Maglajlic et al., 2000; Clark and Spafford, 2001; Glendinning et al., 2000a). This is actually the only example of a reform since the 1980s in which citizens are able to make a binding contract with a provider (6, 2003, p. 241). Although it is discretionary, and has been patchily used, this scheme *does* empower users and carers, by putting them in charge of organizing their own arrangements and enabling them to create their own combinations of informal, voluntary and commercial support. Although the transaction costs for this are high for consumers (Glendinning et al., 2000a, and 200b), especially in hiring personal assistance, it meets several of the criticisms of the main programme for social care.

Finally, it is worth noting that large corporations have made an entry into this field, which was dominated by small family businesses in the 1980s. A recent survey has shown that, of 10,000 homes for elderly people, turning over £10,000 million per year, one-third were corporately owned. The largest of such companies, BUPA, Four Seasons, Southern Cross and Barchester, dominated this market. BUPA ran homes offering 17,000 places, many of which had over 180 residents. Large corporately owned homes were still replacing small family-owned ones, which were closing at a rate of three per week (BBC Radio 4, 2005g).

Social care in the UK illustrates some of the tensions between the elements of the Third Way social policy programme. Because of its model of individual choice, deriving from autonomy, self-ownership, property and mobility, those who need care are a residual and anomalous category. They rely on others, they cannot move easily, and they seldom have the resources to pay in full to meet their needs in markets. The creation by the Conservative government of 'quasi-markets' (Le Grand, 1989), in which care managers means-tested applicants and bought care on their behalf, mimicked commercial relations in unconvincing ways, and has offered little real choice for service users or flexibility of support for carers. Direct payments create highly individualized alternatives to collectivized systems. The question which will be raised in the final part of the book is how these forms of individualism can be balanced by measures encouraging participation and collective action in the social services.

Conclusions

The transformation of citizenship in the affluent First World countries has not been uniformly achieved, but a dominant model, derived from the World Bank blueprint for development, has gradually prevailed – first in the USA, the UK and other Anglophone countries, and then in Europe. This combines a liberal polity, where citizens must aim to be self-sufficient, with a market economy and a civil society made up of 'responsible communities' of active associations.

Substantial minorities are excluded from the mainstream, and hence from the new version of citizenship; these often comprise minority ethnic groups and less skilled and healthy populations. Despite the continuing differences between party political programmes, the main outlines of this liberal-communitarian blend are recognizable in all affluent societies (Seeleib-Kaiser et al., 2005). Germany has been among the last to embrace the transformation openly, though tendencies in these directions have been evident since the mid-1980s (Bleses and Seeleib-Kaiser, 2004).

Through their roles in families and communities, women provide the links between the liberal and communitarian dimensions of the model. Their citizenship mediates between 'independence' and the interdependence of social relationships. Social care illustrates the tensions inherent in their roles. The ethic of care and the non-productivist approach to social policy supply a potential new basis for equality and justice in affluent societies (see chapter 14).

10

'Stalled Well-Being'

The strongest argument in favour of the World Bank's model of development, and the liberal-communitarian approach to social citizenship outlined in the previous chapter, is that they have provided the most reliable bases for improved human well-being for the past 200 years. This is why the Enlightenment formula for social institutions derived from the choices of free individuals still seems convincing; the exchanges between such people in markets, and in voluntary civil associations, have supplied ways of doing things which are functional for subjective happiness and self-assessed flourishing – property, free movement, trade and a consensual political order, derived from an active, self-organizing citizenry.

Why else would a self-styled communist regime in China opt for a vast experiment in organizing a part of its economy on this basis, simply holding the rest of society in a kind of fossilized version of its previous state-led system (see pp. 5–7)? And has not this experiment been spectacularly successful, leading to record growth rates and further gains in human development? It seems only a matter of time, on this optimistic analysis, before the rest of China (and India, Indonesia, Brazil and other huge industrializing countries) is remodelled according to some versions of the same blueprint. Democratization will be slower to arrive in China than in these others but – on this analysis – will surely accompany other manifestations of property ownership, prosperity and liberal individualism.

In this chapter, I shall set out a whole series of doubts about this trajectory and examine their implications for social policy. We have already encountered some indications of the origins of these criticisms. Just as authors such as de Tocqueville (1836) and Durkheim (1896) warned that individualism could turn sour unless it was adequately balanced by collective solidarities, loyalties and principles in social life, so again in recent years a whole number of social theorists and political scientists have pointed out the dangers of a combination of doctrinaire market economics and capitalist enterprise.

For example, in two highly critical accounts of the new model of collective life, *The Market Experience* (1991) and *The Loss of Happiness in Market Democracies* (2000), Robert E. Lane disputes the basic premise of the Enlightenment functionalist formula for institutions conducive to human well-being.

> Why, then, do the constituent individuals [of such societies] not make better use of these instruments and choose paths that will maximize their well-being? The short answer is that people are not very good judges of how, even within the private spheres of their own lives, to increase, let alone maximize, their happiness. . . . The problem is that people often choose of their own accord paths that do not lead to their well-being, they escalate their standards in proportion to their improved circumstances, choose short-run benefits that incur greater long-term costs, fear and avoid the means to their preferred ends, infer from early failures an unwarranted and disabling incompetence. (Lane, 2000, pp. 8–9)

We have already encountered a critique of the consequences of the adoption of the new model, and the overthrow of a protectionist welfare state, in Michael Pusey's (2003) report on middle Australia. Pusey's point of comparison was between the income levels and self-reported well-being of Australian middle-class and skilled working-class individuals, looking back at their childhoods. In this chapter, I shall analyse more systematic comparative evidence on the evolution of well-being under new regimes in the affluent First World countries.

The authors we have quoted from so far are social theorists, and their critiques of individualism and the 'choice agenda' are part of a long tradition, going back to the writings of Karl Marx (1848, 1867), which sees the accumulation of property and profit as a process of alienation from the essential elements of human well-being. The associations of that tradition with state socialism, now discredited partly because its denizens were notoriously miserable compared with their counterparts in capitalist countries – populations in the former Soviet Union republics reported levels of satisfaction with their lives which were less than two-thirds those of people in Denmark, Switzerland, Canada and Ireland, and those in Ukraine only half those levels (Frey and Stutzer, 2002, table 2.2) – have made such criticisms less heeded. But now there has been a new alliance between two hitherto little connected groups of researchers and theorists, arguing for a new paradigm in the measurement and analysis of well-being.

On the one side, economic psychologists have argued for, and brought forward new analyses of, the experiences of pleasure and pain – their causes and contexts. Their aim is to discover the circumstances in which people feel well-being or misery, and that these should be integrated into a coherent theoretical account, using data which are measured in standard ways. This new initiative stems from a specific set of criticisms of the dominance of modern microeconomics in the field of public policy under the current model.

> At present, economic indicators hold the most sway in policy circles. Yet, the economic approach is limited in several ways. First, it focuses on those aspects of life that can be traded in the marketplace. Thus, desirable goods such as love, mental challenge, and stress are given little consideration. . . . Second, the economic view presupposes that individuals will choose the greatest amount of utility for themselves, yet a great deal of evidence now contradicts this proposition. Third, economics assesses variables that are only indirect indicators of something else – subjective fulfilment. (Kahneman et al., 1999, p. xii)

On past form, we might have expected economists to reject these criticisms, none of which is new. However, a large body of opinion is emerging in the community of academic economics which not only accepts but embraces the new evidence and analyses coming from these psychologists. Not only theorists but also leading empirical investigators who have been influential on public policy, such as Richard Layard (2003a, 2005), have declared themselves persuaded by the psychologists' arguments, and thus opened up a new front in the long battle between social and individual perspectives in the social sciences. If what a person actually chooses is no longer to be taken as knock-down evidence of a utility-improving (and hence welfare-enhancing) decision, then the foundations of microeconomics, the new model of social policy and indeed the new world order are destabilized.

We thus face a paradox in social policy in the affluent First World countries. The dominant social science paradigm, which informs the World Bank and Third Way models of human development, is derived from microeconomics and the version of welfare or public economics which prevailed in the 1980s and 1990s – utility maximization, as modified by the group or collective preferences and analysed by the public choice and fiscal federalist schools (see pp. 141–53). But, within economics itself, there is a new movement towards incorporating psychological evidence and social factors which were systematically excluded from the dominant model. The unlikely alliance between psychologists and economists now awaits a response from political scientists, social theorists and social policy analysts (Jordan, 2005). In this chapter, I shall outline the case for such a new response and start to sketch some of the forms it might take.

Subjective and objective well-being

Despite the enormous influence of utilitarian principles on public policy, social scientists have until recently devoted little attention to the study of *happiness*. Jeremy Bentham (1780) advanced the remarkably simple maxim that the aim of government should be to promote the greatest happiness of the greatest number of citizens; and this approach was carried forward by such important liberal theorists as his secretary and executor, John Stuart Mill (1860), and the Fabian School of socialist reformers (Webb and Webb, 1911). However, social scientists virtually stopped trying to define and measure happiness in the early twentieth century. It is to this task that economic psychologists have now returned.

Some model of a trade-off between the intensity and the duration of unhappiness (or pain) and the intensity and duration of happiness (or pleasure) has, of course, been implicit in many aspects of social policy. For example, in allocating scarce medical services, such as choosing who should have a transplanted organ or kidney dialysis, doctors or managers have to decide how to compare the benefits of treatment and the costs of withholding treatment across a number of candidates. This means devising a notional scale of pain and pleasure, in which the intensity of an immediate experience is charted, along with its duration. This has yielded a measure, Quality-Adjusted Life Years (QALYs), with equivalences between years of survival in normal health and years at some lower level of heath (Weinstein and Fineberg, 1980).

Psychologists have explored the relationship between pleasure or pain at a particular moment, as reported by a subject, and overall happiness or well-being, which encompasses all domains of life. This relationship is complex, because subjective assessments of overall well-being rely on memory and evaluation, and may be influenced by very recent events or by current mood. Psychologists have therefore tried to combine *subjective* reports of instant happiness, focused on particular experiences of pleasure and pain, with *objective* measures of how those reports sum together over time, using scales which allow intensity of feelings to be traded off against their duration (Kahneman, 1999, pp. 4–6).

All this assumes that individuals can put a value on each fleeting experience, somewhere on a scale between good and bad, with a neutral point halfway between them, and that a single value can be assigned to very diverse experiences. Experiments tend to confirm that people do evaluate their experiences continuously, but not necessarily consciously (Förster and Strack, 1996); this evaluation strongly influences action to seek or avoid continuation of the experience. However, this also assumes that there is no valid distinction between pleasures and pains, on the one hand, and the *contexts* in which they are undergone, on the other. Preferences (still the basis of this approach) do not distinguish between these aspects; the eating of a favourite food while watching an exciting football match is simply a series of very pleasurable moments. This issue will be analysed in detail in chapter 11.

A problem which is directly addressed in the psychological theory is the idea of a 'hedonic treadmill'. As people's well-being improves (for example, as a result of rising income) they raise their expectations (the assessment of 'neutrality' of experience applies to higher states of welfare), so improvements do not count as benefits (Brickman and Campbell, 1971). The notion of objective measures of well-being contains the proviso that, even if individuals' self-assessed happiness (as an overall evaluation of their life) is not rising, because they are adapting over time, there are ways of showing that their well-being is improving, through a record of their evaluations of a huge series of successive experiences. This, of course, creates a wedge between immediate assessments of utility, which may evoke short-run choices, and long-term assessments, which might influence strategies or investments. The 'hedonic' approach argues that, to counter mistaken evaluations based on faulty memory or adaptation, objective data should be gathered and made available as a better basis for public policy: 'Real-time measures of experience can be obtained, stored without error, and aggregated to yield a measure of objective well-being that is anchored in the reality of present experience, not fallible reconstructing and evaluations of the past' (Kahneman, 1999, p. 22).

In the meanwhile, however, such subjective assessments are all that is available, and there is now a vast body of survey evidence, of comparable data, spanning many countries of the world. This indicates that, in broad terms, people living in affluent market economies describe themselves as happier (as an overall evaluation of their lives) than those in poorer countries. However, as table 10.1 shows, the main feature of the average satisfaction with life in the rich countries is that it is not increasing in line with growing prosperity. By contrast, in the industrializing and less developed countries, growth in national income is usually reflected in growth in subjective assessments of well-being. It fell in the former Soviet bloc, where it reflected the *decline* in GDP per capita in three years.

Clearly there is no easy match between prosperity and self-assessed well-being. Among the poorer countries, China (with a GNP per capita level at $3,291 in 1999) was higher in the table than that level of income would have indicated, as were Nigeria ($744), India

Table 10.1   Average satisfaction with life, 1990–8

Country	1990–3	1995–8
Bulgaria	5.03	4.66
Russia	5.37	4.45
Belarus	5.52	4.35
Latvia	5.70	4.90
Romania	5.88	n/a
Estonia	6.00	5.00
Lithuania	6.03	4.99
Hungary	6.03	n/a
India	6.21	6.53
South Africa	6.22	6.08
Slovenia	6.29	6.46
Czech Republic	6.30	n/a
Nigeria	6.41	6.82
Turkey	6.41	n/a
Japan	6.53	6.61
Poland	6.64	6.42
South Korea	6.69	6.69
France	6.76	n/a
China	7.08	6.83
Portugal	7.10	7.07
Spain	7.13	7.15
Germany	7.22 (West)	7.12 (unified)
Italy	7.24	7.34
Argentina	7.25	7.78
Brazil	7.39	7.15
Mexico	7.41	6.69
UK	7.48	7.46
Chile	7.55	6.92
Belgium	7.67	n/a
Finland	7.68	7.68
Norway	7.68	7.66
USA	7.71	7.67
Austria	7.74	n/a
Netherlands	7.84	7.77
Ireland	7.87	7.88
Canada	7.88	7.89
Sweden	7.97	7.77
Iceland	8.02	n/a
Denmark	8.16	n/a
Switzerland	8.39	n/a

Source: World Values Study Group (1994, 1998)

($2,149) and Brazil ($6,317). Conversely, South Africa ($8,318), South Korea ($8,910), France ($21,897), Germany ($22,404), the UK ($20,883), Japan ($24,041) and the USA ($30,600) were lower in the table than their GNP per capita would have predicted. As the leading theorists of these measurements point out, 'Although people may be happier if they live under improved conditions, the influence is likely to be large at first and then taper off. Expectancies can outstrip reality, even when an economy is growing rapidly – with a net loss of SWB [subjective well-being]' (Diener and Suh, 1999, p. 449).

This phenomenon is particularly clear in the affluent First World countries. As Layard (2003b) points out, time-series data on self-assessed happiness with life shows the phenomenon of 'stalled well-being' in all such states. In the USA, data gathered by Gallup show that self-evaluated happiness has not increased since the 1960s, after a rise during the previous decade. In Japan there is the same lack of any increase, despite a much faster rate of economic growth up to the 1990s (Frey and Stutzer, 2002, pp. 8–10). In Europe, the Eurobarometer statistics show no rise since the 1970s, except in Italy and Denmark (Layard, 2003a, p. 15). It seems as if the close connection between increases in average income per head and improved subjective well-being, on which Adam Smith's thesis, the World Bank model of development, and the Third Way version of social policy and citizenship all rely, holds only in less affluent societies (Frey and Stutzer, 2002, p. 9). In the most prosperous states, the growth of well-being seems to peter out once averages reach a level of about $15,000 per capita, at 2000 prices (Layard, 2003a, p.17).

In all countries, the wealthiest group are also the happiest, according to their self-evaluations. In the USA, 39 per cent of the top quarter of income receivers assessed themselves as 'very happy' in 1975, but only 19 per cent of the bottom quarter; 8 per cent with the high incomes said they were 'not too happy' and 30 per cent with the lowest. But by 1998, when the disparities between these incomes had increased substantially, but both had risen, the proportions were much the same (Layard, 2003b, p. 3); the number who said they were 'very happy' had fallen in both groups.

In the next section, I shall consider theoretical explanations of 'stalled well-being' in the affluent countries. Economists have responded to the challenge set by psychologists to account for this apparent anomaly in the previously reliable correlation between rising average incomes and self-assessed happiness.

Adaptation, rivalry and values

For economists, these phenomena take them back to a major theoretical shift in their discipline, which took place in the 1920s and 1930s.

A. C. Pigou limited his analysis of welfare to aspects which could be measured in terms of money (Pigou, 1920, p. 11). In his account of *The Nature and Significance of Economic Science* (1932), Lionel Robbins turned away from the attempt to incorporate well-being into economic analysis, or indeed the whole question of how individuals come to form preferences. All that was necessary to explain how scarce resources could best be deployed to achieve particular purposes (such as a government's programme or a firm's output) was to assume that each person has a stable set of such preferences.

However, even if preferences are consistent and transitive over a short period of time, they may be adapted over a longer period. Norms of what constitutes an adequate income have risen with increases in earnings, for example, so that even steady rises in salaries leave more people dissatisfied (Lane, 2000, fig. 2.4). As we saw in the previous section, the 'hedonic treadmill' makes people adapt to rising living standards, so that loss of earnings has a substantial negative effect on subjective well-being but small gains have little or no positive effect.

This seems to apply particularly strongly to material aspects of lifestyles (Frank, 1999, ch. 6). The desire for designer and luxury goods is insatiable, and both advertising and rapid changes in fashion mean that expensive items must constantly be replaced. The very nature of consumer markets in affluent countries ensures that these are assessed according to criteria in which they very quickly become not just unsatisfying, but repulsive; the moment an item is no longer trendy, it carries stigma and shame. This is in stark contrast with the situation in the developing world, where sought-after items (such as radios and motorcycles) do have enduring use value, as well as being status symbols.

The second major explanatory factor is the issue of comparisons. Robbins's innovation was to reject these in his account of the necessary assumptions for coherent economic analyses, and this view is certainly consistent with the principle that individuals are autonomous agents, making choices based on their moral sovereignty and on personal utility functions. However, it is obvious that individuals can also incorporate others' preferences into these functions. For example, it is common for teenagers to want to buy what their friends have, or to want to avoid owning what their parents, or other middle-aged people, possess. Once this occurs, another variation of the 'hedonic treadmill' comes into play; what people find satisfying, and what makes them happy, is related to what others have.

Evidence of this phenomenon is now available. For instance, Solnick and Hemenway (1998) found that graduate public-health students at Harvard would prefer to earn $50,000 a year, if others got half that salary, than to earn $100,000 a year where others got more than double that amount. People seem particularly concerned about salaries as a point of comparison, presumably because they measure esteem in some sense (Clark and Oswald, 1996). The situation in affluent countries seems to be that more information is now available about earnings in wider society, and that individuals compare themselves with others across a wider range of social groupings. For example, since more women in the USA are now in the labour market, they are more likely to compare their material situation with that of men, and to be unhappy about it, despite improvements in their relative earnings (Layard, 2003b, p. 8). Another example is citizens of the former East Germany (GDR), whose subjective assessments of their well-being have fallen sharply since they stopped comparing themselves with other Soviet bloc residents and started comparing themselves with West Germans (ibid.).

However, rivalry is not simply a question of comparisons; people compete for scarce resources, and some situations are indeed 'zero-sum' by their nature – winner takes most, or all. In post-war welfare states, one of the sources of rising self-assessed well-being was the creation of large sectors of the economy where rivalry was contained and competition restrained. As Hirsch (1977) pointed out, the public services provided opportunities for 'managed crowding' – new professions in which previously blocked people of intelligence could rise to situations of responsibility in conditions of security, although on modest salaries. The new model of society has not merely cut back this sector in most countries; it has also introduced competitive tendering, performance-related pay, managerialism, and competition between units, all of which deliberately stimulate rivalry between employees.

Furthermore, the 'choice agenda' over public services and the public infrastructure widens the field of rivalry even further. While resourceful people can celebrate their wisdom and skill in finding the best schools for their children or hospital for their parents (they do so endlessly at bourgeois dinner parties), poorer people are not unaware that they are disadvantaged by these same processes. They resent the fact that, even within the institutions which are supposed to promote equality and social justice, their disadvantages are further reinforced. The consequences of this, in terms of intercommunal resentment and antagonistic mobilization, are shown in the case example at the end of this chapter (pp. 180–2).

However, subjective well-being does not relate solely, or even mainly, to material issues. The psychological studies already referred to show that the main constituent elements in self-assessed happiness are personal relationships, health, employment satisfaction and security (Helliwell, 2002). In general, married people are happier than unmarried, healthy than ill or disabled, and employed than unemployed (Frey and Stutzer, 2002, ch. 3), but these very general patterns conceal important detailed variations.

Helliwell (2002) has charted the specific effects on a scale of subjective well-being of these factors across a range of countries (not only affluent states) in terms of loss in happiness. He found the largest effect (4.5 points) to come from marital separation, followed by unemployment (3 points) and subjectively assessed ill-health (3 points), divorce (2.5 points) and widowhood (2 points). Having an income 35 per cent lower than the average caused only 1 point of decline in happiness, whereas having an insecure job caused a 1.5 point fall.

It is obvious, therefore, that wider social and economic relations are more important determinants of happiness than income and wealth alone. Such factors as divorce rates, quality of life in old age, and labour market conditions are not reducible to purely statistical measures; there are qualitative factors at work, and relational aspects to what is at stake (see chapter 12). Rivalry is an economic concept, relating both to competition for goods and to congestion of shared facilities, but it is also a description of how people relate to each other in some situations. Here the factors which protect against destructive rivalry are shared concerns, co-operative practices, and the sense of common purposes.

This is why values, too, are important for subjective well-being. It appears that, even if people cannot always live up to their value commitments, being concerned for the well-being of others is a positive factor in subjective happiness. Not only religious people (Veenhoven et al., 1994) but also those who do voluntary work (Lynn and Smith, 1991) have been found to give more positive evaluations of their well-being than their average compatriots. By contrast, those who watch a great deal of television are less happy than average (Argyle, 1999).

There is a relationship between individualism on the one hand, which correlates with high rates of separation and divorce, and communitarianism on the other, which is associated with lower rates:

> If individualism corrodes family commitments, we should also expect to see greater individualism linked with weaker family bonds across cultures – and we do. The United States is both the world's most individualistic and most divorce-prone nation. Britain is somewhat less individualistic and has barely half the divorce rate. . . . Divorce rates tend to be even lower in collectivist cultures such as Japan. (Myers, 1999, p. 385)

As we saw (pp. 160–1), higher expectations of partners and greater dissatisfaction in relationships are growing fast in the UK; given the salience of this issue for self-assessed well-being, these outworkings of the individualist culture of self-realization, autonomy and choice clearly contribute to stalled happiness ratings. However, the other relevant contributory factor lies in political culture and values – how individual citizens relate to each other, and to their governments.

Trust in fellow citizens

If rivalry and distrust are two factors in stagnant or falling levels of self-assessed well-being in affluent countries, then a political culture of democratic membership, where all citizens are treated with equal respect and feel able to influence the decisions of their government, might be expected to lead to high and rising rates of happiness. Conversely, the notorious failure of state socialist governments to win the loyalty of their citizens, or to extinguish rivalries between them, may help explain very low levels of self-assessed well-being in the Soviet bloc countries. These regimes often took power in states which had experienced years of coups and authoritarian governments that set citizens against each other.

Among the countries with the highest levels of self-assessed well-being are Denmark, Norway, Finland and Sweden (see table 10.1), all of which have very stable political systems with social democratic institutions and relatively egalitarian distributions of income. Political stability is considered to be an important factor in high ratings; in the Dominican Republic in 1962, after the murder of President Trujillo, an all-time record low for subjective happiness was recorded, at 1.6 (Frey and Stutzer, 2002, p. 125). However, African countries such as Nigeria have relatively high levels, despite their political instability – perhaps partly because government is remote for most people in a large low-income state.

The high rating of Switzerland does not fit the Scandinavian model. Switzerland has a very stable political system, but unlike those others is highly diverse (linguistically, and in terms of foreign immigrant populations). It has a very small welfare state and a relatively unequal pattern of income distribution. However, Switzerland has (both nationally and locally) highly participatory democratic institutions, including frequent referenda on many issues, prefaced by lengthy discussions, negotiations and soundings of opinion. Citizens are well informed, and do control political decisions. Frey and Stutzer use evidence of studies

in particular cantons to conclude that 'More extensive political participation rights, as well as more autonomous communes, increase people's
subjective well-being over and above the demographic and economic
factors . . . . [G]ood political institutions do indeed raise happiness'
(Frey and Stutzer, 2002, p. 150).

In recent years, anxiety about declining trust in political elites in
such varied countries as the USA and Japan (Frey and Stutzer, 2002,
p. 127; Lane, 2000, p. 201) has led to considerable political engagement and academic research on this topic and its relationship to trust
among fellow citizens. This is clearly of relevance for social policy,
since the goal of increasing mutual trust and co-operation lay behind
the creation of welfare states (see pp. 124–5), and there are important
policy implications if increased competition under economic restructuring has eroded democratic political culture. The relationship
between individualism, trust, welfare states and political democracy is
complex, as can be seen from the case of Sweden.

Sweden is the country with the longest tradition of social democratic
government and the largest proportion of income transfers and public-
service expenditures. This research has been undertaken partly with a
mind to the implicit accusations of the original social policy ideology –
that deep penetration of government agencies into civil society, high
marginal rates of taxation, large proportions of employment in public
services, and decision-making over collective goods and distributive
shares by representative elites all contribute to passive citizenry and a
hollowing out of the associational life of the community.

The evidence shows that high rates of participation in voluntary
associations of all kinds, stemming from the traditions of social movements and local activism in the nineteenth century, have been sustained through the development of the Swedish welfare state. The
institutions whose scope expanded between the 1940s and 1970s rely
on dense networks of negotiations between state agencies and civil
society groups. Although these mechanisms have declined in
significance, as the 'Swedish model' ran into economic trouble in the
early 1990s, and the country joined the EU, this has not affected membership rates of these associations. As local activism first waxed in the
USA, and then waned after the 1960s, Swedish participation remained
buoyant, and if anything increased towards the end of the century
(Rothstein, 2002, pp. 295–305).

The important point here is that this has occurred despite disillu-
sionment among Swedes about many aspects of corporatist institutional structures for political decision-making in recent years. There
has also been a cultural shift towards more individual autonomy and
moral sovereignty. But this did not undermine collective solidarity;

above all, it did not damage the links between the middle and working classes, or the redistributive systems between genders and age cohorts. Research on these more individualistic members of the Swedish population shows that

> they do *not* show any stronger interest in increasing today's wage differentials, they do *not* evidence any greater tendency to view the poor with a 'they-just-have-themselves-to-blame' attitude, and they do *not* show any stronger tendency to regard their fellow beings in less of a spirit of trust and fellowship. (Pettersen and Geyer, 1992, pp. 28–9)

Rothstein interprets these findings as showing that the new 'solidaristic individualists' are 'willing to give support to other individuals, but also to accept that they have other, different values and want to engage themselves for different causes' (Rothstein, 2002, p. 308). He regards this as a form of reciprocity over lifestyles, which involves a combination of individual autonomy and social responsibility. The question is therefore how this combination, which sounds like the liberal-communitarian blend sought by Third Way regimes in the USA and the UK in the later 1990s, is achieved in Sweden, perceived from the Anglophone countries as an extreme version of a collectivist, high-taxation, regulated, welfare state.

On Rothstein's account, *because* of its welfare-state institutions, Swedish society has achieved even higher levels of trust between citizens and engagement in civic affairs in the 1990s than in the heyday of political corporatism. Commitment to redistribution through universal social insurance provides the framework for mutual security, in which Swedes are able to combine freedom with solidarity (Rothstein, 2002, pp. 323–4). And this is sustained despite the breakdown of trust of specifically designed mechanisms for negotiation over the economy between employers, unions and the state, seen as a 'crisis of democracy' (ibid., pp. 327–30).

However, a caveat should be entered before reaching this conclusion. During the early 1990s, the numbers claiming social assistance in Sweden rose rapidly, from a very low baseline. At a time when countries such as Denmark and the Netherlands were introducing 'activation' measures for such claimants, requiring them to accept low-paid work or training to be eligible for benefits (see pp. 66–7), Sweden had a long tradition of such measures built into its social insurance system. Research on trust in fellow citizens had established that among those receiving state pensions and disability benefits it was only slightly below that of mainstream citizens. But claimants of social assistance displayed levels of trust far lower than those with social insurance entitlements, and those on welfare-to-work schemes the lowest by far, little over half mainstream levels (Rothstein and Stolle, 2001).

This shows that some programmes, even in advanced welfare states, still attract stigma – especially those which are targeted on 'outsiders' and administered in ways that remove autonomy and put citizens under the direction of officials. Groups which feel that they are being blamed for society's ills, or accused of not contributing to the well-being of the body politic, feel alienated and distrustful. In the next section, I shall consider the situation where such feelings are reinforced by ethnic and faith divisions, and eventually by a culture of hostility between the minority and the mainstream.

Case study: intercommunal conflict in France

It is now well recognized in all First World countries that the liberal-communitarian model of citizenship faces particular difficulties where the dimensions of poverty and disadvantage are combined with those of ethnicity and religion. In this situation, rivalry and resentment take on a group as well as an individual aspect, and the bonds between members of a local community, identifiable by skin colour and the symbols of faith, come to carry a group stigma. This challenges the government, and the mainstream members of society, to specify the common core of institutions and values in which citizens are supposed to share. If well-being is related to such forms of trust, reciprocity and membership, then policies are required to make these explicit and implementation to reflect inclusion and empowerment.

Each country faces a specific version of this challenge, but one which has attracted international attention is the case of France, especially in relation to communities of North African, Muslim immigrants, concentrated in forbidding blocks of flats in the northern districts of Paris. Within popular culture, this constitutes a distinctive problematic grouping, resistant to 'integration', with high rates of criminality and 'anti-French' attitudes, especially among young people. In France, the challenge relates specifically to its republican tradition of citizenship, and to Article 6 of the Declaration of the Rights of Man and of the Citizen of 1789 – that all are equal without distinction of race, class, sex or religion, and distinguished only in terms of their virtues and talents. The French language represents the symbol of this common equality among citizens, a very different basis from the ethnic German version, for example. But this also makes it difficult for French people to acknowledge the forms of discrimination which lead, for instance, to having very few people of colour in the National Assembly but a majority in their football team; it also makes suspect any policies directed specifically at ethnic groups or communities, seen as 'partisan for particularisms, in other words hostile to the generous universalism of the 1789 revolution' (Begag, 2004, pp. 17–18).

Within this political tradition, the whole phenomenon of the ethnic ghettos of public-sector housing in northern Paris is perceived as self-exclusion by the members of this community – the refusal to integrate, derived from loyalty to an alien faith and culture, which in turn has generated hostility, deviance and subversion of the republican order. One issue which has focused these concerns has been the Act to ban the wearing of conspicuous religious symbols in state schools, widely seen as directed primarily against the headscarves of Muslim girls. French politicians and officials perceived these as indications of domestic oppression and the inequality of women. The Act was implemented in early 2005; at that moment two French journalists were captured by insurgents in Iraq, who demanded its repeal. The crisis was seen as a test of the political allegiance of French Muslims, the majority of whom dropped opposition to the law in the face of the threat to the lives of fellow citizens.

Social scientific research does not confirm the popular perception that the 'separatism' of the North African minority is a chosen one. Instead, it shows that the creation of 'immigrant ghettos' is part of a twenty-year process of 'segregation from above'. This reflects 'the extraordinary selectivity of residential mobility, revealing the almost infinite anxiety of families and the almost existential importance of place' (Maurin, 2004, pp. 24–5; my translation). As in the UK, this mobility has been partly in search of schools with good examination results, and has left the poorest with no choice but to remain in districts with the least successful outcomes (ibid., pp. 26–8):

> In choosing one's place of residence, one also chooses one's neighbours and the children of one's neighbours, those with whom one's offspring will grow up, will go to school, etc. It is thus because we believe that the quality of the immediate social environment throws the greatest weight on the success or failure of each individual. (Ibid., p. 84; my translation)

People from ethnic minorities are most disadvantaged in this competition for a head start. Maurin's research revealed that being of foreign origin was the factor which most influenced ability to choose to live in a more desirable district – greater than income (ibid., p. 91).

Because of its political traditions, French government devotes few resources to specific programmes for integration – about 500 to 1,000 officials work in this field overall (Begag, 2004, p. 18). But, as in the other affluent countries, local initiatives have attempted to improve trust in official agencies among the residents of disadvantaged minority communities and reduce conflict between them and white, mainstream populations. Comparison between such initiatives in Paris and Chicago have revealed how political culture influences practice, especially over who participates in meetings and how the minority ethnic community is perceived within the body politic.

In Chicago, community safety is the responsibility of the police, in liaison with residents' groups. Local people are invited to monthly meetings, in which they are facilitated to express concerns and discuss all local issues, including those outside the remit of the police force. They also attend courts and advocate on behalf of their communities. Police in turn act as brokers with other government agencies over local issues. In Paris, by contrast, there is no participation by residents of the problem districts. Police meet with other professionals working in the area, to diagnose neighbourhood problems and co-ordinate their response (Body-Gendrot, 2004).

These different practices stem from alternative versions of what citizens have in common, and how to improve trust and well-being. In the USA, the liberal-communitarian model encourages both individuals and communities to find ways of solving problems. Community is not a good in itself, but it can supply resources for members to improve their situations, such as getting jobs or moving. It is a form of membership somewhere between the primary loyalties of family and faith, and national citizenship.

In France, policy and practice are still concerned mainly to reimpose the authority and persuasiveness of the institutions of the republic. Professionals are committed to the universal values of citizenship, and regard residential community and the loyalties of ethnicity and faith as potentially dangerous and subversive of the common good. They stand in a pedagogic relationship to the population, imposing top-down, rational solutions and trying to break down local particularisms.

A crisis in this model was signalled by the riots in the minority ethnic suburbs, first of Paris and then of other cities, in October–November 2005. Young men burned cars and damaged property as a protest against their exclusion from mainstream public life. In proclaiming that 'We hate France, and France hates us', they challenged the republican model of 'integration' and citizenship.

Conclusions

Throughout this book, improvements in well-being have been the standards against which social policies have been judged. Such evaluations seemed unproblematic until recently, because of the unexamined faith which social scientists, politicians and the public placed in the functionalist formula, derived from the Enlightenment philosophers. The pursuit of their own utility, by free individuals in markets, when combined with free association in civil society and the widespread ownership of property, were taken as guarantees of increasing well-being, in line with growing average incomes.

In this chapter we have seen that this set of assumptions has now been shaken by new evidence and theoretical criticism. The concept of utility has been shown not to equate to happiness; people make decisions which lead to misery and regret. Autonomous choices sum together to create patterns and outcomes which are not to individuals' advantage. Many strategies turn out to be self-defeating, especially those driven by rivalry of various kinds. The economic, social and political institutions built out of such choices do not sustain the advance of well-being, at least in the affluent First World countries.

This leaves social scientists (including social policy analysts) with several theoretical dilemmas. Psychological researchers and theorists argue that it should be possible to construct *objective* measures of well-being (see pp. 170–1) which will supply a better basis for public policy (Kahneman, 1999). The same view is echoed by some social theorists who criticize the market-based order of the World Bank and Third Way models (Lane, 2000). But it would be difficult to reclaim governments' powers to organize societies and redistribute resources from a public which has become disillusioned with politics and politicians, partly as a result of the 'stalled well-being' phenomenon itself (Pusey, 2003). The idea of an 'objective' political authority, with the wisdom and power to act in the common interest, has been abandoned throughout the world (except perhaps in China and, in a very different way, in North Korea) in favour of the principle of individual moral sovereignty. It is difficult therefore to see an alternative to a grass-roots mobilization around some new principles for social policies, deriving from a new awareness of more reliable strategies to improve 'objective' well-being.

The doubts about present strategies and institutions presented in this chapter rely mainly on reported self-evaluations from many countries. Subjective accounts of well-being may misrepresent actual pain or pleasure in several ways (see pp. 171–2). Economists who use these to reach conclusions about public policy draw attention to other evidence on stress at work (Blanchflower and Oswald, 2000, table 19), desire for a better work–life balance (Landers et al., 1996), loneliness and fear of crime (Glaeser and DiPasquale, 1999), mental health (Rutter and Smith, 1995), and many others, to argue for institutional changes which would reverse many of the features of the new order. For example, Layard (2003b) argues for taxes which discourage overwork; intrinsic and professional rather than material incentives for workers; limits on advertising and status-related promotions; more income redistribution; greater security at work; reduced geographical mobility; more priority for mental health; and more participatory democracy. Coming from a leading economic adviser to Third Way regimes and post-communist governments, this represents an important new development (Layard, 2003b, pp. 17–18). Even Tony Blair now wants more research into the origins of sustainable well-being (*The Guardian*, 2005a).

Clearly economists need to play a major role in any such shift in social policy, as it is the dominance of their discipline over the other social sciences, and especially politics, which has brought about the new order. As Lane puts it,

> Political and especially democratic theory suffers from the same problems as economic theory: it poses as ends what are really means. Maximizing choice (freedom) is valuable only as the choices contribute to well-being – or human development or justice. Democracy, itself, is a means which derives its value from its contribution to ends – but if the ends are not articulated, the value of democracy rests on uncertain grounds. (Lane, 2000, p. 324)

However, this raises a whole set of huge issues, to be tackled in the final part of the book. The choice of ends is a moral and political one. Even if a reliable route to improved well-being could be found, it would not necessarily be the one prescribed by the route to human development or justice. Would it include the whole world's population, or only certain nations? And would it be ecologically sustainable in the longer term? These are some of the questions which will be tackled in the concluding chapters.

Part III

Global Social Justice: The Big Issues

11

Community, Morality and Belonging

The questions raised at the end of the previous part of this book are uncomfortable ones for social policy analysis, especially for those scholars raised in the post-war welfare-state tradition. In that tradition, questions about the moral goals of society, the appropriate unit of account in assessments of justice, and the ecological sustainability of policies were seldom addressed. It was assumed that the basic institutions of each society (property, markets and democracy) would spontaneously propel it in a certain general direction, and that a combination of welfare economics (Pigou, 1920; Robbins, 1932) and applied social theory (Tawney, 1931; Titmuss, 1968) would steer national government decisions about distributive shares, public services and the regulation of civil order. Third Way theorists, who advocate the 'choice agenda' and individual autonomy, are even more reluctant to tackle questions about the ends of society, though more willing to address global and ecological ones (Giddens, 1998).

In this part of the book, I shall argue that these moral and political questions have now become inescapable, partly because of evidence of 'stalled well-being' in the affluent First World countries, partly because of a resurgence of ethical and religious mobilizations all over the world, partly because of clashes of interest between affluent, newly industrializing and less developed countries over the costs of economic growth, and partly because of the issues of global governance raised by all these other questions.

These issues cut across a tradition of sophisticated comparative analysis of national social policies, established in the wake of Esping-Andersen's (1990) pioneering work. In this tradition, the characteristics and outcomes of institutional design and political struggle are analysed within a framework of how a 'production regime' (the way governments, banks, enterprises and labour forces are co-ordinated) relates to a 'welfare state regime' (Huber and Stephens, 2001). The goal is therefore to find out how ideological factors (such as the neoliberal ascendancy of the 1980s) and social movements (such as the mobilization of women) are reflected in organizational shifts and statistical outcomes.

Research in this tradition now argues that – under the pressures of globalization – differences between party programmes in the affluent states have narrowed (Huber and Stephens, 2001, p. 321). Although the fundamental characteristics of each of the major types of regime remain distinctive, each is adapting towards a more liberal 'production regime' and attempting to balance this with protection for the values and institutions which are central to its 'welfare state regime'. For example, in the Scandinavian social democratic countries, these are income and gender equality and public-service employment; in the Christian democratic countries they are income protection and the family; in the liberal Anglophone ones they are civil society associations.

The question raised in this chapter is whether a more fundamental change, which is not captured by this type of analysis, is under way. It refers back to Karl Polanyi's (1944) account of the transformation of societies by global market forces and the 'second movement' of collective action resisting these processes. As Polanyi showed, the latter movement was diverse and incoherent, containing elements which were atavistic, xenophobic and paranoid, including fascism. Do such phenomena as the rejection of the new European Union constitution by voters in France and the Netherlands in May 2005 indicate a resurgence of racism and paranoia, or the desire for a more idealistic and universal expression of collective identities and purposes?

More generally the resistance to global transformation in the name of morality and community is deeply ambiguous. Does it indicate a retreat into the particularisms of specific religious faiths and regional cultures, or an attempt to balance economic growth with new institutions which spread its benefits to the world's dispossessed? Is it motivated primarily by the need for the affluent states to compete with China, India and Brazil, or does it contain a truly inclusive new moral vision?

Polanyi's 'first movement', towards the more anonymous, neutral systems of markets and states, rejected notions of a 'moral economy' and 'divine order', because they brought conflict and misery. In the sixteenth and seventeenth centuries in Europe, moral reformers and religious enthusiasts tried to reorganize emerging modern societies on ethical and religious lines. The result was two centuries of religious strife, with massive mortality and waste of human potential – one of the most disastrous periods for human well-being. It was brought to an end only by the division of Europe into two *de facto* groupings, Catholic and Protestant nation states, most of which had absolutist rulers. Hobbes's theory of the political authority of the sovereign was under a contractual regime for economic progress, founded on individual human attributes (Hobbes, 1966 [1651]).

In a society with extensive private property and a complex social infrastructure, it is far easier to motivate and steer action in search of material gain than it is to sustain systems of moral obligation. Families have survived and adapted, and faith-based organizations have proliferated and mutated, but overall systems for organizing societies around specific *ends* (moral or political) have ultimately lost out to systems with adaptable *means*. In advanced welfare states, families and NGOs are systems for getting some tasks of social reproduction done, within the overall rationale of the regime.

As a result, it has seemed inconceivable, since the 1960s at least, that any advanced Western society would adopt a moral (still less a religious) set of principles as its organizing framework. With globalization and increasing diversity, with the claims of feminism, anti-racism and other new social movements, this notion became increasingly unlikely. As Robert Lane puts it, the failure of *economism* (the fallacy that higher income automatically increases individual well being) does not imply the validity of *moralism* (because those who advocate obligation ignore its costs in terms of conformity and loss of autonomy). 'If *moralism* is at one pole of the problem, economism is at the other' (Lane, 2000, p. 324).

It therefore came as something of a surprise, not to say a shock, when George W. Bush's second presidential election victory turned on his strong commitment to a set of fundamentalist Christian positions on such issues as gay marriage and abortion. In arguing for 'family values' from a born-again Christian point of view, Bush also confirmed his support for faith-based welfare provision and abstinence-based sex education. In the poll, a decisive 22 per cent of voters, most of whom voted for Bush, declared that they had cast their ballot on 'values issues' of this kind (BBC World Service, 2004).

What was even more striking about this phenomenon was that, in US political terms, these 'values voters' identified themselves as specifically *anti-choice*. They rejected, in particular, the principles of women's choice over abortion rights, and gay people's choice of sexual identity and partnership over lifelong commitment and sharing. 'Family values' were not simply the responsibilities to sustain relationships, as in Third Way, communitarian versions of civil society. They were specifically the adoption of such traditional rules as paternal authority, spousal and filial obedience, the sanctity of life from conception, and the sinfulness of homosexual activity. Within three months, the US government had demanded that the UN drop abortion rights from its declaration on the rights of women (*The Guardian*, 2005b).

Up to this point, the predominant view of the Bush presidency, despite his support for faith-based social policy provision, had been that he balanced neo-liberalism in economic policy with a neo-conservatism in foreign affairs that was largely driven by the post-9/11 moral panic and the 'war on terror'. In the new context of his second electoral victory, neo-conservatism represented a critical reassessment of the whole liberal Enlightenment project. If individualism constructs no reliable set of institutions for membership and belonging, because commitments of all kinds are too instrumental and means-orientated, and because identities and loyalties are not rooted in firm moral principles, then it is not merely poor people, ethnic minorities and other vulnerable groups who have much to fear from the reformist zeal of governments. Large sections of the middle classes, and even elites, whose lifestyles reflect a post-traditional view of intimate and informal relationships (Giddens, 1991, 1992; Plummer, 1995) would find themselves under official scrutiny and disapproval.

We should not suppose that the USA is the only country where some such struggle is taking place in the current global political landscape. For example, in the lead-up to the 2005 general election in the UK, the leaders of the two major political parties expressed doubts about the current rules for abortion (*The Guardian*, 2005b). There are many signs worldwide that the liberal order of individualism and choice in markets, and voluntaristic civil associationalism, is losing its persuasiveness as the most sustainable version of social relations. In the UK, for example, doubts about community cohesion, sparked by inter-ethnic violence in the summer of 2001, have led to new programmes for greater engagement and 'bridging social capital' (Blunkett, 2003, 2004). Since the suicide bombings on the London underground in July 2005, the concept of 'multiculturalism' has come under increased criticism as encouraging a separation that breeds disaffection.

Another clear case of the clash of values was the nomination and eventual rejection as European Commissioner of the Italian politician Rocco Buttiglione in 2004. Mr Buttiglione expressed the view that homosexuality was a sin, and held traditionalist Catholic views on marriage and the primary role of women. In this case, liberal and left-wing objections to his appointment prevailed, but the struggle exposed fundamental divisions about the basis for the European project. Also in that year, the murder of the Dutch film-maker Theo Van Gogh, presumably by Muslim extremists, showed that opposition to forms of liberalism and social criticism which had been commonplace in the Netherlands for several decades were manifesting themselves as a protest movement, perhaps akin to the killing of abortion doctors in the USA.

In this chapter, I shall analyse accounts of community and belonging to explore the implications of morality as the basis for membership. Can ethical and religious principles supply reliable institutions and programmes which might supplant choice and markets as the basis for social policy? This is the first big question for this part of the book.

The 'moral economy'

Systems of obligation, such as kinship, community and religion, are not just rules and proscriptions. They are ways of allocating roles and resources and getting very practical things done. In this sense, they provide specialized *alternatives* to markets and systems of political authority. Systems of obligation can organize a group or community to produce goods and services, to distribute assets and products, and to enforce their regulations. In both the East Asian and Latin American models of social policy, families supply many of the supports and services which are formally organized in Europe and North America.

In affluent market societies, systems of obligation have been relegated to marginal roles, on the fringes of mainstream life. Family, community and faith-based organizations are confined to the private and informal aspects of social reproduction, dealing in issues which are outside the serious business of the economy and polity. The promotion of voluntary organizations (including international NGOs) to greater prominence in the Third Way and World Bank models of social policy has been largely a way for the state to withdraw, leaving much more to firms and 'economic clubs', with the voluntary and community sector either as a residential category or required to act as nonprofit enterprises, accountable to taxpayers via local authorities.

The only exceptions to this rule in affluent societies are those ghettos of deprivation in which neither markets nor the state are really attempting to organize the life of the residents; they are too poor to be worth selling to, and too resistant and needy to supply with decent services.

However, Third Way governments have seen families and communities as potentially important sources of social cohesion and mutual support that might offset the consequences of individualism and commercialism. The more difficult question has been how to stimulate the 'moral economy' and establish a reliable relationship between voluntary associations and public bodies. By tradition, the Anglophone political cultures have set great store on the 'independence' of civil society organizations as a source of autonomy and enterprise among citizens. In the Christian democratic tradition, and especially in Germany, Austria and the Netherlands, the state has both funded and been strongly represented in these bodies, which carry out many of its functions. Some commentators have seen the Third Way as adopting aspects of the Christian democratic approach to social policy in this respect (Huntington and Bale, 2002).

There are several different characteristics of the 'moral economy' which are potentially attractive to policy-makers. We have already seen that it has been linked to such phenomena as trust in fellow citizens and active political participation (see pp. 177–80). In this respect, it plays an important part in policies for 'civil renewal' (Blunkett, 2003). But it is also a potential source of those collective values and practices which might balance individual autonomy and choice, and therefore fill a vacuum in collective life left by economic restructuring.

The difficulty about this direction in policy is that the 'moral economy' is a source of divisions among populations as well as co-operation. This is clearest in the case of ethnic and faith communities. While governments may encourage faith groups to provide schools or welfare agencies for their members, they also need to make links of citizenship between these. In the UK, this was recognized after the intercommunal strife in northern towns in the summer of 2001, resulting in a government-led programme for 'community cohesion' (Home Office, 2002a; Blunkett, 2004).

In countries with a corporatist Christian democratic tradition, the closer links between the state and the 'moral economy' allow scope for more direction of such programmes. Ireland is an interesting example, because the integration between Church and state under the constitution and the development of corporatist systems since the early 1980s have been combined with Third Way programmes for economic liberalization. The most recent phase of this development has been the strong incorporation of the community sector in state-led programmes for development.

The Irish trajectory of social policy is derived from a series of partnership agreements between government, employees, trade unions, farming organizations and (since 1996) the community and voluntary sector. These began in the early 1980s, when Ireland was experiencing unemployment of 15 per cent and stagnant incomes. Its greatest achievements (near full employment and one of the fastest rates of growth in the EU in the first years of the new century) were attributed to holding down wage rates and negotiating reforms in taxation and welfare benefits.

Under the Development Programme of the late 1990s, a Community Support Framework and a Local Development Social Inclusion Programme were set up, for 'the community to work together to identify their own needs and then make a collective response to those needs' through bringing groups, organizations and individuals together to 'participate in the process of analysis, planning and implementing activities to achieve tangible outcomes' (ADM, 1995, p. 1). This built on community development projects, established in 1990, and incorporated from 1991 the EU LEADER programme, which linked social, environmental and economic dimensions of rural development (Kearney et al., 1994), and between 1996 and 1999 the EU URBAN community initiative programme for very disadvantaged urban districts.

In a research project drawing on the experiences of professionals working in these programmes for social inclusion and community development, Doherty (2003) investigated whether these arrangements allowed a truly participatory and inclusive problem-solving culture to emerge, in which organized and unattached (often marginal) citizens could establish reliable means of negotiating agreed outcomes. This tested the notion that some kind of communal collective logic, offsetting the market dynamic of the 'Celtic Tiger's' rapid transformation and growth, could identify and practise a local version of social justice.

Even though the programmes promised to reverse the trend away from participatory and democratic processes of governance in Ireland, by giving all members a stake in just outcomes and incentives to seek agreed solutions Doherty found that the professionals who steered these processes saw marginal citizens as severely disadvantaged in meetings and negotiations. They felt compelled to intervene, if necessarily covertly, to forestall unjust and exclusionary outcomes. Despite their commitment to the ideals of community and participatory democracy, they acted manipulatively, as professional guardians of social justice (ethical guides, as it were). Doherty concluded that communal and participatory approaches required constitutional underpinnings, which protected against the domination of the advantaged over the disadvantaged, and also a guiding hand from professionals with specific ethical responsibilities. On this analysis, community is not only an expensive way of doing things (in terms of time and effort), but also one which is not, on its own, ethically reliable. The 'moral economy' does not always lead to justice among citizens.

Social capital and community

The Third Way programme for community cohesion draws on an approach developed by the World Bank, in its model of economic and social progress, in which NGOs and local community groups act strategically to help poor people link into the larger economy. In that view, people whose strategies orientate towards informal activity for subsistence and survival need to be guided 'to engage society's power structure and articulate their interests and aspirations' (World Bank, 2001, p. 131). A key concept in that process is *social capital* (Dasgupta and Serageldin, 2000).

According to its chief theorist and researcher, Robert Putnam, 'social capital refers to connections among individuals – social networks and norms of reciprocity and trustworthiness that arise from them' (Putnam, 2000, p. 19). In his view, communities with strong networks and norms of this kind experience less crime, better health, higher educational attainment and faster economic growth. The connection with citizenship runs in both directions. In his earlier research (Putnam, 1993), he found that regions of Italy with the densest networks of civil associations (from sports clubs to cultural societies) also had the best-functioning democratic institutions (corruption-free and efficient civic services). These in turn led to greater trust in democracy, more political participation, and more associations – a virtuous circle first identified by the French thinker Alexis de Tocqueville in the USA in the early nineteenth century (Tocqueville, 1968, [1836]).

The notion of social capital and its functions for society is appealing for precisely the same reasons as the ideas of the 'invisible hand' and other Enlightenment explanations of enduring institutions (see pp. 127–8). Simply by interacting together in ordinary, everyday ways, as neighbours, kin and friends, people solve problems in their communities *and* unintentionally give rise to norms and practices of reciprocity and trust (Coleman, 1988). The social institutions created in these ways reduce transaction costs and hence promote efficiency in the economy (Bourdieu, 1986); they thus create a robust civil society and a culture which is favourable for democratic politics. The appeal of the concept for Third Way politicians is that both individual and social welfare are enhanced in these ways, without the direct intervention of government.

It also links together the active citizen as autonomous, morally sovereign, independent economic agent and the notion of a 'responsible community'. In their search for self-development, such citizens

(especially women) will interact with like others in their neighbourhoods – for instance, taking their children to school or leisure facilities – and social capital is an unintended by-product of these
interactions. Rather like Weber's Protestant ethic, it generates both
individual and civic virtues, giving rise to collective as well as private
benefits. For the mainstream, it is consistent with the principle of a
social order constructed out of individual choices and spontaneous,
self-selected groupings (chapters 8 and 9). But for the disadvantaged
minority, it both explains their marginality (shortage of social
capital, or the *wrong kind* of social capital, in deprived districts) and
points towards programmes for empowerment, inclusion and poverty reduction (World Bank, 2001, pp. 34–41).

However, the theory of social capital has to deal with a problem –
how to explain the fact that some close-knit groups and communities,
such as the mafia and criminal subcultures, generate 'bad' social capital.
In these interactions, members of close associations or tightly bound
networks define themselves by opposition to the government, the forces
of law and order, and even democracy itself. No one would deny that
al-Qa'eda, for instance, is an organization with high levels of mutual
trust and reciprocity (even to the extent of self-immolation for the
cause), or that the resistance in the city of Faluja in Iraq involved close
co-operation and mutuality. So how do we distinguish between the
social capital that makes global terrorism feasible and that which pro-
duces prosperity and good governance?

Putnam distinguishes between *bonding* social capital, in which like
individuals, with homogeneous social characteristics, often in a small
district, join together in exclusive associations (in informal economic
niches, or esoteric faith cults), and *bridging* social capital, which ties
diverse and heterogeneous individuals into mainstream economic,
political and social life (Putnam, 2000, pp. 22–3). In policy terms,
bonding social capital may help disadvantaged groups to 'get by' – to
survive in adversity – but bridging social capital enables individuals and
communities to 'get ahead', by linking them into the mainstream and
engaging with the centres of economic and political power (World
Bank, 2001, pp. 34–41). Implicitly, bridging social capital is a way of
connecting individuals and their human capital (education, skills) with
the physical capital owned by firms (factories, offices, technology), as
in the work of Bourdieu (1986). By contrast, bonding social capital is
associated with economic backwardness, even when communities are
mutually supportive (Matthews, 1983; Richling, 1985), because it cuts
members off from wider sources of prosperity and progress. Social
policy should therefore seek to counteract the tendency of bonding
social capital to isolate (and even alienate) disadvantaged communities

from the mainstream, and instead build bridges into the wider civil society and economy.

The challenge for the Third Way model arises from poor communities' tendency to split along ethnic, faith or micro-territorial lines. Partly because of the flight of more resourceful citizens, using the opportunities afforded by affluence, property ownership and the 'choice agenda' (see pp. 141–3), poor communities become polarized. In the USA, urban districts have experienced concentrations of poor black residents, as both white and better-off black households have moved to the suburbs (Wilson, 1989, 1996). Third Way agendas for inclusive citizenship are required to challenge the bonding cultures of these districts, and their survival strategies, as well as the hostility and resentment of one ethnicity or faith community for another (Home Office, 2002a; Blunkett, 2004).

An instructive example of these issues, and a test of Putnam's theory, is the case of Northern Ireland, where Republican Catholic resistance to privation of civil and political rights, and to disadvantaged social citizenship, provoked 'the Troubles' – nearly thirty years of paramilitary activity, in which the Provisional IRA conducted campaigns against the UK government and army and against loyalist irregulars. Here the links between bonding social capital and citizenship (or its absence) were all too explicit; those tied into the IRA or loyalist groups owed their first obligations to the defence of local communities, conceived as exclusive ethnic and faith-based networks.

But the bonds between residents in these districts were as much economic as political and social. Reporting on her research on a very deprived district of West Belfast, controlled by the IRA, Madeleine Leonard described

> a vibrant community with strong network ties and social and economic support structures. Community inhabitants were involved in a host of informal economic activities including working while claiming welfare benefits, self-help, family, kinship and friendship networks, reciprocity and volunteering. (Leonard, 2004, p. 931)

For women, much of this activity was self-provisioning of a very traditional kind. In an earlier account of the same research, Leonard reported that activities such as repairing clothes and making jam were widespread and culturally approved under the regime enforced by the IRA (Leonard, 1999). In other words, the solidarity which was sustained partly by a shared ideology of political resistance, and which avoided stigma in this way (Leonard, 2004, p. 932), was also severely limiting in the identities, roles and relationships it prescribed. Loyalty implied traditional family roles.

Furthermore, Leonard argued that it was an oversimplification to see this social capital as inclusive of all as equal members. Men in particular were selective in their reciprocity, doing favours and informal tasks for others where they could expect these to be returned. Although the political situation in Northern Ireland and the controlling influence of the IRA maintained ideological solidarity, many individuals were excluded from informal economic networks because they could not contribute (Leonard, 2004, pp. 934–5). Other studies have found that there can be deep divisions and distrust within poor communities because of internal circuits of mutual assistance which bond more resourceful residents together, to the exclusion of the most vulnerable (Daly and Leonard, 2002; Williams and Windebank, 1999; Neef, 1992).

In policy terms, the situation in Northern Ireland has been particularly challenging for the Blair government. Under the terms of the ceasefire, Sinn Fein, the Republican political movement which dominates this area of West Belfast, has attempted to build bridges with the wider institutional structures of the province, in line with its strategy for the 'peace process' and power-sharing. However, as Leonard points out, these initiatives have been ambiguous in their consequences. Attempts to absorb informal economic groupings into the formal economy have often put them out of business, as their costs rose, and residents could not afford their services. Alternatively, where they survived it was by trading outside the estate. And the penetration of non-sectarian services, with professional employees living elsewhere, has often displaced local (unqualified) community workers (Leonard, 2004, pp. 935–40).

> Hence, West Belfast continues to be characterised by low levels of economic and human capital. Bridging social capital has had limited success while the rationale for bonding social capital continues to be dismantled. . . . In relation to economic linkages, the West Belfast example demonstrates how bridging social capital benefited individuals rather than communities. (Ibid., pp. 940–1)

Obviously, it could well be argued that West Belfast is a special case, and that the attempt to build bridging social capital is more likely to be successful under less conflictual conditions. Here the evaluation of the Sure Start programme in the UK may provide a fairer test. This initiative had several goals relating to inclusion and empowerment, attempting to link parents and pre-school children in selected deprived districts into various facilities and services, and to engage with them to change both child development and family functioning. So the intensive engagement of professional staff with resident parents and children, and their involvement with each other, was supposed to produce evidence of changes in behaviour which made those in receipt of interventions more capable of entering the 'mainstream' than comparable citizens in non-intervention districts.

Preliminary findings of the evaluation researchers did not uphold much of the optimism behind the massive and expensive programme (now being further extended into many new districts). The only significant difference attributable to Sure Start, found in all local programmes, was 'mothers/principal carers were observed to treat the child in a warmer and more accepting manner than in comparison areas' (NESS, 2004, p. 1). Several other dimensions of parenting and child development showed improvement in several local programmes, but the research was as yet unable to distinguish between 'more successful' and 'less successful' projects (ibid.).

All this makes it clear that the distinction between bonding and bridging social capital does not stand up well to empirical testing. Whereas, in West Belfast, new policy initiatives benefited individuals but not communities, in England and Wales, Sure Start produced an improvement in *bonding* between parents and children, but not reliably in the kinds of behaviour which might improve children's chances in mainstream education, employment or civil society.

In the UK, ideas about how social capital is an essential ingredient in citizenship have been incorporated into official policy and research. The Home Office conducted a 'Citizenship Survey', starting in 2001, which aimed to reveal sources of formal and informal advice about parenting and family issues, participation in civic and social activity and in volunteering of all kinds, attitudes to race and racism, and beliefs on rights and responsibilities. The theoretical framework for the survey was social capital's role 'in contributing to social "benefits" and "costs" ' (Home Office, 2001, p. 4).

But research had already indicated the broad outlines of the situation in the UK. Although associational activity has been maintained, the overall high levels of membership of groups and organizations disguises a big shift in the distribution of activism. As the 'new middle class' of service workers has grown, voluntary organizations have attracted such members; but this has masked a rapid decline in participation of all kinds by the working class:

> the more accurate image is of a nation divided between a well-connected group of citizens with prosperous lives and high levels of civic engagement and other groups whose networks, associational life, and involvement in politics are very limited. . . . The two groups who face marginalization from civil society are the working class and the young. (Hall, 2002, p. 53)

A similar picture emerges from analysis of survey evidence of three cohorts born since the war. Among Class V men born in 1946, and interviewed aged thirty-six, 58 per cent belonged to organizations; for women it was 37 per cent. Among Class V men born in 1970, interviewed aged thirty, only 2 per cent were members of organizations, and among women 6 per cent (Bynner and Parsons, 2003, figure 10.1a).

For both white and minority ethnic deprived communities in the UK, the choice agenda has left them stripped of the kinds of residents who could lead the organized lives of their districts. Polarization has left them uniformly poor and reliant on state benefits and services – but usually with the worst quality of provision. To attribute this to the shortcomings of bonding social capital is to misrepresent a process in which mobile households have joined more desirable districts, leaving ill, disabled, elderly and impoverished immobile residents to rely on each other (Dorling and Thomas, 2003). Informal networks have understandably identified themselves against the mainstream, and used practices regarded by the authorities as deviant (Jordan and Jordan, 2000, chs. 7 and 8).

Balancing rights with belonging

It is clear that social policy relies on the balancing of two essential features of good social relations – individual freedom to choose between alternative versions of a good life, and the substantive, qualitative elements of intimacy, friendship and belonging which actually bind together the disparate elements in any such version. The first set of institutions are associated with liberal systems of rights and rather thin, abstract and neutral definitions of how people should relate to each other, concerned with protecting their scope for self-determination. The second set of features are about the nature of the bonds between them and the kinds of relationships they form. The balancing has much to do with how these features interact in systems which combine exit, voice and loyalty options (Hirschman, 1970).

The critiques of neo-liberalism and economic restructuring which have been outlined in this chapter and the previous one have certain features in common. They all emphasize how market institutions and formal individual liberties discount human emotions, relationships and communities. In Robert Lane's words, his evidence and analysis

create a strong presumption that the way to increase SWB [subjective well-being] in the United States and probably in all advanced Western societies is

> to move from an emphasis on money and economic growth toward an empha-
> sis on companionship. Of course people need and want both material
> resources and companionship, but the needs vary with the relative supplies of
> these two goods. In rich societies, for people above the poverty line, more
> money, as compared with friendship and community esteem, a loving spouse
> and affectionate children, quickly loses its power to make people happy.
> (Lane, 2000, p. 7)

The difficulty is that the neo-liberal model and microeconomic
processes have a logic which cannot take such considerations into
account. As we saw in chapter 8 (pp. 146–7), happiness is an unintended by-product of the search for gain through trade; once the connections between more money and greater subjective well-being are
loosened, the whole edifice is destabilized. But it is far from clear how
the priorities of intimacy, friendship and secure belonging can be
introduced into a system which runs on mobility, creative destruction
and profit.

We saw in the first part of the book that Asian countries, still at the
stage of urbanization and industrialization, have found ways of protecting families (and to some extent communities) in the face of rapid
change and economic growth. But these countries are still at the stage
of development in which rising income does reliably contribute to subjective well-being (i.e. below \$15,000 per capita incomes per year).
Japan, the leading economy of the region, has become more unequal
and unhappy since the 1970s, and suffers all the ills except high
divorce rates of the rich North American, European and Australasian
states (see p. 177).

The Third Way reforms of the 1990s, in the USA, the UK and eventually all over the affluent First World, did attempt to address these
issues. They took seriously two features of the Washington Consensus/
neo-liberal model, also revised in the World Bank (2001) development
plan, which were causing concern. First, there was the exclusion of
marginal communities, such as the ones analysed in the case examples
in chapters 9 and 10. They used community development methods, on
the lines of the Irish projects discussed above (pp. 192–3), to try to
increase social capital formation, build bridges into the mainstream,
and improve the physical and social infrastructure. In this way, they
hoped to improve the morale as well as the living standards of
excluded groups, and to revive the sense of belonging to wider society
(Jordan and Jordan, 2000, chs. 8 and 9).

It is understandable that the attempt to protest against the failure
of the market-driven order and to 'remoralize' society should take the
form of a return to religious traditions. Faiths have shown resilience
in the face of materialism and egoism; they have, like families, adapted

to new conditions and found new ways of giving their members a sense of identity and belonging. Among ethnic minorities and in marginal communities they have protected people from the worst indignities of social exclusion. In upholding spiritual and human values, they have been part of a wider movement to defy the corrosive effects of global economic forces and the transformation of collective life according to economic principles.

But this does not imply that they supply the most viable basis for social policy, either in terms of guiding norms or in terms of service delivery mechanisms. Faiths assume that members share values as well as theological beliefs; they can therefore rely on loyalty to certain common principles as well as solidarity among the faithful. This is their strength in open societies, where people can leave to join other faith groups or secede in splinter groups, and where they also have the capacity to live another whole sphere of their lives in the wider world of the economy and polity. It becomes a weakness where a single faith claims a monopoly of the true values for social relations and comes to provide the ruling institutions of the state. Spanish fascism, Iranian theocracy and Dutch Reformed apartheid all supply recent or current examples of how a faith-based ideology can suppress liberty and pervert justice.

However, political loyalty is also problematic in the present context. The European Union seemed to have created a new sense of identity and belonging, especially among citizens of the older member states. This has been challenged by the referenda in France and the Netherlands in May 2005.

Since the year 2000, there has been intense debate within the European Commission and the EU member states about the future of the European Social Model (ESM) – the combination of labour-market regulation, minimum wages and social insurance schemes which has shown far more continuity in Western Europe than in the Anglophone countries. Whereas the public posture of the governments of member states, and especially France and Germany, was that the European Union consolidated and extended the ESM, behind the scenes a series of directives have been aimed at 'modernizing' and 'liberalizing' it. These tensions exploded when, immediately following the enlargement of the EU in May 2004, the new Commission embarked on a more open programme of reform and restructuring designed to reorientate the Union towards a global competitive strategy.

In France in particular, much of the debate focused on trade in services, with overt fears about competition from the enlargement countries (Ricard, 2005; Rivais, 2005). France had signed up to the 'Bolkestein Directive' in the hope of exporting services to the post-communist countries; now its political elite suffered a backlash from citizens fearful of losing jobs to Central European firms and workers.

The European Social Model was able to make assumptions about the value basis of social protection when the EU consisted of ten or fifteen affluent states; however, since enlargement, these are no longer valid. The interests of all citizens and all workers are no longer automatically served by regulation of employment security, minimum wages and benefits levels. Citizens of the new states are denied access to jobs in all the old member states except the UK and Ireland, except under special dispensations. The liberalization of trade in services raises problems about the goals of social policy (accelerated employment creation or protection of wages and conditions?), the size of the unit among whom protections and benefits are shared (citizens of the enlarged EU or just those of the old Union?) and relationships with the wider world (global well-being or exclusive advantage?). If it is difficult to agree common values and achieve solidarity between members in a continent with a shared history whose constituent states have all applied for membership, how much harder to achieve this on a world scale?

Conclusions

The attempt to introduce religious and moral dimensions into social policy is highly problematic, because present-day societies are diverse and systems of values vary between faiths and communities. But it is also fraught with difficulties because there is no obvious way to combine faith-based or morally cohesive groupings with the collective units brought together by patterns of ownership (capitalist firms), employment (occupational groups and trade unions), residence and neighbourhood associations, and service use ('economic clubs'). The former mainly derive from affiliations of blood, soil and belief; the latter stem from choices in markets and market-orientated public systems. It is clear that a good society must somehow balance these features of social relations, but it is not at all obvious how.

We have considered ways in which Third Way governments have attempted to incorporate micro-social principles into political obligations and citizenship, and some of the reasons why these attempts remain unconvincing. New versions of what it is to be a good citizen, in which individuals are required to be self-responsible and self-developmental, have fed into a culture of individualism, not one of collective concern and communal co-operation (Jordan, 2004). We

COMMUNITY, MORALITY AND BELONGING **203**

have seen why this is so; community is a time-consuming way of getting things done, and the new, flexible economy of creative destruction leaves little scope for this form of action outside the family and the faith congregation.

In the next chapter, I shall draw attention to a neglected issue in social policy analysis, the nature of services, and argue that it provides some clues to the puzzle of how individual rights and communal values might be balanced.

12

The Role of Services in the Social Context

In the previous chapter, I portrayed 'values voting' and the shift towards faith-based services and community development methods as a kind of protest against the 'choice agenda'. Electorates seem to be expressing dissatisfaction with the culture of individualism, mobility and a collective life of 'economic clubs'. In the case of the French political debate, this unease linked free trade in services with the constitution for the European Union, and led to a mobilization for retaining the European Social Model, even at the expense of the development of the post-communist countries. In all these ways, voters and parties seemed to be making a connection between 'stalled well-being' – the failure of self-assessed happiness to grow in line with average incomes – and the decay of human companionship and community. But no convincing model has yet emerged of how a new turn in social policy might balance individual rights and freedoms with the satisfactions of good family, kinship, friendship and associational relationships.

In this chapter I shall outline an analysis of why this gap in the theoretical literature of welfare economics and social policy literature exists, and how the various social science disciplines might collaborate to fill it. There have been clues to the nature of the gap in the accounts of subjective well-being and the critique of microeconomics I have given in chapters 10 and 11. It was noted (p. 170) that the psychological theory of well-being, including the attempt to measure an 'objective' version of pleasure and happiness, does not attempt to distinguish between specific sources of pleasure, and the *context* in which these are experienced. It seeks to show that human beings make single, overall evaluations of their well-being at any moment in time, and only retrospectively separate these out into various elements, such as mood, company and the physical environment (Kahneman, 1999).

However, social policy in particular, and public policy more generally, is centrally concerned with contexts. It cannot prescribe either exactly what people do or how they experience what they do; all it can attempt to achieve is to create a social and physical infrastructure which will influence these experiences. In the post-war era of welfare states, the goal was to build a public infrastructure in which citizens would interact in ways consistent with their status as equal and democratic members, seeking to realize *common* interests. The transformation of citizenship aims to make them more like consumers, seeking to satisfy their *personal* desires and interests in quasi-markets (DSS, 1998, p. 28; Eriksen and Weigård, 2000; Freedland, 2001) – see chapter 10.

I shall argue that it will be impossible to tackle the task of balancing individual rights with companionate and communal values unless a distinction can be made between pleasure in consuming particular items and the context of such consumption. This is because all policy, in every field, influences people's interpretations and beliefs (their values) as well as their behaviour. It affects collective culture, including political culture, as much as strategies of individuals and groups. Preferences and tastes are not given, but deeply shaped by contexts and cultures.

Let me give an example. In 2004, in view of evidence of growing obesity and associated health problems among children, the UK government began to be concerned about the nutritional standards of meals provided in school canteens. In particular, it was concerned about how this affected children from disadvantaged backgrounds, allowed free meals under schemes which waived costs for poor households. The celebrity chef Jamie Oliver undertook to assess the meals provided in a comprehensive secondary school in a relatively disadvantaged district of a London borough (Greenwich). He then attempted to introduce alternative healthy meals, containing fruit and vegetables, within the local authority budget (37p per meal). In the event most children chose not to eat Oliver's meals, and some protested about being denied the former menus (of fatty, salty or sugary food, processed and mass produced, reheated in the school kitchen) (Channel 4 TV, 2005b).

Oliver then visited a primary school in County Durham, a coal-mining district of the UK; in this school, 70 per cent of children received free school meals (at a budget of 44p each). Here again, most children rejected his options, refusing even to *taste* vegetables and fruits, very few of which they were able to identify and name. Those who tasted them blindfold spat them out. Oliver then engaged in intensive interactions with the children, in order to persuade them at least to try his ingredients and meals. By organizing the children to harvest, cook and serve meals, and excluding from his class those who resolutely refused to taste any of them, he eventually managed to get first all his class, and then the whole school, to eat his healthy meals – which they all said they enjoyed. Teaching and kitchen staff declared themselves very satisfied with the experiment, and parents reported much more calm and better concentrated behaviour among the children. When Oliver interviewed the commercial company supplying the largest share of the mass-produced, unhealthy meals to schools in the UK, they resisted his proposals, on the grounds that they interfered with pupils' rights to choose what they preferred.

The point about this example is that the context for choice under the existing systems, together with current diets in poor households, strongly predisposed children not merely to 'choose' unhealthy food, but to refuse even to contemplate eating healthy meals. Oliver was only able to change preferences by changing the whole context – transforming first the class and then the school into a giant production unit for his alternative menu, and using peer pressure to get the most resistant children to try his options. Oliver mobilized a feature of comparative utility calculation not considered in the psychological literature. Just as people incorporate others' preferences into their own in rivalrous and competitive ways ('keeping up with the Joneses'), so also they incorporate others' preferences because they want to share and be friendly with them. Children in particular are keen to express their bonds with others by doing things together.

This idea of adopting others' choices into one's own utility function as an act of solidarity and an expression of common interests applies in many situations. For example, it is a necessary feature of good morale among armed forces and civilians in wartime. Unless citizens want their comrades to survive and overcome, they will lose the will to fight and resist. The team spirit and community solidarity both of children's groups and of nations in wartime are instances of how contexts can be changed by culture shifts (and vice versa). How people perceive their choices, how they choose, and how they evaluate their experiences are all heavily influenced by contexts.

In this chapter, I shall argue that contexts and choices cannot be neatly distinguished, but that it is very important, for the success of social policies, to identify how contexts can be made explicit and overt in order to sustain the quality of relationships and experiences. If all that makes up the context for experiences – the set of values, beliefs and relationships in which they happen, and the physical environment surrounding their occurrence – is ignored, or treated as if it were simply an item of consumption, then the scope for policy will be diminished. I shall also argue that well-being will be reduced and justice rendered incoherent.

For all the sophistication of the analysis of culture (Archer, 1996), this branch of social theory has had little impact on social policy. Some ideas from organizational culture (Ahrne, 1990), and particularly business culture (Buchanan and Huczynski, 1997), have had some influence on public administration and management since the 'managerialist turn' in the public sector (Clarke and Newman, 1997). But there has been little attempt to analyse the interaction between policy and public or political culture, and how the cultural context is relevant for policy outcomes.

I shall argue that this is in large part owing to a remarkable theoretical vacuum in both microeconomics and welfare economics – the absence of a theory of services. In neither of these are services adequately distinguished from commodities or theorized in any distinctive way. Yet (as I shall show) the original definition of commodities, as distinct from services, was fundamental to the whole tradition of economics that underpins both the World Bank model of human development and the Third Way model of society.

I shall show that the failure to identify and analyse the relational nature of services lies behind the inability of social policy to make the necessary distinctions between programmes which aim to influence the context of human action and those which aim to act directly on individuals. As the choice agenda has become the dominant discourse of public-service provision, and individual preferences have come to be the basis for collective groupings, the whole notion of the context for human experience has disappeared from consideration. Hence programmes in Third Way regimes focus more and more on interventions aimed at changing individual behaviour, through advice, counselling or punishment. This is ironic, since the profession most associated with these interventions in the era of welfare states, social work, has been thoroughly discredited and marginalized (Jordan and Jordan, 2000). The Third Way model of social interventions uses the language of social work in its programmes, but calls official practitioners by other names.

I shall argue that a more complete understanding of the contextual significance of services would lead to a very different approach to service delivery. But this understanding could only emerge from an analysis in which economic methods were combined with psychological and sociological ones. At the end of the chapter, I shall sketch a possible future research agenda.

The new perspective adopted in this chapter is the one derived from the distinction between experience and context, and the big issue for social policy is how to link personal experience, enabled through individual rights, with a social context conducive to well-being. 'Values voters' are on the right track in insisting that choice alone, in a consumerist framework, cannot create the institutions for a good society. But the cultural and environmental infrastructure for human well-being is more complex than the neo-conservative approach allows or the communitarian theorists recognize.

The missing economics of services

Following Adam Smith (1976 [1776], pp. 330–1), economics textbooks still state that services are distinguished from goods by being of no lasting value. In the microeconomic tradition, service workers are 'unproductive'; they 'consume and invest industrial products, but produce none themselves' (Bacon and Eltis, 1976, p. 24). 'Goods are physical commodities, such as steel and strawberries. Services are activities such as massages and live theatre performances, consumed or enjoyed only at the instant they are produced' (Begg et al., 1997, p. 2). The examples chosen are revealing. A massage benefits its receiver for a good deal longer than a bowl of strawberries, which is of very short-term nutritional value. More significantly, in the next 625 pages the authors then devote no further space to the distinctive nature of services. Equally, there is no analysis of the economics of services in welfare economics textbooks, such as Barr (2004). The idea that services are of no lasting value has indeed been an enduring one. But it is difficult to maintain this idea in the face of the lifelong benefits of education, some health interventions, and the social care services which sustain people with disabilities.

A more convincing account of the economic distinctiveness of services would start from their *relational* nature. They cannot be given or received without some kind of interpersonal exchange, however brief. Goods are inert objects, which are either consumed or activated for use by humans. The consumption or use of goods does not, therefore, have implications for power, abuse or exploitation of one person by another; any such implications arise from the human processes of their production or deployment – for instance, the use of technologies in war, or in factory or office production. But, because of their relational nature, the production and consumption of services always involves issues of power, abuse or exploitation; and, in this case, the context determines how these issues are played out.

In the modern period, the state's services were seen either as interventions to correct market failure (such as undersupply of schooling for children whose parents could not afford to prepare them adequately for work and citizenship), or as official measures to combat social pathologies, and thus save costs to the state. It took a long time, for example, for reformers to convince governments of the sound economics behind investment in proper sewage systems, waste disposal and clean water supply (Finer, 1950).

So economics did theorize collective services as a contribution to efficiency (improving education and health, and reducing costs associated with environmental pollution), but it did not analyse the relational aspects of services identified above. The fact that services provided the contexts for production and consumption was taken for granted, and not treated as an aspect worthy of economic analysis in its own right. When services came to be reconsidered in the middle years of the twentieth century, it was their political implications rather than their economic ones that were primarily addressed.

Because services were so under-theorized in economics and sociology, the post-war welfare states were not directed primarily at reforming this aspect of social relations. The main targets of new institutional arrangements were rentiers, as unreliable sources of the flows of investment needed for industrial expansion (see pp. 55–7), and capitalists, who could derive a surplus from the labour of their employees but did not have to pay them a living wage. Hence the main instruments of social democratic institution-building were fiscal and monetary management and investment planning; state ownership of key industries such as mining, steel production and railways; and income redistribution. Conservative welfare-state regimes in Europe, such as Germany's, which were deeply influenced by Christian democratic traditions, were more concerned to regulate markets, redistribute incomes and sustain growth for the sake of *family* solidarity and security than to strengthen the power of the state (Esping-Andersen, 1999, table 5.4; Gough et al., 2004, fig. 1.1).

In all this, the expansion of public services was secondary to the goal of modifying capitalist institutions and outcomes. Welfare states were concerned primarily with protection against economic risks in market societies, seen as industrial systems for producing commodities. In the Beveridge Report, for example, the creation of the National Health Service was seen as necessary to achieve that aim (Beveridge, 1942). But, more generally, public services were a forum in which citizens could interact as equals, in a *democratic* context – a political context suitable for the new citizenship (Cole, 1945, p. 29).

What was seen as vitally important was to provide a proper context for the new economic settlement, and services were as much about democratization and the demonstration of equal respect among members as about delivery of technically efficient health care or social work.

The weakness of this model was that it did not ground its advocacy of public services in any economic analysis of their advantages, or link these notions of democratic context with a theory of the relevance of contextual factors in well-being. This was not surprising, given the version of welfare economics prevalent at the time. A. C. Pigou's *The Economics of Welfare* (1920), which was reprinted many times in subsequent decades, and is frequently referred to by Beveridge (1944), has no entries in its index for 'services', 'health' or 'education'. It is concerned mainly with investment, employment, taxation and income shares, in line with the predominant issues for socialists, social democrats and progressive liberals alike.

In a slightly different but parallel way, the expansion of public services in the Scandinavian welfare states in the 1960s and 1970s was justified mainly in terms of the entitlement of citizens to aspects of life quality which were not appropriately delivered by markets. This process of 'decommodification' was identified by Esping-Andersen (1990) as most advanced in social democratic welfare regimes; the state defines a sphere of the lives of its citizens which is not market-dependent (Gough et al. 2004, p. 4). The non-market context for citizen interactions is an important political goal; but, once again, the arguments for this are not framed in terms of an economic analysis of well-being or the role of contextual factors within this.

These missing elements in the creation and expansion of public services left them vulnerable to the kinds of developments in public economics – public choice theory and fiscal federalism – described in chapter 8. Those who wanted to justify the *public* aspects of state services, in terms of direct benefit for well-being, were thrown back on a political justification of their advantages (in terms of equality and democracy) rather than an economic one. It was easy for economists committed to individual choice in the construction of institutions, and to markets as the basis for allocations, to argue the merits of the new approach (see pp. 147–50). As welfare economics shifted towards the new paradigm of methodological individualism and self-selected collective units, advocates for the public sector could not link their defence to a convincing *economic* account of the merits of their contextual advantages.

But public services were also being eroded, not just by these direct attacks on their theoretical bases in Keynesian and social democratic versions of welfare economics, but also by new developments in capitalism itself. Above all, the transformation of advanced First World economies from industrial to service production, with employment in manufacturing shrinking to around 20 per cent of the workforce, saw the rapid growth of new forms of services and service work.

The goal of welfare-state services of providing an overall framework for interaction between citizens, while still substantially realized in the Scandinavian countries, is now completely undermined in the Anglophone ones, where the public sector must strive to meet the norms and standards set by commercial service providers. '[E]xpectations of service quality and convenience have risen – as with the growth of 24-hour banking – but public services have failed to keep up with these developments. . . . [A]s incomes rise, people prefer to own their own houses and investments' (DSS, 1998, p. 16).

This reversal has been achieved through the transformation in the basis for citizenship itself; under the 'new contract' citizens are market-like beings exercising choices in the public as well as the commercial sectors (see chapter 10). But the expansion of private services and employment has supplied a new model of what a service is, in which the contextual features have been totally obscured. Even in the public services, the whole emphasis is now on the technically tailored unit for consumption and aimed at those citizens who have selected this particular commodity. Services have finally received the same attention as goods by being absorbed into the logic of marketed commodities, as items for private consumption from which the relational dimensions have been eliminated. Their shared common aspects have also been denied, except in so far as mainstream service users are allowed to choose with whom to be associated – i.e. to avoid sharing with people who are poor and needy (Cullis and Jones, 1994, p. 300). In all these senses, services have become the same as goods – they have been *decontextualized*, even in the public sector.

This has been possible because of the rapid growth of two kinds of marketed services. The first of these is financial services – the means by which mainstream individuals in affluent First World countries have entered the class of rentiers, as part-time holders of financial assets and property in land. Banks, insurance companies, building societies, mortgage companies and other kinds of financial intermediaries have created a whole new range of products, through which individuals can first gain credit to buy items such as houses and cars, and later (if they are fortunate) acquire holdings in the stock market, private pensions, insurances and the property market. Part of the success of politicians such as Margaret Thatcher and Ronald Reagan in the 1980s was in convincing electorates that it was preferable to pay interest on borrowing from these services, in order eventually to gain private property rights, than to pay taxes, in order to get better social benefits and public services (Jordan, 2005).

The other transformation in First World capitalist economies has been the growth of private services in such fields as retailing, leisure, fast-food outlets, hospitality and catering, and personal services such as cleaning, hairdressing and social care for elderly people. These services were targeted towards the needs of newly affluent sectors of the population and middle-income groups who had little time for self-provisioning, especially two-earner households. They employed mainly women, usually part-time, and often at low wages (Ehrenreich, 2002; Abrams, 2002). But their main selling point was that they catered for specific preferences through their 'flexibility' and range of alternative 'packages', made possible by the employment terms of their workers. The idea of 'individual service', coming from corporations in the USA, was quickly influential worldwide; the 'Have a Nice Day' approach to the marketing of services set a universal standard of pseudo-personalization of commercial service 'customer care' in which the human skills of low-paid staff were converted into corporate assets.

The end result of all these processes is that services are produced, sold and consumed as items of individual utility and preference. Neither firms nor public agencies see it as part of their function to supply an overall context in which citizens can experience the quality of their interactions as an element in their well-being. If experiences of sharing (in a pop concert, a theatre or a sports event) are positively evaluated, this is to be interpreted as contributing to an individual unit of pleasure, not to some intrinsically shared experience. Corporate logos and public agency slogans proclaim commitment to satisfying individual tastes, and any collective dimension, positively interpreted, is seen as enhancing individual utility. As we have seen (p. 170), even the new psychological analysis of well-being fails to distinguish the contextual element (Kahneman, 1999).

Individualism and the growth of services

I do not intend the above analysis to imply that services are *intrinsically* contextual or collective. They are ambiguous, because they can be either used or experienced as individual and private or contextual and public (Jordan, 2005). The relational element in them means that they are inescapably *social*, in the sense that they involve communication between people, necessarily laden with exchanges of value and power (Goffman, 1972; Rawls, 1989). But these may be interpreted and experienced as personal exchanges, as communal, as commercial or as public and political, depending on contextual factors. And the focus of the exchange may be the consumption of the service itself (as in buying a session at a hairdresser) or on the cultural collective and contextual elements (as in singing in an amateur choir). Services directly relevant to human development and well-being, and to justice between citizens, can also be treated in either of these ways.

For example, many of the services which in affluent countries are provided by professionals, either commercially or through public agencies, in Africa and South Asia are still organized on a communal, informal, traditional basis, among kin, villages or tribes. What we in affluent countries call 'welfare' or 'social care' is still the province of relationships among such groups, where power is very unequally distributed and deference must be paid to traditional holders of status and authority (Wood, 2004). Because neither markets nor states supply reliable income or services, but the most resourceful and well-connected members of communities may get substantial income from the former, or power from the latter, vulnerable individuals must seek protection from leading figures, in patron–client relationships. In the poorest countries, the protections available to very poor people can extend very little outside the family, while those of the rest may rely on warlords or corrupt politicians. In slightly less adverse situations, wider connections are relevant:

> within 'community' we can include clans and lineages which offer social actors crucial identities as well as the social frame within which rights of allocation of scarce resources occur, such as land, water, access to pasture, places to build homesteads, and so on. This would apply with equal force to, say, northern Pakistan and rural East Africa. (Wood, 2004, p. 75)

Obviously, it is inappropriate to call these arrangements 'services' – they are, as it were, all context and no individual component. People must constantly negotiate with powerful others to sustain their claims to an identity and a place within a social infrastructure, where modern commercial and political intrusions have merely widened differentials of wealth and authority. Access to 'care' depends on who one is within these systems of power and obligation.

But private, commercial services are at the opposite end of the scale from these. Increasingly, they are designed to enhance individual distinctiveness or to progress personal development and self-fulfilment. In line with the redefinition of citizenship in terms of projects of self and independence, these services cater for the mainstream or higher-income groups who are committed to the 'realization' of their inner potential. So lifestyle gurus, style coaches and personal trainers, for example, cater for people who want to enhance their expression of their individuality; and even group therapies and quasi-religious experiences are linked to the members' powers to get in touch with their 'true selves'.

In the light of this shift towards a collective culture of individualistic self-exploration it is not surprising that the UK Yellow Pages revealed that between 1992 and 2002 there had been an increase of over 500 per cent in listed aromatherapists and cosmetic surgeons, compared with a decline of 59 per cent in greengrocers (BBC Radio 4, 2004c).

The avowed aim of personalized, individualized, 'tailor-made' services, both in the commercial and in the public sector, is to improve subjective well-being – to make people feel happier about themselves and their lives, to be more effective and successful in their relationships, and to meet their needs in precise ways, rather than provide 'one size fits all' services. But this process of individualization ignores the possibility that people need a balance between the personal and the collective in their lives, and that even a very rich supply of pleasurable, chosen experiences can add up to very little meaningful satisfaction if it has no overall context. In stark contrast with the African and Southern Asian case, Anglophone citizens have services which are all content, with no contextual infrastructure for interpreting individual experiences and making sense of them.

Kahneman and his colleagues (1999) are unable to distinguish between these components of well-being in their analyses of the psychology of pleasure and pain, and this may be part of the human tragedy. As individuals, we merely seek what is experienced as pleasurable, without being able to distinguish adequately between the positive factors which stem from eating chocolate and those which come from being a supporter of the side winning the match we are watching together. We rely on collective culture and the institutional order of our organized social life to make these distinctions for us – to categorize and make sense of our world for us (Douglas, 1987). If we live in an individualistic culture, we will simply be unable to recognize contextual features as significant.

The new services which have made up capitalism's adaptation in post-industrial economies have a stake in expanding the scope of individualization (which leads to increased consumption of private, marketed services) and containing the scope of collective, contextual ones. So long as the consumption of personalized services continues to be a feature of the rivalrous quest for position and status, profits in these branches will continue to be healthy.

But there is another reason why the growth in service employment and consumption may be associated with 'stalled well-being' in the affluent countries. In the Lewis model for economic growth (see p. 31), wages rise because workers move from low-productivity rural work to higher productivity industrial employment; this is still the trajectory in newly industrializing countries such as China, Malaysia and Brazil. But only some of the components of the service economy of affluent countries are susceptible to productivity growth. The number of people whose hair can be cut and styled in a day has probably not increased since about 1820 (Gershuny, 1983), and the number of frail elderly and disabled people who can be cared for by a care assistant has also not increased over time.

Hence, although people in affluent countries have more to spend on services, the wages of service workers cannot grow from increased output per hour. Economies with a large service sector suffer from the 'Baumol cost disease' (Baumol, 1967; Baumol et al., 1985); the price of services constantly rises in relation to that of goods. And because competition between service providers (commercial and public) cannot take the form of improved productivity, it tends to take that of increased work intensity. The reports of Barbara Ehrenreich (2002) and Fran Abrams (2002) on their experiences of service work (retailing, house and hotel cleaning, waiting tables, working in care homes) supply evidence of exactly such processes, as low-paid women workers were under constant surveillance and pressure to do more and to be 'flexible' (i.e. dispense with breaks, safety standards and other protections in the workplace).

Because of the Baumol phenomenon, the service economy is more subject to forms of zero-sum rivalry than the industrial economy; wages can only rise in one firm or sector if they fall in another. This helps explain the stress and reported dissatisfaction with work experiences, especially in the Anglophone countries (Bunting, 2004), as workers (particularly women) strive to please their supervisors (usually other women) and employers (usually men) at the expense of their health and well-being. This phenomenon is avoided in Sweden, where most of the increase in service work has been in the public sector, and women's wages have benefited from the national agreements under which they are sustained by transfers from the industrial sector.

Conclusions

In this chapter, I have traced the current difficulties for governments in balancing individual rights with shared, convivial contexts – a big issue for the twenty-first century – to two gaps in the theoretical literature of the social sciences. Psychologists studying well-being have not distinguished between the immediate sensory and emotional pains and pleasures of specific experiences and the background contribution of the social context to the interpretation of those experiences. This inability to distinguish between specific experience and context may stem from some long-term heritage of human perception. But it is crucial for social policy's development in the current century. For example, we need to be able to analyse which features of the low levels of well-being in poor African countries are derived from very low incomes and individual capabilities, and which from the insecure, arbitrary and clientelist social relations of those countries (Wood, 2004; Bevan, 2004b). It seems fairly obvious that an increase in individual rights, incomes and capabilities would be the best way to improve well-being in such situations, but we also need to know which features of the social context might best be strengthened and enhanced, and which suppressed and minimized. For example, would the spread of market relations and capitalist production increase insecurity and clientelism more than it would increase individual rights and capabilities? Research might be focused on trying to answer this question.

Second, I identified the gap in the economic analysis of how services help to supply the context to material consumption and individual choice, without which they become meaningless and unsatisfying. Services have been neglected in economic analysis, because opponents of collectivism saw them as indistinguishable from goods, and hence susceptible to the same principles of individual utility maximization. 'Stalled well-being' signals that they require economic analysis in their own right, as determinants of well-being.

Both neo-liberal and Third Way models of society neglect the human dimensions of relatedness – intimacy, the quality of family and friendship relationships, community as convivial association (rather than social control), and citizenship as belonging and solidarity. In restructuring institutions for the expression of individual choice, they have neglected the role of services in providing interpretative frameworks for these choices. This has become much more important in a service economy, where more aspects of individuals' lives rely on interactions with others in paid roles, as childminders, style coaches, fitness trainers, counsellors, aromatherapists and cosmetic surgeons. If each of these experiences is part of a fragmentary series of disparate choices, each individually satisfying, but with no common themes other than 'self-realization', individuals may suffer stress, and their well-being may decline. This may explain the higher levels of self-assessed happiness among people who are practising members of a faith, people who do voluntary work, and people who are physically active in leisure organizations, compared with those who are none of these things (Argyle, 1999). Another research agenda might set out to investigate whether these effects can be measured.

Finally, the 'personalization' of public services, which breaks up the contextual, infrastructural nature of welfare-state collective institutions and intentionally mirrors the individualistic basis for commercial services, may well be contributing to the fragmentation of communal and solidaristic networks and the loss of links between disparate populations. Social work as a profession tried – even in its pre-welfare-state, voluntaristic origins, in charitable interventions – to balance the counselling and advice of individuals with methods which promoted community cohesion and mutuality (Jordan and Forsythe, 2002). Third Way social policy does pursue a community development agenda as well as an individualized one, but the issue of how to combine them effectively remains unresolved.

In particular, policy on children and young people is faced with disturbing evidence of increasing psychosocial disorders (Rutter and Smith, 1995) and delinquency and deviance (Rutter et al., 1998) – individuals from a broad spectrum of families whose well-being is measurably jeopardized. How can targeted services which address their personal distress and behavioural problems be set against universal services which supply a context for integration, membership and security? Under the liberal-communitarian social policy agenda, far more attention has been devoted to therapeutic and resocialization interventions than to contextual questions. There is another research agenda here.

All these aspects of social relations, political culture and social policy have co-existed with an alarming rise in abuse within official organizations of the state, or of First World states abroad. At the same time as the new model of citizenship emphasizes the sanctity of the individual, as a unique being who owes him- or herself a duty to realize true potentials (Jordan, 2004, ch. 3), there are more and more alarming instances of violent abuse of prisoners and detainees. In the UK, in a single week, a public investigation heard of young prisoners being put together in cells as employees of a private security company bet on the outcome of a 'gladiatorial contest' between them (BBC Radio 4, 2005h); and an undercover investigation showed detainees in a centre for asylum seekers being verbally racially abused, assaulted and sexually assaulted (BBC 1 TV, 2005a). This was soon after the photographs from Abu Ghraeb and Camp Breadbasket in Iraq, which led to prison sentences for military personnel, and even sooner after allegations of torture at Baghram in Afghanistan and Guantanamo Bay in Cuba (Channel 4 TV, 2005c).

The big issue around individualization in social policy is the danger that, in focusing on the personality and behaviour of the 'target', it encourages blame and punishment if the programme to change these is unsuccessful. In settings such as mental hospitals and prisons, these dangers become magnified out of all proportion. Once prisoners and detainees lose the status of beings who can be improved through therapy, they may instead be seen as sub-human. Without a *political* context for individual rights, old prejudices and practices resurface. Only if there are cultures and institutions which uphold a set of common standards, for staff and inmates alike, are such regimes protected from sliding into abuse and torture.

13

Interdependence, Development and Justice: A Cosmopolitan World Order

The big issue identified in the previous chapter – the balance between individual rights and the quality of social relations in the collective context – leads directly to the second big issue for the new century. What should be the nature and size of the collective units in which membership, sharing and belonging are located? And, as a set of questions within this one, should the same units supply the basis for services such as education, health and social care, and for redistribution of resources between members for the sake of justice?

We have already encountered several aspects of the analysis of policy decisions which are relevant for the investigation of these questions. In relation to economic efficiency, the public choice and fiscal federalist schools of thought recommend overlapping 'clubs' and jurisdictions for different collective goods (see pp. 150–3). Under the GATS, national governments in the affluent countries now pursue strategies to enable service firms based in their territories to win contracts for supplying health, education, prisons and other facilities in many states (see pp. 89–90). This implies something like the fiscal federalist model for services, with multinational corporations' strategic plans promoted by national policies, including those of developing states (Paranagua, 2005), under the guidance of the WTO's agency the IFC (see pp. 99–100) (Dodd, 2002).

But the previous chapter pointed out that the growth of measurable well-being cannot be reliably linked, in the long term, to the expansion of a service economy with a commercial logic (pp. 210–12). The sources of human happiness seem to lie within such forms of life as partnership, parenthood, kinship, friendship and community. These thrive on different sources of nourishment from economic efficiency. They rely on bonds between people, rather than individual autonomy and choice. But they are highly problematic as a basis for larger-scale societies, and their principles do not readily carry over from face-to-face relationships into the more abstract systems which link strangers in political units (Jordan, 1998, chs. 2 and 3).

Disappointingly, although the literature on cosmopolitanism and global governance, in which the appropriate size of the social and political unit of decision-making is debated, refers extensively to social issues (income redistribution, the development of human capacities, etc.), social policy analysis takes little account of these debates. For example, David Held (2004, box 5, p. 164) includes the relief of poverty, education and health among the priority measures for a 'new global covenant', but the literature on social policy in a global context – with the exception of Deacon (1997, 2003) and contributors to the journal *Global Social Policy* such as Day (2002) – tends to neglect this dimension. While criticizing the assumptions of organizations such as the IMF and WTO, Gough and his colleagues (2004), for instance, confine their comments on the possibilities of a 'global welfare regime' to the last two pages of their book, and do not mention the debates on cosmopolitanism and the basis for global governance.

In this chapter, I shall consider how the perspectives of the theories which regard individual choice and mobility as the best basis for collective units and institution-building might be reconciled with those which emphasize the priority of equality and justice among members. Many of the latter see the growth of interactions between citizens of many different states in cosmopolitan associations and organizations as a pathway towards a 'global public sphere', in which non-government organizations (NGOs) with a more ethically informed and qualitative global view of well-being and development can influence governance and decision-making (Bohman, 1996, 1997, 1999; Dryzek, 1999). Others insist that it is globalization itself, bringing economic interdependence, which requires governments to act together and to create global institutions for solving collective problems (Falk, 1995, 1998; Held, 1995, 2004).

New initiatives by international financial organizations, such as the ones spawned by the United Nations Finance for Development Conference of 2002, give clues as to the current direction of change in the evolution of such institutions (Day, 2002), while the wars in Afghanistan and Iraq, and the Israeli–Palestinian peace process, indicate that the world superpower, the USA, is willing to use influence (and if necessary force) to achieve a national model of governance which it sees as consistent with the new world order. In the UK, too, the government has been active in trying to link global policy on debt with better governance, especially in Africa.

To do justice to these issues, the study of social policy must adopt perspectives on efficiency and equity which move beyond the national standpoint taken in the vast majority of texts. A truly interdisciplinary approach to the big issue of the appropriate size of units for the funding and provision of services, and the redistribution of resources, must recognize and reconcile the logics of international competition between firms for market shares in these fields (chapters 5 and 6) and the values and practices which sustain collective life in groups and communities (chapters 11 and 12).

It is far easier to state the general principles which should guide the 'global covenant' for good governance than to specify how these should be implemented in administrative units and service delivery systems. For example, Held states that the guiding ethical principles should be 'equal moral worth, equal liberty, equal political status, collective decision-making about public affairs, amelioration of urgent need, development for all, environmental sustainability' (Held, 2004, box 5, p. 164).

In somewhat similar terms, the United Nations Finance for Development Conference at Monterrey, Mexico, in 2002 produced a document, the 'Monterrey Consensus', which affirmed the ethical principles which should underlie these policies.

> . . . we commit ourselves to promoting national and global economic systems based on the principles of justice, equity, participation, transparency, accountability and inclusion.
> . . . Freedom, peace and security, domestic stability, respect for human rights, including the right to development, and the rule of law, gender equality, market-oriented policies, and an overall commitment to just and democratic societies are also essential and mutually reinforcing. (United Nations, 2002, articles 9 and 11)

Here at once we also recognize a difference of emphasis, because whereas Held stresses the need for 'regulating global markets', and even 'taming global markets' and 'privileged access for developing countries where fledgling industries require protection' (Held, 2004, box 5, pp. 164–5), the Monterrey Consensus states firmly:

> . . . we reaffirm our commitment to trade liberalization and to ensure that trade plays its full part in promoting economic growth, employment and development for all. (United Nations, 2002, article 26)

In practice, specific issues constantly reveal the tension between these two sets of principles. For example, the BBC *Panorama* programme showed that the Ugandan government wants to regulate the export of second-hand clothes from the UK to that country, on the grounds that it is a form of 'social dumping' which is ruining the Ugandan textiles industry, a potential source of growth and exports. But currently most Ugandans buy such imported clothes, which are inexpensive, from market stalls, and are rather satisfied with them (BBC 1 TV, 2005b). The situation may be improved in the long term by the decision of the World Trade Organization that protection given to the US cotton industry is illegal in its terms (BBC World Service, 2005e). This might provide new export opportunities for Ugandan-grown cotton products, but it does not supply a clear principle to decide the question about second-hand imports from the UK, organized by well-intentioned NGOs.

In setting out a framework for analysing the implications of these issues for social policy, I shall also introduce another dimension, which is missing from the debates in public economics and political theory. As we have seen in part I of this book, mobility and migration are prominent strategies for individuals and households faced with very limited choices in a particular economic environment. How do transnational movements of population influence the principles of equality and justice that apply to relations between all groups worldwide (Jordan and Düvell, 2002, ch. 10)? How can we evaluate the immigration policies of affluent First World countries in the light of the regimes for ethical institutions proposed by the various schools of thought on global governance? This will provide the case example at the end of this chapter, which aims to show that migration regimes cannot be excluded from the study of social policy.

Globalization, human development and well-being

The first question is whether more frequent transnational interactions of all kinds and greater interdependence are themselves contributing to a potential improvement in human development and well-being, or whether they are intrinsically destructive of the quality of life of all social units. Some social movements, notably the anti-capitalist, anti-globalization and global justice movements, argue emphatically that the attempt to integrate the world economy through the Washington Consensus has led to long-term harm to all these progressive projects. In effect, they pit themselves as representatives of Polanyi's 'second movement' of transformation against the drive towards One Big Market (Polanyi, 1944; see pp. 79 and 90). Their economic and ethical arguments will be assessed in the following chapter (pp. 239–45).

In one view of the history of social policy, it has always consisted of a series of new and larger-scale collective institutional solutions to problems emerging at a smaller-scale level of organizations. According to Abram de Swaan,

> the dilemmas of collective action may be understood as a transitional phenomenon, as a phenomenon which occurs in the process of transition from a collection of interdependent but unco-ordinated human beings to a co-ordinated association, which may effectively impose its policies upon constituent members. (Swaan, 1988, p. 26)

In this perspective, a set of collective actors (such as towns and cities in late medieval Europe), faced with an issue such as 'vagrancy' between them, created new measures of transcendent collectivization as a common solution. He suggested that a similar process was becoming visible in relation to economic migration from post-communist Eastern Europe (Swaan, 1994, pp. 105–10). The early twenty-first century might be seen as such a transition from national to global institutions. Such a view seems implicit in Held's contention that new challenges of social vulnerability call for 'a number of new global institutional tools to foster both the supply of public goods and the public nature of decision-making about them' (Held, 2004, p. 103). This would represent both a new version of 'social democracy at a global level' (ibid.) and a solution to problems of 'institutional competition, overlapping jurisdictions, the excessive costs of inaction, etc.' (ibid., p. 102).

However, at the same time as this drive to a higher level of collectivization is taking place, so is one towards greater devolution to local units, with budgetary control and powers of governance – 'economic clubs' (see pp. 141–53). Such units may well be confined to a small locality, be focused on a particular collective good (such as health care), and have governance by members who represent managers, workers and service users (Blears, 2003). While it is possible to see this fragmentation of welfare states as 'inclusive subsidiarity' in governance (Held, 2004, pp. 100–2), the economics of club formation and membership selection tend towards 'zoning' – the exclusionary segregation of the poorest and neediest (Cullis and Jones, 1994, pp. 297–301).

The question to be investigated is how international organizations, national governments and transnational firms interact to create the institutions for social policy to be made and implemented. The evolution of global institutions (such as the WTO) can influence governments to contract with firms to provide services for certain citizens (see chapter 3). But if governments select members who are eligible for services (through migration controls) and firms select members through the fees they charge, international organizations have very limited influence over the rules governing the memberships of such units. Global co-ordination cannot achieve the outcomes prescribed by fiscal federalist analyses, still less require units to include poor people, and achieve social justice.

In part I of this book, we saw that globalization is not inherently damaging to human development. The most successful among the 'productivist' regimes of South-East Asia have been able to harness the forces driving the integration of the world economy to make gains in the productivity, income and capabilities of their citizens commensurate with the profits of multinational enterprises, at least during the industrialization phase of their development (chapters 1 to 3). Although there may be evidence, from Japan in particular, of longer-term limitations on this model's contribution to well-being (Gough, 2004), the continuing economic success of the Special Economic Zones in China demonstrate its potential for rapid transition from poverty. Hence globalization has not simply compounded inequalities. Even though some regions, such as sub-Saharan Africa, have fared very badly, the number in the world living in the very poorest conditions seems to have declined slightly (Held and McGrew, 2003, part III). In distributional terms, the picture is mixed. For example, in India, as in China, urban and coastal areas have witnessed growth of average incomes, while rural and inland areas have stagnated (CEPR, 2002). Developing countries as a whole are not losing out in world trade (Held, 2004, pp. 8–9; Moore, 2003, p. 169), though some are faring much better than others.

We have also encountered many examples of failures in global governance, especially those of the IMF, the World Bank and the WTO, such as the East Asian financial crisis, the Russian crisis, and the collapse of the Argentinian economy (see pp. 72–5). The Washington Consensus model of liberalization and privatization also spawned programmes for health care and educational restructuring with negative and regressive effects in many developing countries (chapters 5 and 6). It is not obvious how these adverse, and sometimes catastrophic, features of economic integration through markets and capitalist institutions can best be minimized and the logic of their transformations modified. Held's recommended structures are consciously adaptations of post-war, social democratic welfare states and Keynesian economic management mechanisms to the global scale – an extended collectivization of the settlement between the productive forces in the global economy achieved by co-ordination between nation states.

From this perspective, the task of global governance is to rediscover institutions to *embed* liberalism and capitalism in a global political and social system – 'a grand social bargain whereby all sectors of society agree to open markets . . . but also to contain and share the social adjustment costs that open markets inevitably produce' (Ruggie, 2003, pp. 93–4). But – like the World Bank Development Plan – this confident recommendation becomes much woollier when specific models are sought:

> experimentation with suitable domestic institutions and maturing of internal economic integration need to be combined with sound macroeconomic policy and some aspects of external market integration. (Held, 2004, p. 53)

> these requirements can be generated in a number of different ways. . . . There is no single model of a successful transition to a high growth path. Each country has to figure out its own investment strategy. (Rodrik, 2001, p. 22)

The lack of a clear-cut model and the emphasis on local conditions, on specific institutional paths and on sequencing and timing (Stiglitz, 2002, pp. 73–8) all imply that nation states need to have a good deal of control over processes of adjustment, such as trade and capital market liberalization. But only China has hitherto had the economic muscle to resist pressures for rapid transformations among the developing countries, and those with large foreign debts have no leverage at all. The consequences of compliance with the demands of international financial institutions in every continent have been discouraging (Milanovic, 2003, p. 679).

This requirement for local knowledge, historical sensitivity and fine tuning also sits uneasily with the idea of pooling political sovereignty. The notion of a 'global covenant' – an international social settlement on the model of post-war national settlements – demands an ' "unbundling" of the relationship between sovereignty, territoriality and political power' (Held, 2004, p. 87). Notions of transnational business associations, NGOs and public bodies forming regional and global policy regimes beg questions about power and autonomy, which are central to all collective action problems. We have encountered these in relation to European Union social policy on the issue of trade in services (see pp. 93–4).

The economic logic of fiscal federalism is far more specific than this. It has a clear economic analysis of the costs and benefits, in terms of efficiency, of organizations to supply each collective good to a population – but not how to specify the constituency for these groupings, whether local, national, regional or global (see pp. 150–2). Firms will respond to this logic of collective provision (developing land or providing services) within whatever the terms allowed them under contracts with local, national or regional governments, and will recruit staff and attract members without reference to criteria for equity, unless these contracts specify otherwise.

It is this imprecision of the overall model for global governance, together with the clarity of the economic logic of fiscal federalism, which is most challenging for social policy on this big issue. What general principles, if any, can be applied to the analysis of the best size for units, and the best mode of governance for balancing individual rights with quality of life considerations?

Cosmopolitan citizenship and a global civil society

The arguments for a global regime which collectivizes the institutions of national social democratic welfare states are open to two possible criticisms. One is that these institutions have proved inadequate to the tasks of organizing societies of diverse autonomous, mobile individuals, or commanding their loyalty, *within* such states. The Third Way's new 'social contracts' or 'covenants' in the USA and the UK in the 1990s were focused on taxing less mobile factors of production and coercing the poor and dependent, while giving free rein to transnational finance and industrial capital. They have largely reneged on the attempt to achieve collective solidarities based on common interests – so how might these be pulled off on a global scale?

The second criticism is that any such institutions – organized, for example, through a democratized United Nations – would reflect the economic forces driving globalization rather than a genuine cosmopolitan community. It would express the need for a kind of forum for corporatist negotiations between capital and labour at the global level, with perhaps some representation for transnational NGOs. It would therefore suffer from many of the weaknesses identified by critics of (for example) the European Union – a deficit of genuine democratic participation, or mass loyalty to its institutional arrangements.

The problem of linking political and administrative structures for a social settlement, capable of redistributing resources and supplying public goods, to a cultural community which gives it vitality and substance again goes back to the Enlightenment period. Adam Smith pointed out that capitalists were always in danger of becoming pure transnational opportunists, with no real roots in any such community, unless their political loyalties could be engaged. Because a merchant 'is not necessarily the citizen of any particular country', '. . . a very trifling disgust will make him remove his capital, and together with it all the industry which he supports, from one country to another' (Smith, 1976 [1776], III. iv. 24).

Smith saw the solution to this as drawing the commercial class into national politics and the ownership of land. Immanuel Kant, starting from the recognition of a need for international law, sought ways of being hospitable to strangers in any land as the ethical basis for a 'cosmopolitan constitution', based on 'universal rights': 'the peoples of the earth have thus entered in varying degrees into a universal community, and it has developed to a point where a violation of rights in one part of the world is felt everywhere' (Kant, 1970 [1801], p. 107).

So the issue for cosmopolitan theorists of 'universal community' is to show how globalization does not simply create a transnational elite of commercially minded nomads which 'comes to have more in common with each other than it does with the more rooted, ethnically distinct members of its own particular civil society' (Falk, 1994b, pp. 134–5) – a phenomenon we have encountered in the work-permit holders coming to the UK from Poland and India (Jordan and Düvell, 2002, ch. 9; 2003, ch. 3). To balance both this and the corporatism of the Third Way model, several theorists have – following Habermas (1987, 1996) – emphasized the importance of communication, based on local associations and networks, being reflected in interactions in a 'cosmopolitan public sphere' (Bohman, 1996, p. 191). This comes from below, and occurs when such organizations from different countries begin to meet and debate common issues: 'Contrary to a global aggregate audience, a cosmopolitan public sphere is created when two or more limited spheres begin to overlap and intersect' (Bohman, 1998, p. 213).

These ideas are also reflected in the theory of 'discursive democracy', where decisions result from communicative deliberation between stakeholders rather than instrumental negotiation between representatives of interest groups (Dryzek, 1990, 1999, 2000). In the work of Habermas himself, commitment to a cosmopolitan constitution which transcends nationalism (and hence defensive paranoia and aggressive racist or faith-based mobilizations) combines with the creation of this kind of global public sphere, with a 'cosmopolitan matrix of communication' leading to 'world citizenship' (Habermas, 1996, p. 514).

The obvious advantage of these notions as the link between an institutional order of restraint, co-operation and redistribution and a cultural community with ethical substance and real social bonds is that they seem to be free from the divisive and partisan elements which make up traditional faith-based and ethnic solidarities. A global public sphere, if it were to come into existence, would have somehow to operationalize the ideal of stakeholders with a common interest in a shared ethical order, but not be so committed to alternative versions of this utopia as to turn the public sphere into a seventeenth-century battleground. After all, the world order based on a balance of power between competing nation states came into being in the second half of that century precisely to end that nightmare (see pp. 150–1).

So how might that negative outcome be avoided? Gerard Delanty argues that a cosmopolitan public sphere, leading to cosmopolitan *citizenship*, could come into being through a balance between the polis (active political participation) and the cosmos (membership of a world cultural community). Globalization on its own tends to turn the citizen into a consumer (Touraine, 1997, p. 68) and global civil society into 'a network of functional interdependencies . . . above all finance, technology, automation, manufacturing industries and the service sector' (Zolo, 1997, p. 137). But a cosmopolitan public sphere, in which the imaginary and uncriticized aspects of collective identities can be reflected on and transformed into self-awareness, might transcend nationalism and exclusive community. In this form of cosmopolitan citizenship no group is excluded, and all share in 'a pluralist world of political communities'.

> The cosmopolitan moment occurs when context-bound cultures encounter each other and undergo transformation as a result. Only in this way can the twin pitfalls of the false universalism of liberalism's universalistic morality and the communitarian retreat into the particular be avoided. (Delanty, 2000, p. 145)

The big question, of course, is whether existing international institutions show any signs of evolving into forms in which cosmopolitan citizenship and the culture of a cosmopolitan public sphere could find expression. In particular, Held's model requires the United Nations to develop into a deliberative and legislative body, reflecting this global communicative matrix, under a constitution for international security and human rights (Held, 2004, chs. 9 and 10).

He holds out considerable hope for progress towards this outcome, based on a number of current initiatives. For example, the UN Secretary General, Kofi Annan, launched an appeal in 1999 for 'corporate leadership in the world economy' – a Global Compact, in which companies embraced nine universal principles concerning human rights, labour standards and the environment, to 'manage global growth in a responsible manner' in the interests of diverse stakeholders, 'so that all people can share in the benefits of globalization, not just a fortunate few' (UN, 2001). The Global Compact Office organizes annual policy dialogues on the 'challenges of globalization', 'to encourage action networks between labour and civil society organizations in pursuit of innovative solutions to complex problems'. The notion that firms may become the primary agents with responsibility for maintaining universal standards and virtues (O'Neill, 2000, pp. 21–2), via a 'social learning network' in which good practice will drive out bad through competition (Ruggie, 2003, p. 113), is one of Held's examples of how the market might be reframed or 'tamed'.

The Finance for Development (FfD) Conference and Monterrey Consensus represented another such initiative by the UN, and with the compliance of the international financial institutions. While reasserting the claims of trade and capital market liberalization, the conference could not impose its redistributive recommendations (such as 0.7 per cent of GDP as a target for overseas development aid) on nation states or require companies to comply with ethical standards. But Day claims that its 'deliberative influence' in the direction of cosmopolitanism can make a substantial contribution to the 'socialization of global politics':

> The use of high-level roundtables with participation from civil society and business at FfD represented a significant aspect of the Conference that was thoroughly novel. . . . Instead of seeing its lack of influence as being the result of domination by powerful self-serving elites, it could be that UN global conferences might prove to be an evolving model on which global governance would, after confidence was established, be founded. (Day, 2002, p. 312)

These authors claim to detect a global version of the liberal-communitarian regime evolving in UN institutions – a set of systems for balancing the rights of autonomous and mobile economic actors (individuals and firms) with those of settled communities and a diversity of associations. But it is important to notice that the form these arguments take is not the functionalist one of Hume or Adam Smith (that these institutions are the unintended side-effects of the self-interested choices of people with limited ethical horizons). It is more like the Kantian one of moral beings willing the universalization of their personal principles. Most of the writing on these topics is aspirational, and does not specify in detail the political forces which might bring these outcomes into being.

This is even more the case with those authors who argue for radical redistribution in favour of the world's poor. As we have seen in chapters 7 to 9, globalization and the Third Way model have been associated with pressures on national governments to make redistribution more conditional, reduce spending on public services, and lower tax rates on mobile factors of production (Swank, 2001) – to be more 'competitive' in the global marketplace. The hope of those who argue for more generous aid to the poorest countries is that the rhetoric of 'targeting' in domestic social policy can be deployed in the international arena, so that help can be given to those in most need (Kelly, 2002).

Hence those who argue that principles of social justice should be applied without regard to political borders (Pogge, 1994, 2002) can point to the very modest transfers which would be necessary in order to bring about a large improvement in the welfare of the neediest. Proposals such as a 'Tobin tax' on speculative currency transactions rely on appeals to the sense of responsibility and inclusiveness of citizens of affluent First World states.

This has seemed idealistic in the face of more moralistic and conditional attitudes towards transfers among citizens – far stronger support for benefits for retired and disabled people and 'hard-working families' than for lone parents or unemployed people (Hills and Lelkes, 1999). But the response to the Indian Ocean tsunami in late December 2004 showed that huge public generosity for the least fortunate could be mobilized under certain circumstances. The question of whether this represented a new manifestation of a cosmopolitan consciousness of social justice will be an important one for the near future.

Citizenship, redistribution and borders

An obvious test of the idea of cosmopolitanism is to consider migration policies and controls, to see whether evidence of this new spirit and new institutions is recognizable. But significantly there is no consensus, even among progressive thinkers, about what an egalitarian regime for the optimization of global well-being would look like. For instance, Philippe Van Parijs, a distinguished philosopher and advocate of the universal right to the means for self-actualization (Van Parijs, 1995), is quite clear that restrictions on the mobility of labour and capital have historically captured the benefits of economic development in some states, so that inequalities in national income per head represent a form of such historical 'citizenship exploitation'. Because of the unequal distribution of assets worldwide, individuals gain advantages simply from where they were born. When trade between rich and poor countries occurs, this is 'an exchange of labor today for access to capital produced in the past' (Roemer, 1983, p. 42).

Differences in productivity between countries can be equalized *either* by moving people (and their human capital) *or* by moving money. Roemer showed that – in his model – either free movement of people or free movement of money could lead to rates of wages and profits being equal and in equilibrium in the world as a whole, but only if borders were completely closed to movements of the other factor. This led Van Parijs to conclude – after allowing for cultural factors such as the work ethic and natural factors such as climate and mineral resources – that global justice would best be served by free movement of money, to avoid the human distress of migration. But this implies strict border controls if each country is to achieve a just internal distribution of resources and income:

> There is no way in which such systems could survive if all the old, sick and lazy of the world came running to take advantage of them. The reduction of domestic wealth or job exploitation, it seems, clashes head on with the reduction of citizenship exploitation. (Van Parijs, 1992, p. 164)

This unequivocal view is not unique among liberals. John Rawls himself, in his last major book, insisted that 'a people's government' (i.e. a democratic state) must take responsibility for its territory and the size of its population. Government ministers and officials 'cannot make up for their irresponsibility in caring for their land and its natural resources by conquest in war or by migrating into other people's territory without their consent' (Rawls, 1999, p. 39). In his theory, the institutions of justice emerge from a contract between citizens in a society whose membership is fixed (Rawls, 1993, p. 277). He endorsed Walzer's view that an absence of immigration controls would lead to internal restrictions of movement and closure of organizations (Walzer, 1983, pp. 31, 61–2) which were inconsistent with a society's first principles of justice (Rawls, 1999, p. 39n.).

These views are diametrically opposed to the ones advanced by Rainer Bauböck in his analysis entitled *Transnational Citizenship* (1994). For Bauböck, although states would continue to provide the basic units of political membership and democratic voice, accelerated migration implied that 'citizenship will have to become transnational by reaching beyond boundaries of formal membership as well as territorial residence' (1994, p. viii), as societies become more cosmopolitan. This was the only way in which citizenship could remain equal and inclusive under conditions of globalization.

Bauböck argued that states are a mixture of systems – polities, economies and societies – with overlapping membership systems. Global cities (Sassen, 1991) are examples of open systems (see pp. 41–3). Political membership is the principle out of which collective decisions are generated to regulate such complex processes and interactions, but it need not be the dominant system. Political participation is optional, and many residents in global cities are not voters. Just as cultural and religious communities span national borders, so increasingly does political citizenship, so it is misleading to base theories of justice on either civic republican or communitarian versions of membership rights (Bauböck, 1994, pp. 103–4, 171–5).

Consequently, Bauböck saw human rights as universalized rights of citizenship extended to the transnational level, first discursively and then institutionally (1994, p. 239). This implied that freedom of movement across borders was a goal of policy, and the pathway to it lay in extending individual citizenship rights beyond national memberships and territories (ibid., p. 327). Migration between states should not be enforced, but nor should voluntary border crossings be restricted: 'In liberal democracy the primary role of territorial boundaries of states is not to control human mobility but the organization of local populations as polities which democratically control the political power to which they are subject' (ibid., p. 328).

These drastic disagreements about the significance of migration for justice in a world still made up of such states are discouraging for the prospects of a cosmopolitan world order. It is not simply a conflict of views about the means of achieving a fair distribution of resources between members of the world community. It is also a dispute about the ends of social policy, because Van Parijs's principles presuppose that justice is a question to be determined among a fixed population of people with a shared history, occupying a territory with certain natural resources, whereas Bauböck argues that it is a matter to be negotiated between a diverse population of people, some of whom have moved to work or join cultural associations, and do not plan to stay. In the latter view, principles of justice must always be neutral between the claims of nomads and settlers (Jordan and Düvell, 2003, ch. 5).

But both mobile and immobile populations are now deeply interdependent in many ways, and all are influenced by global regimes as well as national ones. Institutions affecting the justice of the outcomes of their interactions include trade rules, international relations and investment flows. This implies that the principles of justice governing distributions of resources and the provision of public goods should be transnational in their reach:

> If it is possible to justify them to persons in all parts of the world and also to reach agreement on how they should be adjusted and reformed in the light of new experiences or changed circumstances, then we must aspire to a *single*, *universal* criterion of justice, which all persons and all people can accept. (Pogge, 2002, p. 33)

I shall now examine whether, in practice, any such principles are emerging under conditions of globalization in relation to rules for migration, asylum and settlement.

Case study: migration regimes

Despite the divergence of perspectives about the role of migration in global social justice outlined in the previous section, two facts about societies in the early twenty-first century are inescapable. The first is that migration is a strategy strongly favoured by many resourceful and risk-tolerant individuals all over the world, and that this has been the main factor in creating cosmopolitan cities and multiethnic societies. The second is that, often while conducting nationalistic or racist rhetoric about the threat posed by immigration, political leaders have adopted pragmatic responses to the spontaneous movement of populations and have sought to *manage* migration flows to their national advantage. In this section I shall consider the implications of new migration regimes for social policy.

One of the paradoxes of migration policy in the affluent First World countries is that, as labour markets have become more regulated and wage rates have risen, immigration provides the scope for 'flexibility' in the use of labour power (Jordan and Düvell, 2002, ch. 3). Particularly in continental Europe, 'guest worker' schemes have, since the 1960s, supplied unskilled labour recruits who would do jobs which were too unpleasant, or required unsocial hours or frequent relocations. By the 1990s, as unemployment rose in these countries, new schemes for recruiting workers from the former communist states were also expanding. For example, in Germany in 1998, there were a million labour-market recruits, mostly from these countries, more than half for seasonal jobs (Cyrus and Vogel, 2003, p. 232). Although their rules were quite different, similar phenomena were seen in the USA, which attracted a stream of migrant workers from Latin America, the Caribbean and East Asia (Castles and Miller, 2003; Stalker, 2000), and in Japan, where workers were recruited from Korea, Brazil and the Philippines (Tachibanaki, 1994). Indeed, as Sciortino (2004) argues, one way of comparing welfare regimes in OECD countries is to analyse which kinds of immigrant workers (both legal and irregular) they attract.

As might be expected under conditions of globalization, the main driver for migration flows is the strategic action of firms in deciding what to produce and where, and recruiting staff on a global basis. A large proportion of the foreign workers in any country are simply transferred there by multinational employers, whether these are managers and professionals from the firm's base in a First World country moving to a less developed one or skilled workers shifted in the opposite direction (Sassen, 1988).

Despite the rhetoric in the 1990s of tighter control over immigration (which was focused mainly on asylum flows from civil conflicts and repression in the Balkans, the Caucasus, the Middle East and Africa), migration regimes now recognize the economic advantages of immigration to deal with skills shortages and bottlenecks in labour supply. The European Commission announced a strategy for co-ordinating migration control systems, which consisted partly of enabling recruitment for these purposes, and partly of agreeing co-operation over restricting asylum and irregular migration (European Commission, 2000). But the decision of all but two member states (the UK and Ireland) not to allow free movement of workers from the accession countries immediately after enlargement in 2004 indicated a preference for schemes of selection of immigrants for specific sectors of the labour market, on short-term schemes.

The UK government simultaneously announced a more proactive approach to recruitment from all over the world, seeking 'the brightest and best' in what the immigration minister defined as a competitive situation (Roche, 2000), and emphasizing the contribution of migrants to economic dynamism and growth (Glover et al., 2001). Research during that period found that all UK immigration control agencies, but especially the small but highly efficient Work Permits (UK), saw their role as facilitating recruitment by businesses, for the sake of the efficient functioning of 'UK plc' (Jordan and Düvell, 2002). This agency was able to process firms' applications, if they had used the system before, in about ten days. The immigration control officials in Germany (Cyrus and Vogel, 2003), Italy (Triandafyllidou, 2003) and Greece (Psimmenos and Kassimati, 2003) were much more conscious of protecting the employment and wages of workers in their own countries when making their decisions.

As a result of this proactive approach, the numbers recruited under the work-permit scheme in the UK rose from 76,000 in 1999 to 119,000 in 2003 (Home Office, 2004, table 1.4). During the same period, numbers of recruits under other schemes, such as seasonal workers and au pairs, also increased, and new channels for highly skilled and self-employed workers were created (Home Office, 2002b). Because of low pay, organizational change and alternative opportunities, a recruitment and retention problem for the public services in the UK in the early years of the century meant that the largest category of work-permit holders were doctors, nurses, teachers, social workers and other public-service professionals (Salt and Clarke, 2001). But, at the same time, the government took vigorous measures to deter asylum claims, to process them more quickly, and to remove unsuccessful applicants.

This reflects the fact that humanitarian protection is an anomalous category in the management of migration flows which governments are now attempting. If the primary aim of policy is to facilitate international business, by creating a global labour market in skilled occupations and allowing spontaneous movement of enterprising and highly qualified individuals in search of better rewards (see pp. 134–5), then forced migration from political persecution represents a systems failure. Hence the goals of sorting out political problems at source, arranging asylum in the first safe country, and settling claims quickly (European Commission, 2000). Hence also the rigid separation of the immigration status of asylum seeker from those of labour market recruits, entrepreneurs or students. In the UK, the rights of asylum seekers to do paid work have been removed, on the grounds that claims will be settled before these would have become operational under old rules.

The enlargement of the EU also offers an important insight into the dynamics of migration under present conditions. As one of only two countries in the Union to offer free movement for workers from the accession states, the UK might have expected a large influx, but in fact only a few hundred thousand from the post-communist countries have registered as foreign labour (Channel 4 TV, 2005d). Opening the borders has not significantly increased labour flows, because of the many factors which tie people to family, community and the security of 'insider advantages' in their home society (Fischer et al., 2000). Rights to free movement, as an example of individual freedom through exit options, are generally balanced by the quality of social relations, even in a much poorer society. Migration regimes are a good test of liberal-communitarian values in relation to this balance.

The UK government is consistent with its declared values in relation to labour recruitment but not to asylum migration, where it has used nationalistic rhetoric of exclusion, even as numbers of applications have fallen to their lowest rates since the early 1990s. In other European countries, and in Australia, the 'protection' of national employment standards has precluded free movement; but special measures of recruitment have supplied employers with the flexibility they demanded.

Conclusions

In this chapter, I set out to examine the big issue of the nature and size of social units appropriate for belonging, sharing and solidarity – both political, and for the supply of specific services such as health, education and social care. In particular, I assessed the arguments of those who propose that larger political units can solve collective action problems associated with globalization, and can steer it in the pathways of human development and social justice. These analyses turned out to rest on several different sets of principles, derived from alternative perspectives.

If the issue is defined as how to establish collective institutions to 'embed' global capitalism, replacing the Washington Consensus by something like a global version of the Third Way, liberal-communitarian model of nation states, then it is possible to see progress towards this outcome in the World Bank Development Plan and initiatives such as the Global Compact for Corporate Leadership of the World Economy and the Monterrey Consensus. But these institutions are rather tenuously linked with the informal systems, communal networks and associative solidarities of societies worldwide, and it is unclear how they can readily balance individual rights with the quality of social relations through their policies and regulatory codes.

Alternatively, and starting from the perspective of societies as overlapping political, economic and social systems, we examined theories about the evolution of 'cosmopolitan citizenship' and a global public sphere. These analyses directly address the problem of rival versions of the good society, derived from faith- or culture-based ethical principles, and how they might be transcended to give rise to a politics of global democratic contestation within parameters of common interest. These approaches might complement those derived from the institution-building perspective, by providing the social movements and political mobilizations which could contribute human substance to their deliberations.

These latter theories focus on the issues of voice in global governance; but individual rights – especially in the economy and the sphere of personal relations – rely at least as much on exit options. It is fundamental to any system of organization of the services relevant for quality of life that members have the chance to leave one unit for another, where they can improve their well-being or personal development. Yet these rights, so emphasized in the Third Way liberal-communitarian model of autonomous citizenship, do not apply to movement between states. The dominant logic of migration management is the recruitment of staff by transnational firms or by public agencies within wealthier countries.

Indeed, both forced migration through persecution and conflict (such as that in Central Africa and Sudan) and irregular economic migration provide the scope for the most coercive actions of governments in the democratic countries of the world. Asylum seekers and irregular migrants are routinely detained in prison-like camps without judicial hearings, denied rights to work or choose their place of residence, and given levels of support well below those for citizens (Jordan and Düvell, 2003, ch. 4). In the newly industrializing countries, the situation is even worse. In February 2005, the Malaysian government used more than 20,000 soldiers, police officers and immigration officials, and another 300,000 'volunteers' who had been promised cash rewards, in 'Operation Firm', to round up and deport irregular migrant workers, mostly from Indonesia. If they overstayed an amnesty, they faced a fine of up to a year's salary, a whipping with a rattan cane, several months in gaol, and a ban from re-entering for the rest of their lives (*The Guardian*, 2005d).

It is not just that this does not sound much like cosmopolitan citizenship; it also undermines any economic or ethical foundations for decisions about the optimum size of social units. The economic theory of fiscal federalism, which underpins many of the reforms of public services worldwide, relies on exit rights (either to move to another jurisdiction, or to join another organization) as a way of revealing preferences for collective goods (see pp. 149–53). However, there is no way to design the optimum membership system for any such goods without settling the logically prior question of the constituency available for selection (by these methods).

If migration management systems prevent free movement across political borders, the issue of the size of constituencies for goods such as health care, education and social services can never be rationally settled (Jordan and Düvell, 2003, pp. 54–5). It is left to the power of governments, and the fees charged by service-provider firms, to determine who can join which collective units.

Cosmopolitanism offers the prospect of global social justice between citizens of a single global unit. But as long as national governments can decide who can become citizens, and firms can decide what fees to charge for services, being a citizen of the world means little in terms of entitlement to a share of health care, education or income. If the size of subsidiary units is determined by migration politics and the economics of clubs, international organizations may reinforce inequalities and injustices, as they often did during the period of the Washington Consensus. This points towards more radical redistributive policies, which will be addressed in the next chapter.

14

Sustainable Development

The third big issue for the twenty-first century is in many ways more fundamental than the first two. It is how to reconcile the demands of social justice among members of the whole world's population with the requirement for sustainable use of finite resources and the collective solution to the problems (such as global warming) already caused by economic development. Social policy analysis in the welfare-state tradition has only recently recognized these issues as central to its concerns – for example, over justice between generations (Beckerman and Pasek, 2001) and between the citizens of countries at different stages of the development process (Dobson, 1998, 1999).

Issues of environmental sustainability were not directly addressed in the economic literature of development, but started to appear in analyses by dissident and heterodox authors such as Mishan (1967) – see p. 115 – and Nordhaus and Tobin (1972). It was only in the 1990s that systematic scepticism about the long-term benefits of growth-orientated economic policies began to be expressed, building on the publication of *The Limits to Growth* (Club of Rome, 1972) and the UK Pearce Report *Blueprint for a Green Environment* (DoE, 1989). These analyses drew together historical, scientific and economic evidence of the negative impacts and disappointing outcomes of the pursuit of economic growth, and argued for an entirely new approach to human development and well-being (Douthwaite, 1992).

The impact of these new perspectives was to redirect attention from the search for growth towards underlying issues of resource ownership, productive dynamics and income distribution, raising once more the questions about the logic of capitalism which had driven Marxist theory at exactly the moment when Soviet-style state socialism was collapsing. These ideas have supplied the lifeblood for new social movements committed to the critique of capitalist growth-orientated policies, and reasserting the claims of human values, the sanctity of nature and our ecological heritage, and global justice. This has raised new possibilities for an 'anti-capitalist' approach to social policy, which will be explored in this chapter.

In relation to the issues of cosmopolitanism and international governance discussed in the previous chapter, it also confronts social policy with one particularly difficult problem. Social democratic welfare states were uncritically 'productivist' in their economic basis (Offe, 1992); they rested on contracts or truces between capital and organized labour over the management and distribution of economic growth. In the 1990s, all First World countries evolved into service economies, earning much of their income through a financial sector which invested in developing countries and an industrial sector with many branches in such economies worldwide. The most successful of those countries from an economic standpoint, and especially China (the largest), are unashamedly productivist in their approach to human development and well-being. Any reorientation of global social policy towards ecological and growth-limiting strategies will necessarily clash with the policies adopted by 'communist' China and the other industrializing states.

So the agenda for sustainability in global governance is up against fundamental problems not fully recognized in the analyses of Held (2004) or Delanty (2000), or in the World Bank approach to development (Sen, 1999; Stiglitz, 2002). In the absence of any consensus among the leading economic analysts in the affluent countries, it is not easy to see how political leaders in China, India, Brazil or Indonesia will be persuaded to limit growth or set environmental priorities for economic policies which really address the big issues raised by this perspective. Instead, the likelihood is that the global trajectory of policy will continue to be, as it is at present, productivist and growth-orientated, but with attempts at co-ordinated crisis-management. Even in the latter field, the refusal of the US government to sign the Kyoto Protocol on global warming, or accept the scientific analysis on which its terms were set, points up the limitations of this approach.

One of the difficulties in bringing these new perspectives to bear on global social policy or the programmes of particular states arises from the fact that the other two big issues have not been resolved, or even researched sufficiently thoroughly to provide convincing evidence. There are still fundamental disputes about the factors which go to make up individual well-being and the relative contributions of material commodities and convivial relationships. Furthermore, the sketchy evidence available suggests that different laws apply to different stages of development. In the phase of industrialization, which still applies to China,

India, Brazil, Indonesia and the majority of the world's population, the model derived from Adam Smith and Arthur Lewis seems still to work – subjective well-being does increase with average national income (Frey and Stutzer, 2002, pp. 8–10; Layard 2003b, 2005).

Radical critics of economic growth argue that, even at this stage of development, it usually does more to harm than to benefit people's well-being. For instance, Douthwaite (1992) claimed that in the UK the fastest measurable improvements in human development occurred in the period between the outbreak of the First World War and the late 1940s – an era of very slow economic growth (see also Sen, 1999, pp. 49–51). He also pointed out that equality of incomes and physical endowments was greatest in UK society in 1949, before the productivist welfare state introduced its combination of sustained growth and public welfare services (Douthwaite, 1992, chs. 4 and 7). He commended Ireland, at the time of his book still a relatively unsuccessful economy, but a society with a good quality of life, especially in rural districts, as a model of well-being, because it scored higher in terms of subjective happiness and quality of life than many far richer countries (ibid., ch. 14).

However, this view is difficult to impose, retrospectively as it were, on developing countries. How are we to tell Chinese urban flat-dwellers who until fifteen years ago still carried water for cooking and washing from a distant standpipe, and used a communal district bath-house, that private water supplies, showers and toilets do not contribute to their well-being (BBC World Service, 2005d)? And how can we rebut the evidence from South Korea, Malaysia and Thailand that growth has greatly enhanced educational attainment, life-expectancy and child health?

The second big issue also influences the power of anti-growth arguments to provide a convincing case against productivist welfare regimes. The goals of economic growth and material gain have provided a rather reliable basis for collective solidarities in all parts of the world, transcending ethnic and religious divisions, regional rivalries and intercommunal conflicts. It is all very well to emphasize the importance of community and the sense of belonging for quality of life (Douthwaite, 1992, ch. 8), but loyalties of blood, faith and soil have been incapable of supplying a basis for the wider solidarities between diverse populations which are necessary for national (let alone global) compacts and covenants. Ireland (and especially Irish women) eventually rejected 'de Valera's dream' of a traditional, Catholic, rural community, because it stifled individual freedom.

Growth and productivist welfare institutions, which still supply the basic elements of the liberal-communitarian national model for social policies, and the World Bank Development Plan have simply been the most *politically* sustainable kinds of regimes under conditions of economic globalization. This being so, it is argued against the radicals, it is better to look for ways of balancing individual rights with small-scale communal arrangements rather than attempting to overthrow existing political settlements and international institutions. Something like a technical fix for the problems of the productivist model is recommended (Huber and Stephens, 2001, pp. 325–31).

But this rebuttal simply refocuses attention on the issues which the radicals insist on raising once again – ownership, dynamics and distribution. Even the original economic theorists of growth never claimed that it led to well-being or justice, rather than increasing *choice* (Lewis, 1954a, 1954b). If choice is defined purely in terms of commodities which can be divided up into private portions and given a price, this leads to a perverse way of calculating welfare gains that allows natural resources to be depleted to the point of exhaustion, and human life itself to be sacrificed for material gain. So property, markets and money incomes should not provide the fundamental units of the calculus of well-being, or a system for linking the allocation of resources with human development and social justice.

Thus the critique of productivist welfare and growth-orientated social policy directly challenges the notion of individual choice, property and mobility as the bases for well-being. It raises far deeper issues over distribution, and the institutions which might allow sustainable development. It has mobilized large groups of people in anti-capitalist and social justice movements at events such as the European and Global Social Fora. These movements do not share a coherent view of an alternative to capitalism and growth, but they do demand a more thoughtful and fundamental re-examination of the issue of sustainability and the future basis for social policies.

In this chapter I shall also return to some of the issues of redistribution between rich and poor countries raised at the start of the book. Economic growth has always promised to improve the condition of the poor; after 250 years of global markets it is still promising this to impoverished minorities in affluent countries and a majority of poor people worldwide. The generosity of donors to the tsunami appeal funds after the disaster of 26 December 2004, and the deliberations of Tony Blair's Africa Commission, have revived interest in the issues of aid and investment funds for the poorest countries. The principle of fair trade is prominent in talks leading up to a new WTO round agreement (Oxfam, 2002). But none of this really addresses the question of whether capitalist growth is consistent with a sustainable distribution of resources and the fair distribution of incomes.

I shall conclude this chapter with an analysis of whether a particular institutional system for income redistribution – the Basic Income principle – might provide a basis for *both* justice between members of the world's population *and* sustainable development. This points the way towards a radical transformation of the ends of social policy, as well as the means.

Capitalism, property and growth

The anti-capitalist and anti-productivist analyses claim that the model derived from Smith and Lewis has a built-in logic which is unsustainable, given finite natural resources. It will never reach down to the poorest parts of the world's population, because before it gets near doing so it will have destroyed the planet. The logic of capitalist production requires firms to borrow money in order to build factories and install machinery; since this has to be repaid from profits, production must constantly expand. In order to remain competitive, firms must replace equipment with more efficient new technologies, and must therefore pay both interest on ever-renewed or increased loans to rentiers and dividends to shareholders (Hutchinson et al., 2002, ch. 3). Since land and raw materials enter the production schedule as costs to be minimized, and conservation measures cannot come into the calculations on which profits are based, the logic of growth uses up finite resources with no regard for the long-term future or for wider social needs.

It is important here to distinguish between *capitalism* and *markets*. Markets are nothing more than systems for exchanging anything which can be given a price. In this sense, even the most harsh forms of state socialism, or the greenest forms of communal production, use markets, because individuals are able to choose the particular bundle of goods that they will have for day-to-day consumption (no system allocates everyone exactly the same combination of bananas, chicken wings and bracelets). But capitalist firms have an interest in getting customers to desire more choice over more fields of consumption – dwellings, means of transport, heating and cooling apparatus, communications systems and entertainments, as well as personal adornments, food and drink. So capitalist production seeks to expand people's perception of their personal needs and the material goods on which their sense of well-being depends. All this encourages high levels of use of materials, and especially of fossil fuels and other non-renewable sources of energy production, as intrinsic features of capitalist development.

Furthermore, the capitalist firm is intrinsically expansionist and exploitative, as recent economic theory acknowledges. Firms are concentrations of resources and power. Although microeconomics insists on treating them as individuals, they are collective entities, pursuing a collective logic. In the newly developed theory of the firm, Oliver Hart acknowledges,

> Given its concern with power, the approach proposed . . . has something in common with Marxist theories of capitalist–worker relationships, in particular the idea that an employer has power because he owns the physical capital the worker uses (and therefore can appropriate the worker's surplus). (Hart, 1995, p. 5n.)

A firm is a hierarchy of authority which uses its accumulated productive resources to extract such surpluses from workers for the sake of profits. Firms are organized to get things done according to their priorities. The size and structure of business corporations is a direct reflection of the kind of power needed to implement managers' strategies in owners' interests. Those with power will shift their operations, switch suppliers or use resources in whatever way gives them greatest advantage in competition with others.

Hart shows that firms will only contract with independent suppliers or partners where they can be quite sure that the contract can be specified in such a way that these others cannot frustrate or delay their purposes. If the other party can withdraw without completing its part in the deal, or simply put off completion, then neither side will invest in the technology needed to do the job in the most cost-efficient way. In this situation, it is usually most profitable for the larger firm to take over the smaller, or to employ the staff of an independent co-operative – to absorb them into its authority structure, so it can make decisions about what they do (Coase, 1937). Employees lose the 'threat power' which independent producers have (Hart, 1995, p. 32).

Capitalism's collective logic stems directly from the property rights on which it is based, as Marx asserted. The reason why ownership of buildings and machines matters so much is that 'ownership is a source of power when contracts are incomplete' (Hart, 1995, p. 29). As a contract cannot cover every detail and contingency which may arise, it is the owners (or managers on their behalf) who decide. The capitalist therefore has a key power advantage under this system of production, choosing the size and shape of the firm, the deployment of resources and the chain of command (ibid., p. 44). Even if the firm consists of an office and furniture, these assets 'glue' the business together (ibid., p. 57), and the owner can walk away with all the resources if the firm shuts down, whereas independent producers who contract together keep their productive resources when they stop collaborating (ibid., p. 58).

For all these reasons, the collective power of commercial corporations (and cartels) can only be countered by the collective power of labour organizations, political authorities, communities or social movements, each of which has a different kind of logic for its collective action. Because labour organizations are so much less mobile and flexible than firms, they have proved incapable of balancing the power of commercial companies once the institutions of welfare states have been breached by global business and finance. Can any other form of organization balance that of corporations, and what different systems of production might give people alternatives to waged labour under the authority of owners who treat them as commodities entering into the costs of productive processes?

Clearly the state has taken a different role under the liberal-communitarian model than it did in the old welfare-state one; it no longer holds capitalist firms to a bargain with itself and organized labour. Instead, it forces citizens, as workers, to demonstrate willingness to work for employers, calling this 'reciprocity' (see pp. 156–7). In return for this, it hopes that transnational capital will recognize its territory and population as providing suitable sites for productive investment. This reinforcement of the power of capital is then partially compensated by some forms of targeted redistribution (tax credits and means-tested benefits) and 'social investment' (public spending on health care and education, to the extent of their public or social benefit – see pp. 115–16 – mainly in terms of increased productivity). This is essentially a modified version of productivism, with 'weak equality and strong reciprocity' of these specific kinds (Fitzpatrick, 2003, p. 95).

Governments would have to change direction in order to bring about a global switch towards sustainable, non-productivist models, or at least to balance growth with conservation in the medium to long term. But what political and economic forces might push them to do so? Ever since Locke justified the change from a society based on common holdings of natural resources to one of private property in the factors of production (because this shift made everyone, even the poorest, better off), the 'productivity principle' and economic growth have supplied the basis for approaches to distributive justice. Property entitlement is derived from people's contribution to increased value, and value is measured in terms of contribution to productivity, all calculated in monetary prices (see pp. 126–8). But, with the end of the era of welfare states, ordinary people seem to have lost their last claim to property as the fruits of their labour under the protection of the state, rather than as the source of interest payments to rentiers and dividends for shareholders.

But, as we have seen (pp. 70–1), this is not necessarily the case. A very large proportion of shareholdings in business firms of all kinds (including banks) are owned by pension funds; they are the accumulated property rights derived from past labour contributions by ordinary workers. Globally they have been calculated as adding up to $13,000 billion (Blackburn, 1999, 2002), and as representing a potential form of 'collective property' to counter that of capitalist enterprises (Aglietta, 1998; Self, 2000). In the UK, for instance, pension funds own more than half of the stock of nationally based companies, so they could exercise a decisive influence on policies if the individuals they comprised insisted that they did so. Similarly, high rates of savings in the East Asian industrializing countries put the combined individual rentiers there who sustain the US economy in a strong position to influence the policies of the superpower (see pp. 77–8).

So the idea that the world economy, and hence social policy, is driven by individual choices in markets is an illusion. It is driven by the collective logic of firms, which mobilize collective property, and could in principle be offset by the collective pressure of those who are ultimately the owners, some of whom are already collectivized in various forms of funds. If the latter were to combine with governments, which still own very substantial public assets (despite privatization programmes), the logic of capitalist growth could in principle be radically modified. In which directions, and according to what principles, might this be steered? And how could individuals who are part-time rentiers be turned into a social and political movement for global justice?

Sustainability, justice and future generations

We have seen that one reason why social policy has been subservient to programmes aimed at maximizing economic growth is that the analysis of individual choices in markets cannot recognize a social context, or put an economic value on the way in which services contribute to quality of life (chapter 13). We have also considered the feminist critique of productivist welfare regimes, that they cannot recognize or cost informal caregiving in family and community, and hence they favour the priority of increased material consumption over the priority of an 'ethic of care' (pp. 157–61). The critique of Green theorists must therefore be combined with these other elements, to create a 'non-productivist' alternative to the liberal-communitarian model of a national welfare regime and the World Bank model of global development.

As Tony Fitzpatrick (2003) points out, the elements of such a model are already available in the philosophical and policy literature, but at present not in a notion of 'reproductive value', which

> refers to the emotional and ecological foundations of economic value, that upon which economic value is founded, but which it can never fully incorporate or commodify, since care and sustainability imply forms of activity so extensive that they can never be completely quantified or reduced to economic criteria. . . . Economic value . . . cannot acknowledge this dependency, since no economy is wealthy enough to fully compensate for the emotional and ecological costs that it creates. (Fitzpatrick, 2003, pp. 98–9)

For these reasons, Fitzpatrick argues, the liberal-communitarian model (which he calls the New Social Democracy) can improve the relative position of women (through paid work, mostly part-time) and the environment (through technological fixes), but it can never take the step from a productivist to a non-productivist logic. Following Jackson (2002), he argues that 'stalled well-being' is a direct result of being stuck on the threshold of this paradigm shift, still measuring development in terms of GDP rather than an Index of Sustainable Economic Welfare (ISEW). This would insist on both market and informal production and reproduction taking account of ecological costs and personal and interpersonal benefits.

Such a model does not necessarily entail drastic cuts in material living standards, or anti-growth measures, but it does imply that some priority must be given to the well-being of future generations. There is a trade-off between the immediate needs of people who are destitute in today's global economy and the requirement to conserve resources and deal with risks for the sake of our descendants. The former priority is especially clear at a time when peasants in Afghanistan and Colombia have no economic alternative to producing heroin and cocaine, and large proportions of the populations of Muslim countries are so disaffected with global capitalism's cultural standards that they support international terrorism. The costs of drug control and security measures must also be factored into any policy equation aimed at achieving sustainable justice.

So Fitzpatrick argues for a contractual basis for basic individual rights and the rules governing distributive shares, a modified version of Rawls' (1971) conception of justice, but one which includes the elements of *time* (say two centuries of development) and is representative of the generations spread over this period, who know their situation in their time-zone. Any post-productivist principles should take account of facts such as the evidence that environmental damage is greatest in the first stage of industrialization and urbanization, and is then reduced (Panayotou, 1995); that non-renewable fossil fuels are of no intrinsic or aesthetic value as resources other than to provide energy for human development; and that there is a likelihood of new technologies being discovered, both as substitutes for fossil fuels and for cleaner production processes (Fitzpatrick, 2003, pp. 147–9).

All this means that the focus of the non-productivist design for justice (both between present rich and poor members of the world's population, and between all of these and future generations) shifts to issues of ownership and distribution, rather than simply to growth *versus* conservation of resources. We saw in chapter 1 that the distribution of land is already crucial for determining who benefits from the development process (pp. 23–5). It also affects intergenerational justice, because poor landless people in countries such as Brazil, Indonesia and Papua New Guinea have been cutting down rainforests to gain a bare subsistence. One possible approach to ownership of land in particular is that proposed by Roemer (1993) and Unger (1987), where certain assets, such as land, are held in common, but those who use or develop them are entitled to an income (a 'rent') from this for the period of their lives; on their death such rights return to the collective.

This is one form of 'social dividend', derived from 'ecosocial property rights', which balances the requirement of long-term conservation with that of short-term development. The idea of a social dividend derived from natural resources is not entirely novel; all citizens of Alaska, one of the United States, get an annual income from taxes raised from the exploitation of the oilfield there by private companies (Fitzpatrick, 1999, pp. 147–9). The proposed measure would combine this with a more sustainable property regime. The whole system of property, taxation and redistribution proposed by this scheme relates closely to the basic income scheme discussed below (pp. 249–54).

This implies that policies to improve the well-being of today's poor people and policies to conserve resources for the well-being of future generations can be reconciled, so long as their *convergence*, under trade-offs of this kind, is the goal of governance strategies. As Fitzpatrick (2003, p. 144) put it, 'justice can only trump sustainability, or vice versa, if the objective is to allow the two principles to eventually converge.' Taxes should ensure that the utilization of resources both contributes to just distributions among present populations and encourages the development of substitutes for those (such as fossil fuels) which can potentially be used for present benefit without long-term harm (ibid., pp. 147–8).

In the liberal-communitarian and World Bank models, all these ideas are visible in embryonic form, but they have not been joined together in coherent ways to make up a set of convergent strategies, with principles under which decisions about. trade-offs can be debated and decided. Instead, there are a mish-mash of crisis measures to stave off global threats (such as climate change and deforestation), taxes or trading systems to address specific forms of pollution (such as carbon emissions), exhortations about energy-saving priorities, a minor emphasis on redistribution of land (World Bank, 2001, pp. 47–55), and some stirrings of interest in the question of intergenerational justice and contract (Beckerman and Pasek, 2001).

One clear reason why no coherent approach has yet emerged is that the liberal-communitarian and World Bank models link property to productivity and growth in line with Locke's theory and the functionalist formula for increased autonomy, choice, consensual government and well-being (see chapter 7). So, for example, the concept of social dividends is now acceptable within this model, but only as a way of trying to get poorer people in affluent countries a start in saving and property ownership. Mainstream proposals for funds to be established, using tax revenues to transfer to each citizen a bond or savings account (Ackerman and Alstott, 1999; Nissan and Le Grand, 2000; Kelly and Lissauer, 2000), have now been accepted by governments. The Blair administration in the UK has adopted the principle in the form of 'baby bonds', which will give each child born in the country a sum of money to create a Child Trust Fund, which will not become available until they reach the age of eighteen (BBC Radio 4, 2005i).

The rationale behind this measure is framed in terms of improving incentives for saving, instilling the habit of saving, and providing the foundation for encouraging young people from all backgrounds to partake in an 'enterprise culture' and self-responsibility. It is completely consistent with a model which runs on capital accumulation and growth, eventually leading to a population with property holdings to support themselves in old age. But, as we have seen above, this form of property for part-time rentiers could, if transformed, have radical implications if these funds were to be collectivized as a political mobilization rather than remaining passive holdings (Huber and Stephens, 2001, p. 326).

What such new measures do in a small way is subvert the strong resistance to redistributive schemes of all kinds carried over from the neo-liberal and Washington Consensus models. This was founded on the objection to generous social insurance systems (such as the Christian democratic ones, with their high replacement rates under the European Social Model) that discouraged flexible labour markets and employment creation, and also on objections to means-tested social assistance, which trapped households in unemployment and poverty because they had built-in disincentives to take formal work. They are legitimate, in the eyes of the liberal-communitarian and World Bank model, because they are employment-friendly, enterprise-friendly and 'inclusive' (as are tax credits – see pp. 77–80).

Before a transition towards a non-productivist strategy could start, there would have to be a broader acceptance of the advantages of redistribution for the sake of fundamental policy goals. Redistribution would have to be recognized as necessary for improved well-being – for overcoming the phenomenon of stagnating subjective evaluations of happiness. This is exactly what the leading economist Richard Layard now recommends (Layard 2003c; 2005). He argues that redistribution should be one of the central measures to reverse the drift towards increasing rivalry and fear in competitive market societies. The fact that Layard's work was mentioned in relation to Tony Blair's press conference on measuring well-being and discovering ways to improve it (*The Guardian*, 2005a) suggests that this hope is not entirely unrealistic.

Case study: the Basic Income proposal

Social policy analysts with a broad perspective on the liberal-communitarian model recognize that it is in many ways transitional between welfare states and a new institutional order that will better address these issues. But rather than adopting new principles, they recommend a range of specific technical measures to tackle aspects of injustice or unsustainability. For example, Esping-Andersen concedes that poor people in First World countries are trapped in unpleasant, low-wage work by tax credits (because they must take such jobs or have their benefits entitlement terminated, and because they gain little from extra hours' work or pay rises, as their credits are removed and they pay income tax on each additional unit of earnings). But he concludes that this injustice can be mitigated by putting a time limit on the enforcement of low-paid work of this kind (Esping-Andersen, 1999, pp. 180–90).

Huber and Stephens are concerned that pension fundholders could subvert their own stakes in the new model if they, like Swedish workers in the 1970s, mobilized to increase their shares of national income. But they do not recognize that enforced fundholder passivity gives very little priority or space for political mobilizations of any kind, or even for civic action to improve quality of life, by workers and claimants. 'Activation' is one-sided – for work, but not for well-being (Huber and Stephens, 2001, p. 326). Gough recognizes that the gains in human development and well-being achieved by the East Asian newly industrializing countries are at risk from the WTO's and World Bank's programmes for liberalization of trade in services, but recommends the modified productivism of the South Korean regime (Gough, 2004, p. 200).

The problem about such *ad hoc* measures is that they do not supply a coherent response to the set of issues identified in this chapter; particular policies may make specific aspects of the productivist model more damaging to the interests of the poor, of future generations, or of the environment. But one principle claims to address all these simultaneously, and has gained support from theorists of equality and justice (Van Parijs, 1995; Barry, 1997), from feminists (Pateman, 1988; Lewis, 2003) and from environmentalists (Fitzpatrick, 1999), as well as historians of economic thought (Van Trier, 1995) and scientists (Roberts, 1983). This is the Basic Income (BI) proposal – that each citizen of (or resident in) a jurisdiction should have an unconditional, tax-free allowance, provided for a period of time (a week, month or year), which would allow each basic autonomy and economic security, irrespective of work or household status. It would replace social insurance and social assistance benefits, tax allowance and tax credits.

This principle would develop and institutionalize two identifiable features of social policy in the liberal-communitarian model of First World states and one feature of the World Bank productivist model of the more successful East Asian regimes. We have seen (pp. 77–80) that tax credits, paid through the treasuries in the USA and the UK, have brought about partial integration of the income tax and income maintenance systems. Such changes foreshadow an eventual full integration, leading to a Negative Income Tax system in which all residents either are paid a credit, or have tax deducted from their pay, according to their household income from the previous period (Jordan et al., 2000, ch. 2). (As we have seen (p. 79), UK households earning up to £21,200 a year now pay no net tax; but individuals earning over £25,000 a year, who are supposed to pay 40 per cent of earnings, avoid much of this through complex concessions. Such integration would simplify tax collection.)

However, this would consolidate three injustices in the tax credit approach to income maintenance. The first is that, as noted above, people who get credits face disincentive to improve their earnings (a 'poverty trap'). The second is that certain groups – especially students and those who give full-time care to family members, or do full-time community, cultural or political work without pay – would not be eligible for credits. The third is that, in the USA and the UK, the priority for paid work and 'activation/reciprocity' has led to the value of credits rising much faster than that of benefits paid to those outside the labour market (Jordan et al., 2000, ch. 2). A Negative Income Tax could mean that people incapable of work, through illness, disability or age, would eventually get no more than those who could increase their income by earning.

These injustices could be mitigated by modifications of a Negative Income Tax scheme, under which specific contributions such as those of carers, or roles such as student or retired person, gave eligibility for credits. The idea of a partially conditional Basic Income of this kind (a 'Participation Income') has been suggested as a transitional measure (Atkinson, 1995). The UK Secretary of State for Work and Pensions, Alan Johnson, has indicated that he is favourably impressed by arguments for a Citizen's Pension, which would adopt the principle of a universal allowance for all *retired* residents, irrespective of the social insurance contribution record, as a way of rectifying the present injustice to women who have looked after children or relatives during their working years, and the complexities of existing systems, including 'pension credits' (*The Guardian*, 2005e).

Once the principle of Basic Income is adopted for any group – that individuals are entitled to an allowance which recognizes their value and need, irrespective of work contribution or family role – this represents an important breakthrough and a shift from the productivist ethos. It gives all the freedom, which has hitherto been enjoyed only by those with property incomes, for people to decide for themselves how to allocate time and energy between paid and unpaid activities. At present, compromises between the ethics of income-generation for 'independence', of care for members of the unit, and of effort to improve the quality of life or physical environment of a community have to be negotiated between partners or generations of a family, to the disadvantage of members (usually women and young people) without a stake in occupational or private pensions or other employment-related or property assets (Jordan et al., 1994).

The BI proposal is technically identical with the social dividend embodied in 'baby bonds' or the Alaska scheme (p. 247), except that it is paid weekly or monthly rather than in an annual or once-for-all lump sum. Its first advantage is that it has none of the disincentives and injustices of tax credits or Negative Income Tax, because all would face the same rate of tax deductions on their initial earnings or income from savings. By giving recognition to carers, and allowing priority to be given to cultural, political and environmental work, it meets the criticisms and aspirations of several disadvantaged groups and socially progressive causes through a single measure (Fitzpatrick,

1999). Potentially, it can address issues of sustainability, well-being and intergenerational justice at any stage of economic development. For example, a social dividend through land redistribution might be more appropriate than a lump sum or weekly income in less developed economic contexts.

The effects of BI on productive and social relations would vary enormously with the set of other measures which accompanied it. For example, there would be a trade-off between the rate at which BI was paid and the effects on labour supply for formal employment. Other policies would have to attend to issues of sustainability and resource use. The measure could be combined with new initiatives to stimulate informal activity at a local level – increased participation in voluntary and community projects for collective well-being (Jordan and Jordan, 2000, chs. 6–9; Jordan and Travers, 1998).

The question which is seldom addressed by BI advocates is linked to the second big issue for the new century – the size of the social unit. If it is seen as a scheme for social justice among citizens of a nation state, a National Basic Income (NBI) could be paid at a much higher rate in affluent than in developing countries. If it were seen primarily as a way of redistributing basic security and autonomy among the whole world's population, a Global Basic Income (GBI) would be the appropriate approach to justice. It could be administered by a United Nations agency, and would obviate the problems of aid to poor countries, which ends up in the pockets of governments rather than individuals.

We have seen (p. 231) that one of the foremost advocates of BI favours a national scheme of redistribution behind borders closed to immigration (Van Parijs, 1992). One argument for this is that only the solidarities derived from common interests among citizens would sustain the levels of trust and goodwill necessary for an unconditional system. Another argument is that, if BI is supposed to encourage *engagement* among members of a democratic society, this needs to be perceived as taking place in a *political* context, of which BI is one expression. Finally, an NBI could be paid at a rate which greatly reduced the need for any means-tested complexity and stigma, housing allowances being perhaps the only exception (Parker, 1988). A GBI would be quite inadequate to meet the living costs of citizens in affluent countries, so these features of income maintenance schemes would still remain.

The case for a GBI is clearly based on criteria of greatest need – the potential to alleviate global poverty and take pressure off threatened environments and fragile systems of governance. It would give the citizens of the poorest countries a stake in their societies, and protect them from the worst features of exploitation by capitalist firms and domination by corrupt governments and local traditional patriarchs. If combined with the right measures for strengthening local communities, it would provide a balance between individual autonomy and collective capacity.

But none of these would resolve the dilemmas of transnational mobility. Even if fewer people migrated from developing countries under a GBI regime than do today, there would have to be rules about how they qualified for the other income entitlements and services available in richer countries. In an NBI system, there would be pressure for immigrants to gain citizenship, to qualify for rights to this allowance (Jordan and Düvell, 2003, ch. 5). Any proposed solution to these issues would have to balance the needs and rights of settled populations with those of the nomadic migrants encouraged by aspects of the global economy.

The obvious compromise would be for all variants of the BI to contain a global element, the GBI (paid to all the world's population) topped up by regional (e.g. EU) and national elements. But even this would require rules of fairness to apply that would allow individuals who crossed borders to retain their home entitlements until they qualified for what was provided by the host country (Bauböck, 1994, p. 219). The argument for retaining a system of distinctive nation states with political boundaries of membership would be to create a variety of democratic polities, with different cultures and institutional systems of engagement and belonging. But individuals should, as much as possible, have freedom to choose between these alternatives through regimes of free movement (ibid., chs. 12 and 13).

The BI proposal is one of the few opportunities for movement forward on the agenda for non-productivist social policy outlined by Fitzpatrick (2003, chs. 6 and 7). The liberal-communitarian and World Bank models are already up against tensions and contradictions which demand solutions. As Iversen and Wren (1998) point out, governments are having to decide which two options of a trilemma to choose, with no possibility of having all three. Either they opt for employment growth and budgetary restraint, at the expense of equality of incomes, as the Anglophone countries have done since the early 1980s; or they choose equality of incomes and budgetary restraint, as the European Christian democratic regimes did until the late 1990s, but at a cost of high unemployment; or they sacrifice budgetary restraint, as the Scandinavian social democratic states did until the early 1990s.

The BI approach offers a path towards greater income equality which allows employment to be redistributed *by choice* among a wider potential workforce – probably with the present overworkers (Bunting, 2004) able to share more with the present underemployed – and permits those outside the labour market to combine *some* paid work with more unpaid, but quality-of-life enhancing, activity. Until some experiments with the scheme are tried, it will be difficult to say which policy mix can best achieve the synthesis of goals described in this chapter, combined with fiscal prudence. But the possibility of achieving a policy programme acceptable to environmentalists, feminists and even anti-capitalists (Dean, 2005, ch. 10) must eventually either appeal to some political entrepreneurs or present itself as a solution to technocrats in search of a long-term fix for their recurring dilemmas (Jordan et al., 2000, ch. 1).

Conclusions

The third big issue for social policy, identified at the start of this chapter, embraces the other two, and projects the problems of sustainable social justice into the long-term future. I have argued that capitalism, and the productivist principles which support it under the liberal-communitarian and World Bank models, cannot reconcile the various aspects of this issue without decisive collective action. The logic of capitalist growth has shown itself unable to take proper account of quality of human life or the conservation of finite resources, and it cannot have regard to the well-being of future generations. But it should be possible, with wise leadership and the engagement of political movements in debate and decisions, to build freedom in markets and achieve economic progress which takes account of the needs of the most vulnerable present populations, and those of people not yet born.

The evidence that capitalism cannot spontaneously resolve these issues is available from its history, and from current politics. In the past, firms organized to resist the scientific data on damage to health from the production of asbestos and other materials, and the consumption of tobacco. They now mobilize to resist the data proving a connection between carbon emissions and global warming, and the harms done by exploitation of natural resources. The US government has sided with capitalist interests in the negotiations on emissions, undermining the attempts to reach agreed global targets – the USA contributes 21 per cent to the output of these worldwide.

The argument used by the Bush presidency is that it is better to follow a productivist logic in the USA, keeping manufacturing and consumption high there (where it can be monitored and regulated), rather than impose stricter limits at home and let these same activities be pursued in unregulated and even more rampantly productivist China or India (BBC Radio 4, 2005i). It also argues that the focus should be on finding cleaner, more efficient methods of production and consumption. This at least shows that the US administration feels the need to respond to the arguments for sustainability put forward by the rest of the world – to be held to account, in ways which would be more difficult in dealing with banks and manufacturing companies, which follow a purely commercial logic.

If such a dialogue is to lead to constructive and effective policies – the Bush presidency quotes the control of smog in the industrialized countries as a precedent – the pressure from mass movements, NGOs and the more radical governments of the world will all be needed. The arguments put forward in this chapter suggest that it is important to present redistribution for the well-being of today's poor people, and growth through conventionally productivist approaches in the newly industrializing countries, as ultimately reconcilable with justice for future generations and environmental sustainability. The notions of convergence of long-term goals and trade-offs are likely to be more persuasive than principles leading to zero-sum conflicts.

Above all, for redistributive social policies and ecologically sound trajectories to be reconciled in programmes which command majority democratic support, it is important to show that they are consistent with individual liberty and choice. The BI proposal is valuable in this respect, because it is supported by libertarians (Steiner, 1992) as well as socialists (Gorz, 1997). The danger otherwise is that redistribution and sustainability come to be associated with protectionism and backward-looking forms of authoritarianism.

Finally, the World Health Organization (WHO) has had some notable achievements in its programmes to eliminate killer childhood illnesses worldwide. Measles has been confined largely to the Indian subcontinent by inoculation programmes, and the goal was to eradicate it by the end of 2005. Polio, which was rampant in tropical countries and killed or disabled millions, is similarly in rapid retreat. Most striking was the fact that the programme 'Kick Polio Out of Africa', launched by President Nelson Mandela in 1996, had succeeded in confining the disease to a small area of Nigeria and Niger by 2002 – despite the civil wars and conflicts raging at this time from Sierra Leone and Liberia, across Central Africa to Somalia and Sudan. The disease then broke out again from this enclave and affected fourteen countries, but a new thrust by the WHO aimed to eliminate it altogether by the end of 2005 through vaccination in every remote area (BBC World Service, 2005f).

All this suggests that global collective action can be effective, even in countries afflicted by social relations of extreme insecurity and violence (Wood, 2004; Bevan, 2004b). But how does this square with the other major forces in global development – the commercialization of public services and the fiscal federalist agenda? This will be the topic of the final chapter.

Conclusions

The optimistic tone of the previous chapter should not disguise the challenging nature of the big issues facing social policy (as an academic discipline and a branch of politics) in this century. The conclusion from my analysis of the third issue was that the liberal-communitarian and World Bank models of development and well-being are transitional. They might evolve into a sustainable, non-productivist global system for justice between diverse and unequal populations which takes account of the claims of future generations. But the forces which could accomplish such a transformation are still largely latent or passive. The combination of the capitalist collective logic and the productivism of the present models combines to keep them that way.

As we have seen in chapter 12, resistance mobilizations against these dominant models currently take the form of traditional moral, religious and nationalist protests against the instrumentalist individualism and economic functionalism which underpin these orthodoxies. What Islamic global terrorism (along with Iraqi insurgence) and American neo-conservatism have in common is an appeal to solidarities of blood, faith and soil, and to a politics of obligation and self-sacrifice. Each of these mutually hostile mobilizations feeds on fear of the other, and this drives both governments and international organizations to consolidate systems of security and enforcement, including abusive regimes in prisons and detention centres. They raise the spectre of risks which justify coercion and restriction of individual rights, directed mainly at migrants and minorities (Fitzpatrick, 2003, ch. 3; Jordan and Düvell, 2003, ch. 4).

The other barrier to the development of forces for transcending the limits of the two models is the anxiety generated by global mobility and markets. Free movement and free trade are intended to erode the advantages of 'insiders' in labour markets, and cartels of companies, by competing away their 'economic rents' (see pp. 39–40). This threatens established interests among both workers and entrepreneurs, but especially the former, because businesses are more flexible and mobile than their staff, especially service workers, who rely on cultural competences and local knowledge which do not easily transfer to other regions, let alone other societies.

Hence the anti-capitalist movement is not simply, or even primarily, a mobilization to transcend existing models and accomplish true global justice. It also comprises many protectionist groups, defensive coalitions and backward-looking ideologies. We have encountered some of the dilemmas of such mobilizations in relation to the French campaign against the 'Bolkestein Directive' on free trade in services in the European Union (see pp. 201–2). Because the threat to job security and public-sector provision is seen to stem from EU enlargement, and particularly from the post-communist countries of Central Europe, this took the form of a movement to reject the proposed new EU constitution. But the *'non'* vote by left-wing radicals put them in the same lobby as supporters of the Front National, the anti-immigrant party of Jean-Marie le Pen.

A fundamental problem, not adequately addressed in this text so far, is therefore how the provision of a context for individual choice, especially in the infrastructure of collective services, can co-exist with the drive towards including the whole public sector of nation states in the liberalization of trade conditions. In chapters 5 and 6 we saw that affluent First World governments (including the French) had subscribed enthusiastically to the GATS agenda in the hope of gaining substantial earnings abroad by exporting services. But the same enthusiasm does not extend to welcoming Polish, still less Turkish, service providers into their public sectors (Leparmentier, 2005); political leaders have been put on the defensive, as resistance mobilizations have spread from France to Germany, Belgium and Sweden.

This doublethink applies to individuals and households also. Autonomous, mobile and self-responsible citizens of affluent countries have been eager to take up opportunities to travel abroad for medical and dental treatments, going as far afield as India and South Africa from the USA and Europe (see pp. 93–4). They have also moved to countries where they can live more cheaply and pleasantly, while bending the rules under which they are entitled to state incomes and services in their home lands (pp. 134–5). But the same people, and many other citizens, would be quick to protest if they found that migrants from poor countries were taking places in schools, hospitals and care homes in the public sectors of their states of origin (especially if those interlopers were black). By the same token, there is easy tolerance of the staffing of health facilities by doctors and nurses poached from poor countries, but outcries by UK citizens if 'asylum seekers' and 'illegal immigrants' take 'their' places on waiting lists.

So the logic of capitalist firms seeking profits worldwide and that of individuals using exit opportunities to go abroad to work in or use social services both clash with the logic of the collective solidarities from which public provision is funded, the contexts for individual choices are forged, and the political culture of democracies is founded. The first big issue for the new century, the balance between individual rights and shared collective contexts, and the second big issue, the optimum size of collective units, demand clear principles to resolve these apparent contradictions.

The Basic Income proposal, discussed in the previous chapter, would do much to reduce these tensions. By giving people a clear stake in national membership (NBI) or global sharing (GBI), it would provide a firmer basis for solidarities and greater motives for staying (and means to stay) within specific public systems. But there would still be a need to distinguish between those services which could properly be opened up for commercial competition, those which could justifiably be supplied by public–private partnerships, and those which should on principle remain within the government sector.

The problem is not so baffling as it at first sight appears. The distinction between the public benefit from collective provision and the private advantage that accrues to individuals can be applied to this issue. Once a standard of health and education is accepted as intrinsic to the public life of the political community – because it supplies the basic capabilities for citizenship (Sen, 1985) – it should be as much a fundamental right for all members as the Basic Income itself. In effect it becomes part of the BI, but given in kind. It also becomes part of the cultural context of a democratic way of life.

Once this aspect of the social services is defined, costed and funded from public expenditures by each society, the question of how best to provide it is a separate one. Some aspects of preventive and environmental health services, for example, may best be supplied by international organizations (such as the WHO in Africa – see pp. 255–6) or international NGOs. Public services have a better record in supplying basic education in most countries than they do in medical services. In many developing societies, far too many resources have gone into expensive hospital care and too few to low-tech community services. But the record of commercial companies is even worse in this respect (see pp. 95–8). Health provision seems to be a case where partnership should involve international, government and voluntary agencies.

There is nothing in the GATS agenda to stop a government, committed to funding education, health or social care to a certain level, from specifying contextual features of the services it chooses to finance which strongly favour employing its own staff. Conversely, there is little in the evidence of the performance of international companies in these fields to indicate that they are suitable to provide universal, basic services to all the citizens of a society, in a context of citizenship, mutuality, engagement and sharing.

This implies that there will be certain aspects of specialized, technical or high-cost services which can be contracted out to commercial firms or left for them to provide on a competitive basis. Where the advantages from postgraduate education (in business studies, for example) or specialized treatments (such as cosmetic surgery) are mainly private, it makes sense for these to be marketed in these ways.

The fiscal federalist model allows for the fact that, as incomes rise, people tend to want more choice over aspects of service consumption. But the evidence of 'stalled well-being' from affluent societies indicates that international organizations and governments concerned with improving the quality of life of individuals, as well as sustainable social justice, would do well to ensure that such choices are always made in a meaningful collective context. Rivalry and the search for positional advantage through shifting membership of service 'clubs' has not led to greater happiness under neo-liberal and Third Way regimes (see chapter 11). For these reasons, the requirement of social justice is for governments to define and supply the services to which all their citizens are entitled as the means to full membership. Firms can then compete to supply additional levels of service and recruit individual members from a much wider international constituency (see pp. 150–1). This would lead to a pattern of 'overlapping economic clubs' for such services as argued by these theorists (Casella and Frey, 1992; Oates, 1999).

The other related issue left in the air in the previous discussions is the reconciliation of cultural cosmopolitanism and the sense of community and belonging. Examples have been given of both transnational economic nomadism (with little priority given to citizenship, participation and membership) and exclusive local community, either privileged, through the purloining of superior amenities by affluent groups, or deprived, through the self-exclusion of disadvantaged ones (see pp. 180–4 and 196–9). Cosmopolitanism, of the kind advocated by Delanty (2000), is not consistent with either of these forms. It requires a political culture of mutual engagement between members of diverse groups, all of whom recognize common interests in negotiated solutions to shared issues and aspirations.

Here again, a Basic Income which gave all citizens a material stake in their society, and allowed immigrant workers to be treated with respect (as holders of rights from their own countries, or sharing in a GBI entitlement), would allow services to include the goal of engagement between such groups in their remit. In the liberal-communitarian model, the basic services for health, education and social care have been organized around principles of cost-effective delivery to individual consumers, leaving contextual and participatory priorities to community development and social inclusion projects. In chapter 12 (pp. 215–18) I argued that services are most effective when they can combine both these elements.

But another dimension of change might be a 'politics of needs interpretation' (Dean, 2005) – a democratization of the service work and service use, in which people identify, claim and help to create services in a participatory process (Fitzpatrick, 2003, ch. 9). Women and ethnic minorities in particular would have new opportunities to mobilize in action to negotiate about responsibilities and co-operation (Fraser, 1989, 1997). This process, although at present speculative, sounds more consistent with Delanty's cosmopolitan citizenship than the commercial or faith-based alternatives. It might bring aspects of the World Bank model into a First World context.

Cosmopolitanism is, after all, already a feature of the social services in many countries. In the UK, for example, around 40 per cent of health-service professionals come from abroad; two-thirds of new doctors registered in 2004 came from other countries. But – as in all the issues discussed here – there is a tension between the opportunities that this recruitment has provided for citizens of poorer countries to earn more and gain valuable professional experience, and the adverse effects on their home countries. In all, 50 per cent of Ghana's and almost 90 per cent of Zimbabwe's trained doctors, among 12,500 African doctors and 16,000 African nurses, work in the UK. The training of all these staff cost African governments an estimated £270,000; but it would have cost the UK £2.7 billion to train these doctors itself (BBC Radio 4, 2005h). Cosmopolitan citizenship and democratic dialogue are conducive to global justice; robbing poor countries of their human capital is not.

Global justice will not happen spontaneously, through individual choices and some variant of the functionalist formula. It requires an active process of political pressure and action in the name of a coherent set of principles. This book has argued that social policy, as a method of analysis, can contribute to this process if it embraces new insights, perspectives and research programmes from a broader range of new social scientific developments.

References

6, P. (2003), 'Giving Consumers of British Public Services More Choice: What Can Be Learned from Recent History?', *Journal of Social Policy*, 32(3), pp. 239–70.

Abrams, F. (2002), *Below the Breadline: Life on the Minimum Wage*, London: Profile Books.

ABS (Australian Bureau of Statistics) (1990), *Average Weekly Earnings in Australia, 1941–1990*, Cat. No. 6350.0, table 1.

ACC/SCN (2000), 'Nutrition Throughout the Life Cycle', Report No. 4 on the World Nutrition Situation, Geneva: ACC/SCN.

Ackerman, B. (1980), *Liberalism and Social Justice*, New York: Columbia University Press.

Ackerman, B., and Alstott, A. (1999), *The Shareholder Society*, New Haven, CT: Yale University Press.

Ackerman, B., Rose-Ackerman, S., Sawyer, J. W., and Henderson, D. W. (1974), *The Uncertain Search for Environmental Quality*, New York: Free Press.

Ackers, L., and Dwyer, P. (2002), *Senior Citizenship? Retirement, Migration and Welfare in the European Union*, Bristol: Policy Press.

ADM (Area Development Management Ltd) (1995), *Integrated Local Development Handbook*, Dublin: ADM.

Aglietta, M. (1998), 'Capitalism at the Turn of the Century: Regulation Theory and the Challenge of Social Change', *New Left Review*, 232, pp. 41–90.

Ahrne, G. (1990), *Agency and Organization: Towards an Organizational Theory of Society*, London: Sage.

Archer, M. S. (1996), *Culture and Agency: The Place of Culture in Social Theory*, Cambridge: Cambridge University Press.

Argyle, M. (1999), 'Causes and Correlates of Happiness', in D. Kahneman, E. Diener and N. Schwartz (eds), *Well-Being: The Foundations of Hedonic Psychology*, New York: Russell Sage Foundation, pp. 353–72.

Aslund, A., and Warner, A. (2002), 'EU Enlargement: The Consequences for the CIS Countries', paper presented at the conference 'Beyond Transition', CASE Foundation, Warsaw, 12–13 April.

Atkinson, A. B. (1995), *Public Economics in Action: The Basic Income/Flat Tax Proposal*, Oxford: Oxford University Press.

Audit Commission (1986), *Making a Reality of Community Care*, London: HMSO.

Audit Commission (1992), *The Community Revolution: Personal Social Services and Community Care*, London: HMSO.

Bacon, R., and Eltis, W. (1976), *Britain's Economic Problem: Too Few Producers*, London: Macmillan.

Ball, S. J. (2001), 'Labour, Learning and the Economy: A "Policy Sociology" Perspective', in M. Fielding (ed.), *Taking Education Really Seriously: Four Years' Hard Labour*, London: Routledge.

Barber, M. (2001), 'High Expectations and Standards for All, No Matter What: Creating a World Class Education Service in England', in M. Fielding (ed.), *Taking Education Really Seriously: Four Years' Hard Labour*, London: Routledge.

Barr, N. (ed.) (1994), *Labour Markets and Social Policy in Central and Eastern Europe: The Transition and Beyond*, Oxford: Oxford University Press.

Barr, N. (2004), *The Economics of the Welfare State*, 4th edn, Oxford: Oxford University Press.

Barrientos, A. (2004), 'Latin America: Towards a Liberal-Informal Welfare Regime', in I. Gough et al., *Insecurity and Welfare Regimes in Asia, Africa and Latin America*, Cambridge: Cambridge University Press, pp. 121–68.

Barry, B. (1997), 'The Attractions of Basic Income', in J. Franklin (ed.), *Equality*, London: Institute for Public Policy Research, pp. 157–71.

Bauböck, R. (1994), *Transnational Citizenship: Membership and Rights in International Migration*, Aldershot: Edward Elgar.

Baumol, W. (1967), 'The Macroeconomics of Unbalanced Growth', *American Economic Review*, 57, pp. 415–26.

Baumol, W., Batey-Blackman, S., and Wolf, E. (1985), 'Unbalanced Growth Revisited: Asymptotic Stagnancy and New Evidence', *American Economic Review*, pp. 806–17.

BBC 1 TV (2005a), *Real Story: Detention Undercover*, 2 March.

BBC 1 TV (2005b), *Panorama: Fair Trade?*, 6 March.

BBC Radio 4 (2004a), 'Christmas in Many Bethlehems', 25 December.

BBC Radio 4 (2004b), *News*, 30 October.

BBC Radio 4 (2005a), *News*, 4 January.

BBC Radio 4 (2005b), 'Japanese Reflections', 15 January.

BBC Radio 4 (2005c), *Sunday*, 16 January.

BBC Radio 4 (2005d), *Business News*, 11 February.

BBC Radio 4 (2005e), *News*, 15 January.

BBC Radio 4 (2005f), *News*, 22 January.

BBC Radio 4 (2005g), *You and Yours*, 16 January.

BBC Radio 4 (2005h), *News*, 2 March.

BBC Radio 4 (2005i), *News*, 4 January.

BBC Radio 4 (2005j), *Today*, 15 March.

BBC World Service (2004), *News*, 4 November.

BBC World Service (2005a), *World Briefing*, 19 March.

BBC World Service (2005b), *News*, 3 February.
BBC World Service (2005c), *News*, 22 February.
BBC World Service (2005d), *Outlook (in China)*, 11 March.
BBC World Service (2005e), *News*, 21 March.
BBC World Service (2005f), *Health Matters*, 15 March.
Beck, U. (1992), *Risk Society: Towards a New Modernity*, London: Sage.
Beck, U. (1994), *The Reinvention of Politics: Rethinking Modernity in the Global Social Order*, Cambridge: Polity.
Beck, U., and Beck-Gernsheim, E. (1995), *The Normal Chaos of Love*, Cambridge: Polity.
Beck, U., and Beck-Gernsheim, E. (2002), *Individualization*, London: Sage.
Beckerman, W., and Pasek, J. (2001), *Justice, Posterity and the Environment*, Oxford: Oxford University Press.
Begag, A. (2004), *L'Intégration*, Paris: Le Cavalier Bleu.
Begg, D., Fischer, S., and Dornbusch, R. (1997), *Economics*, 5th edn, London: McGraw-Hill.
Bentham, J. (1843 [1780]), 'An Introduction to the Principles of Morals and Legislation', in *The Works of Jeremy Bentham*, ed. J. Bowring, Edinburgh: Tait.
Bertrand, A., and Kalafatides, L. (2002), *OMC, le pouvoir invisible*, Paris: Fayard.
Besley, T., and Burgess, R. (1998), 'Land Reform, Poverty Reduction and Growth: Evidence from India', Development Economies Discussion Paper Series, no. 13, London: Suntory Centre.
Bevan, P. (2004a), 'Conceptualising In/security Regimes', in I. Gough et al., *Insecurity and Welfare Regimes in Asia, Africa and Latin America*, Cambridge: Cambridge University Press, pp. 88–120.
Bevan, P. (2004b), 'The Dynamics of Africa's In/security Regimes', in I. Gough et al., *Insecurity and Welfare Regimes in Africa, Asia and Latin America*, Cambridge: Cambridge University Press, pp. 202–54.
Beveridge, W. (1942), *Social Insurance and Allied Services*, Cm 6404, London: HMSO.
Beveridge, W. (1944), *Full Employment in a Free Society*, London: Allen & Unwin.
Bhagwati, J. N., and Wilson, J. P. (1989), *Income Taxation and International Mobility*, Cambridge, MA: MIT Press.
Blackburn, R. (1999), 'The New Collectivism: Pension Reform, Grey Capitalism and Complex Socialism', *New Left Review*, 233, pp. 3–65.
Blackburn, R. (2002), *Pension Power*, London: Verso.
Blair, T. (1996), Speech to the Labour Party Conference, October.
Blair, T. (1998), *The Third Way: New Politics for the New Century*, Fabian Pamphlet 588, London: Fabian Society.
Blair, T. (2001), Speech on Public Service Reform, http//www.number10.gov.uk/news.aso?Newsld
Blanchard, O. (2002), 'Labour Market Flexibility and Labour Market Institutions', paper presented at the conference 'Beyond Transition', CASE Foundation, Warsaw, 12–13 April.

Blanchflower, D. G., and Oswald, A. (2000), *Is the UK Moving up the Well-Being Rankings?*, NBER Working Paper, Cambridge, MA: NBER.

Blears, H. (2003), *Communities in Control: Public Services and Local Socialism*, London: Fabian Society.

Bleses, P., and Seeleib-Kaiser, M. (2004), *The Dual Transformation of the German Welfare State*, Basingstoke: Palgrave.

Blunkett, D. (2003), 'Active Citizens, Strong Communities: Progressing Civil Renewal', Scarman Lecture to the Citizens' Convention, 11 December.

Blunkett, D. (2004), 'New Challenges for Race Equality and Community Cohesion in the Twenty-First Century', speech to the IPPR, 20 June.

Body-Gendrot, S. (2004), 'Integration of Disadvantaged People in French and US Cities', paper presented at the conference 'Professionals between People and Policy', Utrecht, Netherlands, 8 October.

Bohman, J. (1996), *Public Deliberation, Pluralism, Complexity and Democracy*, London: MIT Press.

Bohman, J. (1997), 'Deliberative Democracy in Effective Social Freedom: Capabilities, Resources and Opportunities', in J. Bohman and W. Rehg (eds), *Deliberative Democracy: Essays on Reason and Politics*, London: MIT Press, pp. 321–48.

Bohman, J. (1998), 'The Globalization of the Public Sphere', *Philosophy and Social Affairs*, 24(2/3), pp. 199–216.

Bohman, J. (1999), 'International Regimes and Democratic Governance: Political Equality and Influence in Global Institutions', *International Affairs*, 75(3), pp. 499–513.

Böhning, W. R. (1972), *The Migration of Workers in the United Kingdom and the European Community*, Oxford: Oxford University Press.

Bolton, G. (1990), *The Oxford History of Australia: 1942–1988*, Melbourne: Oxford University Press.

Borja, J., and Castells, S. (1997), *Local and Global: The Management of Cities in the Information Age*, New York: Earthscan.

Bourdieu, P. (1986), 'The Forms of Capital', in J. Richardson (ed.), *Handbook of Theory and Research for the Sociology of Education*, New York: Greenwood Press, pp. 241–58.

Boutellier, H. (2004), *The Safety Utopia: Contemporary Discontent and Desire as to Crime and Punishment*, Amsterdam: Kluwer.

Bowles, S. (2000), 'Globalization and Economic Justice', Benjamin H. Hibbard Memorial Lecture, Department of Economics, University of Massachusetts, Amherst, 1 March.

Bowles, S., and Boyer, R. (1990), 'A Wage-Led Employer Regime: Income Distribution, Labor Discipline and Aggregate Demand in Welfare Capitalism', in S. Marglin and J. Schor (eds), *The Golden Age of Capitalism: Reinterpreting the Postwar Experience*, Oxford: Clarendon Press.

Breman, A., and Shelton, C. (2001), 'Structural Adjustment and Health: A Literature Review of the Debate, its Role Players and the Presented Empirical Evidence', *WHO Commission on Macroeconomics and Health*, Working Paper WG6:6, Geneva: WHO.

Brickman, P., and Campbell, D. T. (1971), 'Hedonic Relativism and Planning the Good Society', in M. H. Apley (ed.), *Adaptation-Level Theory: A Symposium,* New York: Academic Press, pp. 287–302.

Brueckner, J. K. (2000), 'Welfare Reform and the "Race to the Bottom"': Theory and Evidence', *Southern Economic Journal,* 66(3), pp. 505–25.

Bryan, B., Dadzie, S., and Scafe, S. (1985), *The Heart of the Race: Black Women's Lives in Britain,* London: Virago.

Buchanan, D., and Huczynski, A. (1997), *Organizational Behaviour: An Introductory Text,* 3rd edn, Harlow: Prentice Hall.

Buchanan, J. M. (1965), 'An Economic Theory of Clubs', *Economica,* 32, pp. 1–14.

Buchanan, J. M. (1967), *Public Finance in a Democratic Process,* Chapel Hill: University of North Carolina Press.

Buchanan, J. M. (1980), *The Economics of Politics,* Ann Arbor: University of Michigan Press.

Buchanan, J. M. (1994), *Ethics and Economic Progress,* Norman: University of Oklahoma Press.

Buchanan, J. M., and Tullock, G. (1962), *The Calculus of Consent: Logical Foundations of Constitutional Democracy,* Ann Arbor: University of Michigan Press.

Bunting, M. (2004), *Willing Slaves: How the Culture of Overwork is Ruling our Lives,* London: Allen Lane.

Bynner, J., and Parsons, S. (2003), 'Social Participation, Values and Crime', in E. Ferri, J. Bynner and M. Wadsworth (eds), *Changing Britain, Changing Lives: Three Generations at the Turn of the Century,* London: Institute of Education, University of London, pp. 261–94.

Capital Strategies (2001), *Business of Education Report,* London: Capital Strategies.

Casella, A., and Frey, B. (1992), 'Federalism and Clubs: Towards an Economic Theory of Overlapping Political Jurisdictions', *European Economic Review,* 36(2/3), pp. 639–46.

Castells, S. (1996), *The Rise of the Network Society,* Oxford: Blackwell.

Castles, F. C. (1985), *The Working Class and Welfare: Reflections on the Political Development of the Welfare State in Australia and New Zealand, 1890–1980,* Sydney: Allen & Unwin.

Castles, S., and Miller, M. (2003), *The Age of Migration: International Population Movements in the Modern World,* 3rd edn, Basingstoke: Palgrave.

CBI (Confederation of British Industries) (2000), *In Search of Quality in Schools: The Employers' Perspective,* London: CBI.

CEPR (Centre for Economic Policy Research) (2002), *Making Sense of Globalization,* London: CEPR.

CERI (Centre for Educational Research and Innovation) (2000), *Schooling for Tomorrow: Trends and Scenarios,* Paris: CERI/OECD.

Challis, D., and Davies, B. (1986), *Case Management in Community Care: An Evaluated Experiment in the Home Care of the Elderly,* Aldershot: Gower.

Channel 4 TV (2005a), *News*, 17 March.

Channel 4 TV (2005b), 'Jamie's School Dinners', 24 February, 2 March and 9 March.

Channel 4 TV (2005c), 'Is Torture a Good Idea?', 28 February.

Channel 4 TV (2005d), 'Let 'Em All In', 7 March.

Chowdorow, N. (1978), *The Reproduction of Mothering*, Berkeley: University of California Press.

Clark, A., and Oswald, A. (1986), 'Satisfaction and Comparison Income', *Journal of Public Economics*, 61, pp. 359–81.

Clark, H., and Spafford, J. (2001), *Piloting Choice and Control for Older People: An Evaluation*, York: Policy Press/Joseph Rowntree Foundation.

Clarke, J., and Newman, J. (1997), *The Managerial State: Power, Politics and Ideology in the Remaking of Social Welfare*, London: Sage.

Club of Rome (1972), *The Limits to Growth*, London: Earth Island.

Coase, R. H. (1937), 'The Nature of the Firm', *Economica*, 4, pp. 386–405.

Cohen, G. A. (2000), *If You Are an Egalitarian, How Come You Are So Rich?* Cambridge, MA: Harvard University Press.

Cole, G. D. H. (1945), 'A Retrospect of the History of Voluntary Social Service', in A. F. C. Bourdillon (ed.), *Voluntary Social Services: Their Place in the Modern State*, London, Methuen, pp. 11–30.

Coleman, J. (1988), 'Social Capital and the Creation of Human Capital', *American Journal of Sociology*, 94, pp. 95–120.

Common, R., and Flynn, N. (1992), *Contracting for Care*, York: Joseph Rowntree Foundation.

Cornes, R., and Sandler, T. (1986), *The Theory of Externalities, Public Goods and Club Goods*, Cambridge: Cambridge University Press.

Correa, C. M. (2002), 'Public Health and Intellectual Property Rights', *Global Social Policy*, 2(3), pp. 261–78.

Cox, R. H. (1998), 'From Safety Nets to Trampolines', *Governance*, 18(1), pp. 28–47.

Cox, R. H. (1999), 'The Consequences of Welfare Reform: How Conceptions of Social Rights are Changing', Norman: Department of Political Science, University of Oklahoma.

Cox, R. H. (2001), 'The Social Construction of an Imperative: Why Welfare Reform Happened in Denmark and the Netherlands, but Not in Germany', *World Politics*, 53, pp. 463–98.

Cruikshank, B. (1994), 'The Will to Empower: Technologies of Citizenship and the War on Poverty', *Socialist Review*, 23(4), pp. 29–55.

Cruikshank, B. (1996), 'Revolutions Within: Self-Government and Self-Esteem', in A. Barry, T. Osborne and N. Rose (eds), *Foucault and Reason: New-Liberalism and Rationalities of Government*, London: UCL Press, pp. 301–50.

Cullis, J., and Jones, P. (1994), *Public Finance and Public Choice: Analytical Perspectives*, London: McGraw-Hill.

Cyrus, N., and Vogel, D. (2003), 'Work-Permit Decisions in the German Labour Administration: An Exploration of an Implementation Process', *Journal of Ethnic and Migration Studies*, 29(2), pp. 225–56.

Daly, M., and Leonard, M. (2002), *Against the Odds: Family Life on Low Income in Ireland*, Dublin: IPA.

Dasgupta, P., and Serageldin, I. (2000), *Social Capital: A Multifaceted Perspective*, Washington, DC: World Bank.

Davis, A., Ellis, K., and Rummery, K. (1997), *Access to Assessment: Perspectives of Practitioners, Disabled People and Carers*, Bristol: Policy Press.

Davis, M. (1990), *City of Quartz: Excavating the Future of Los Angeles*, London: Vintage.

Davis, P. (2004), 'Rethinking the Welfare Regimes Approach in the Context of Bangladesh', in I. Gough et al., *Insecurity and Welfare Regimes in Asia, Africa and Latin America*, Cambridge: Cambridge University Press, pp. 255–86.

Day, A. (2002), 'The Prospects of a Cosmopolitan World Order: Investigating the 2002 United Nations Finance for Development Conference', *Global Social Policy*, 2(3), pp. 295–318.

Deacon, B. (1997), *Global Social Policy: International Organizations and the Future of Welfare*, London: Sage.

Deacon, B. (2003), 'Global Social Governance Reform', in B. Deacon et al. (eds.), *Global Social Governance*, Helsinki: Ministry for Foreign Affairs of Finland.

Dean, H. (ed.) (1995), *Parents' Duties, Children's Debts: The Limits of Policy Intervention*, Aldershot: Ashgate.

Dean, H. (2005), *A Short Introduction to Social Policy*, Cambridge: Polity.

Delanty, G. (2000), *Citizenship in a Global Age: Society, Culture, Politics*, Buckingham: Open University Press.

DfES (Department for Education and Skills) (2001), *Schools: Achieving Success*, London: DfES.

DfES (Department for Education and Skills) (2004), *Every Child Matters*, London: HMSO.

Diener, E., and Suh, E. M. (1999), 'National Differences in Subjective Well-Being', in D. Kahneman, E. Diener and N. Schwartz (eds), *Well-Being: The Foundations of Hedonic Psychology*, New York: Russell Sage Foundation, pp. 434–52.

Dobson, A. (1998), *Justice and the Environment*, Oxford: Oxford University Press.

Dobson, A. (ed.) (1999), *Fairness and Futurity*, Oxford: Oxford University Press.

Dodd, R. (2002), 'Health in Poverty Reduction Strategy Papers: Will the PSBR Process Mean Better Health for the Poor', *Global Social Policy*, 2(3), pp. 343–8.

DoE (Department of the Environment) (1989), *Blueprint for a Green Environment* (Pearce Report), London: Earthscan.

DoH (Department of Health) (1998), *Modernising Social Services: Promoting Independence, Improving Protection, Raising Standards*, Cm 4169, London: HMSO.

Doherty, P. K. (2003), 'Managing Participation in an Age of Diversity', PhD thesis, University College Cork, Ireland.

Dorling, D., and Thomas, B. (2003), *People and Places: A 2001 Census Atlas of the UK*, Bristol: Policy Press.

Douglas, M. (1987), *How Institutions Think*, London: Routledge & Kegan Paul.

Douthwaite, R. (1992), *The Growth Illusion: How Economic Growth has Enriched the Few, Impoverished the Many, and Endangered the Planet*, Dublin: Resurgence/Lilliput.

Drèze, J., and Sen, A. (1995), *India: Economic Development and Social Opportunity*, Delhi: Oxford University Press.

Dryzek, J. (1990), *Discursive Democracy: Politics, Policy and Political Science*, Cambridge: Cambridge University Press.

Dryzek, J. (1999), 'Transnational Democracy', *Journal of Political Philosophy*, 7(1), pp. 30–51.

Dryzek, J. (2000), *Deliberative Democracy and Beyond: Liberals, Critics, Contestations*, Oxford: Oxford University Press.

DSS (Department of Social Security) (1998), *A New Contract for Welfare*, Cm 3805, London: HMSO.

Durkheim, E. (1933 [1896]), *The Division of Labour in Society*, ed. M. Wittich, New York: Free Press.

Dworkin, R. (1981), 'What Is Equality? Part II: Equality of Resources', *Philosophy and Public Affairs*, 10, pp. 283–345.

Dworkin, R. (2000), *Sovereign Virtue: The Theory and Practice of Equality*, Cambridge, MA: Harvard University Press.

Dwyer, P. (2000), 'Movements to Some Purpose? An Exploration of International Retirement Migration in the Union', *Education and Ageing*, 15(3), pp. 253–77.

Dwyer, P. (2004), 'Agency, "Dependency" and Welfare: Beyond Issues of Claim and Contribution', in H. Dean (ed.), *The Ethics of Welfare*, Bristol: Policy Press, pp. 135–54.

Eckersley, R. (ed.) (1998), *Measuring Progress: Is Life Getting Better?*, Collingwood, Victoria: SCIRO Publishing.

Edinvest (1999), 'Financial Aid to Students in Private Establishments', *Edinvest Bulletin*, October.

Edinvest (2000), *Edinvest Bulletin*, December.

Eduventures.com (2001), *A Global Education Market?* Boston: Eduventures.com.

Edwards, S. (1995), *Crisis and Reform in Latin America: From Despair to Hope*, Oxford: Oxford University Press.

Ehrenreich, B. (2002), *Nickel and Dimed: Undercover in Low-Wage America*, London: Granta Books.

Eisenstein, H. (1984), *Contemporary Feminist Thought*, London: Allen & Unwin.

Ellis, K. (2004), 'Dependency, Justice and the Ethic of Care', in H. Dean (ed.), *The Ethics of Welfare: Human Rights, Dependency and Responsibility*, Bristol: Policy Press, pp. 29–48.

Ellis, K., and Rogers, R. (2004), 'Fostering a Human Rights Discourse in the Provision of Social Care for Adults', in H. Dean (ed.), *The Ethics of Welfare: Human Rights, Dependency and Responsibility*, Bristol: Policy Press, pp. 89–110.

Elshtain, J. B. (1981), *Public Man, Private Woman: Women in Social and Political Thought*, Oxford: Martin Robertson.

Elshtain, J. B. (1998), 'Antigone's Daughters', in A. Phillips (ed.), *Feminism and Politics*, Oxford: Oxford University Press, pp. 369–81.

Elster, J. (1985), *Making Sense of Marx*, Cambridge: Cambridge University Press, pp. 28–9.

Enthoven, A. C. (1986), 'Managed Competition in Health and the Unfinished Agenda', *Health Care Financing Review* (annual suppl.), 7, pp. 105–20.

Eriksen, E., and Weigård, J. (2000), 'The End of Citizenship? New Roles Challenging the Political Order', in C. McKinnon and I. Hampsher-Monk (eds), *The Demands of Citizenship*, London: Continuum, pp. 13–34.

ERT (European Round Table) (1998), *Job Creation and Competitiveness through Innovation*, Brussels: ERT; www.ert.be.

Esping-Andersen, G. (1990), *The Three Worlds of Welfare Capitalism*, Cambridge: Polity.

Esping-Andersen, G. (ed.) (1996), *Welfare States in Transition: National Adaptations in Global Economies*, London: Sage.

Esping-Andersen, G. (1999), *Social Foundations of Postindustrial Economies*, Oxford: Oxford University Press.

Etzioni, A. (1988), *The Moral Dimension: Towards a New Economy*, New York: Free Press.

Etzioni, A. (1993), *The Spirit of Community: The Re-invention of American Society*, New York: Touchstone.

Etzioni, A. (1999), *The New Golden Rule*, New York: Fontana.

European Commission (1993), *European Social Policy: Options for the Union*, Green Paper COM (93) 551, Brussels: European Commission.

European Commission (1994), http://mkaccdb.@9.int

European Commission (1996), *Accomplishing Europe through Education and Training: Study Group on Education and Training Report* (Reiffers Report), Brussels: European Commission.

European Commission (2000), *Communication from the Commission on a Concerted Strategy for Immigration and Asylum*, COM 757, final, Brussels: European Commission.

Falk, R. (1994a), 'The Making of Global Citizenship', in B. Steenbergen (ed.), *The Conditions of Citizenship*, London: Sage.

Falk, R. (1994b), *On Humane Governance: Towards a New Global Politics*, Cambridge: Polity.

Falk, R. (1995), 'The World Order Between Inter-State Law and the Law of Humanity: The Role of Civil Society Institutions', in D. Archibugi and D. Held (eds), *Cosmopolitan Democracy: An Agenda for a New World Order*, Cambridge: Polity, pp. 163–79.

Falk, R. (1998), 'The United Nations and Cosmopolitan Democracy: Bad Dream, Utopian Fantasy, Political Project?', in D. Archibugi, D. Held and

M. Köhler (eds), *Re-Imagining Political Community: Studies in Cosmopolitan Democracy*, Cambridge: Polity, pp. 309–31.

Fawcett, J. (1989), 'Migration Linkages and Migration Systems', *International Migration Review*, 23, pp. 671–80.

Fédération des Infirmières et Infirmiers du Québec (2000), '*L'Organisation des services: des modèles a repenser*', mémoir présenté à la Commission d'étude sur les services de santé et les services sociaux, 26 October.

Finer, S. E. (1950), *The Life and Times of Sir Edwin Chadwick*, London: Allen & Unwin.

Fischer, P. A., Holm, E., Malmberg, G., and Straubhaar, T. (2000), *Why Do People Stay? Insider Advantages and Immobility*, HWW Discussion Paper 112, Hamburg: Institute of International Economics.

Fitzpatrick, T. (1999), *Freedom and Security: An Introduction to the Basic Income Debate*, London: Macmillan.

Fitzpatrick, T. (2003), *After the New Social Democracy: Social Welfare in the Twenty-First Century*, Manchester: Manchester University Press.

Flynn, N. (1996), 'Managing in the Market for Welfare', in T. Harding (ed.), *Who Owns Welfare? Questions on the Social Services Agenda*, Social Services Forum Policy Series 2, London: NISW.

Foldvary, F. (1994), *Public Goods and Private Communities: The Market Provision of Social Services*, Aldershot: Edward Elgar.

Förster, J., and Strack, F. (1996), 'Influence of Overt Head Movements for Valenced Words: A Case of Conceptual Motor Compatibility', *Journal of Personality and Social Psychology*, 71, pp. 421–30.

Foucault, M. (1988), 'Technologies of the Self', in L. Martin (ed.), *Technologies of the Self*, London: Tavistock.

Frank, A. G. (1979), *Dependent Accumulation and Underdevelopment*, New York: Monthly Review Press.

Frank, R. H. (1999), *Luxury Fever: Money Fails to Satisfy in our Era of Excess*, New York: Free Press.

Fraser, N. (1989), *Unruly Practices: Power, Discourse and Gender in Contemporary Social Theory*, London: Routledge.

Fraser, N. (1997), *Justice Interruptus: Critical Reflections on the Post-Socialist Condition*, London: Routledge.

Freedland, M. (2001), 'The Marketization of Public Service', in C. Crouch, K. Eder and D. Tambini (eds), *Citizenship, Markets and the State*, Oxford: Oxford University Press, pp. 90–110.

Frey, B., and Stutzer, A. (2002), *Happiness and Economics: How the Economy and Institutions Affect Well-Being*, Princeton, NJ: Princeton University Press.

Friedman, M. (1975), *Unemployment versus Inflation? An Evaluation of the Phillips Curve*, London: Institute of Economic Affairs.

Gershuny, J. I. (1983), *Social Innovation and the Division of Labour*, Oxford: Oxford University Press.

Giddens, T. (1991), *Modernity and Self-Identity, Self and Society in the Late Modern Age*, Cambridge: Polity.

Giddens, T. (1992), *The Transformation of Intimacy: Sexuality, Love and Eroticism in Modern Societies*, Cambridge: Polity.

Giddens, T. (1994), *Beyond Left and Right: The Future of Radical Politics*, Cambridge: Polity.

Giddens, T. (1998), *The Third Way: The Renewal of Social Democracy*, Cambridge: Polity.

Giddens, T. (2004), *Sociology*, 4th edn, Cambridge: Polity.

Glaeser, E. L. and DiPasquale, D. (1999), 'Incentives and Social Capital: Are Homeowners Better Citizens?', *Journal of Urban Economics*, 45(2), pp. 354–84.

Glendinning, C., Halliwell, S., Jacobs, S., Rummery, K., and Tryer, J. (2000a), 'Bridging the Gap: Using Direct Payments to Purchase Integrated Care', *Health and Social Care in the Community*, 8(3), pp. 192–200.

Glendinning, C., Halliwell, S., Jacobs, S., Rummery, K., and Tryer, J. (2000b), 'New Kinds of Care: How Purchasing Services Affects Relationships in Giving and Receiving Personal Assistance', *Health and Social Care in the Community*, 8(3), pp. 201–11.

Glover, S., Gott, C., Loizillon, A., Portes, J., Spencer, S., Srinivasan, V., and Willis, C. (2001), *Migration: An Economic and Social Analysis*, RDS Occasional Paper 67, London: HMSO.

Gluck, C. (1985), *Japan's Modern Myths: Ideology in the Late Meiji Period*, Princeton, NJ: Princeton University Press.

Glyn, A., Hughes, A., Lipietz, A., and Singh, A. (1990), 'The Rise and Fall of the Golden Age', in S. Marglin and J. Schor (eds), *The Golden Age of Capitalism: Reinterpreting the Post-war Experience*, Oxford: Clarendon Press, pp. 39–125.

Goffman, E. (1972), *Interaction Ritual: Essays on Face-to-Face Behaviour*, London: Penguin.

Gorz, A. (1997), *Misères du présent, richesse du possible*, Paris: Galilee.

Gott, R. (2005), *Hugo Chávez and the Bolivarian Revolution*, London: Verso.

Gough, I. (2004) 'East Asia: The Limits of Productivist Regimes', in I. Gough et al., *Insecurity and Welfare Regimes in Asia, Africa and Latin America*, Cambridge: Cambridge University Press, pp. 169–201.

Gough, I. and Wood, G., with Barrientos, A., Bevan, P., Davis, P., and Room, G. (2004), *Insecurity and Welfare Regimes in Asia, Africa and Latin America: Social Policy in Development Contexts*, Cambridge: Cambridge University Press.

Gould, E., and Joy, C. (2000), *In Whose Service? The Threat Posed by the General Agreement on Trade in Services to Economic Development in the South World*, Development Movement Report, www.wdm.org.uk/cambriefgs/WTO/Inwhoservice.htm

Gregory, R. (1996), 'The Shann Memorial Lecture: Growing Locational Disadvantage in Australian Cities', Discussion Paper 96–14, Canberra: Australian National University.

Gregory, R. (1998), 'Competing with Dad: Changes in Intergenerational Distribution of Male Labour Market Income', paper presented at the conference 'Income Support, Labour Market and Behaviour', Australian National University, Canberra, 24–5 November.

Griffiths, R. (1988), *Community Care: Agenda for Action*, London: HMSO.

The Guardian (2001), 'International News', 15 October.

The Guardian (2005a), 'Blair's Green Antidote to Beating the Blues', 8 March, p. 9.

The Guardian (2005b), 'Leaders Join Forces to Cool Abortion Row', 16 March, p. 8.

The Guardian (2005c), 'Home News', 14 January.

The Guardian (2005d), 'Malaysia Drives Out Illegal Workers', 28 February.

The Guardian (2005e), 'Johnson Favours Citizens' Pension', 11 February, p. 12.

Habermas, J. (1987), *The Theory of Communicative Action*, Vol. 2: *Lifeworld and System*, Cambridge: Polity.

Habermas, J. (1996), *Between Facts and Norms: Contributions to a Discourse Theory of Law and Democracy*, Cambridge: Polity.

Hall, P. A. (2002), 'Great Britain: The Role of Government and the Distribution of Social Capital in Contemporary Society', in R. D. Putnam (ed.), *Democracies in Flux: The Evolution of Social Capital*, Oxford: Oxford University Press, pp. 21–58.

Harding, T. (1992), *Great Expectations . . . and Spending on Community Care*, Social Services Policy Forum Paper 1, London: NISW.

Hardy, B., Young, R., and Wistow, G. (1999), 'Dimensions of Choice in the Assessment and Care Management Process: The Views of Older People, Carers and Care Managers', *Health and Social Care in the Community*, 7(6), pp. 483–91.

Hart, O. (1995), *Firms, Contracts and Financial Structure*, Oxford: Clarendon Press.

Hatcher, R. (2002), *The Business of Education: How Business Agendas Drive Labour Policies for Schools*, Stafford: Socialist Education Association.

Hayek, F. A. von (1960), *The Constitution of Liberty*, London: Routledge & Kegan Paul.

Hayek, F. A. von (1976), *The Denationalization of Money*, London: Institute of Economic Affairs.

Hayek, F. A. von (1978), *New Studies in Philosophy, Politics and Economics*, London: Routledge & Kegan Paul.

Hayek, F. A. von (1979), *The Counter-Revolution of Science*, Indianapolis: Liberty Press.

Hayek, F. A. von (1982), *Law, Legislation and Liberty*, London: Routledge & Kegan Paul.

Heckscher, E. (1950 [1919]), 'The Effects of Foreign Trade on the Distribution of Income', in H. S. Ellis and L. A. Metzler (eds), *Readings in the Theory of International Trade*, Philadelphia: Blakiston, ch. 13.

Held, D. (1995), *Democracy and the Global Order: From the Modern State to Cosmopolitan Governance*, Cambridge: Cambridge University Press.

Held, D. (2004), *Global Covenant: The Social Democratic Alternative to the Washington Consensus*, Cambridge: Polity.

Held, D., and McGrew, A. G. (eds) (2003), *The Global Transformation Reader*, 2nd edn, Cambridge: Polity.

Helliwell, J. F. (2002), 'How's Life? Combining Individual and National Variables in Explaining Subjective Wellbeing', in *Social Capital, Poverty, Mobility and Wellbeing*, Rusel Papers, Civil Series 5/2002, Exeter University, Department of Politics.

Hemerijk, A. (2001), 'Prospects for Effective Social Citizenship in an Age of Structural Inactivity', in C. Crouch, K. Eder and D. Tambini (eds), *Citizenship, Markets and the State*, Oxford: Oxford University Press, pp. 134–70.

Herring, B., and Pauly, M. V. (2001), 'Premium Variation in the Individual Health Insurance Market', *International Journal of Health Care Finance and Economics*, 1(1), pp. 43–58.

Higgins, J. (1981), *States of Welfare: Comparative Analysis of Social Policy*, Oxford: Blackwell.

Hills, J., and Lelkes, O. (1999), 'Social Security, Selective Universalism and Patchwork Redistribution', in R. Jowell et al. (eds), *British Social Attitudes*, Aldershot: Ashgate.

Hirsch, F. (1977), *Social Limits to Growth*, London: Routledge & Kegan Paul.

Hirschman, A. O. (1970), *Exit, Voice and Loyalty: Responses to Decline in Firms, Organizations and States*, Cambridge, MA: Harvard University Press.

Hirschman, A. O. (1981), 'Exit, Voice and the State', in *Essays in Trespassing: Economics to Politics and Beyond*, Cambridge: Cambridge University Press, pp. 246–65.

Hobbes, T. (1966 [1651]) *Leviathan*, ed. M. Oakeshott, Oxford: Blackwell.

Home Office (2001), *Citizenship Survey*, London: Home Office.

Home Office (2002a), *Community Cohesion, Report of the Independent Review Team Chaired by Ted Cantle*, London: Home Office.

Home Office (2002b), *Secure Borders, Safe Haven: Integration with Diversity in Modern Britain*, London: HMSO.

Home Office (2004), *Immigration Control Statistics: UK in 2003*, London: Home Office, Statistical Unit.

Hood, N., and Young, S. (1979), *The Economics of Multinational Enterprise*, London: Longman.

Huber, E. (2002), *Models of Capitalism: Lessons from Latin America* University Park: Pennsylvania State University Press.

Huber, E., and Stephens, J. (2001), *Development and the Crisis of the Welfare State*, Chicago: University of Chicago Press.

Huntington, N., and Bale, T. (2002), 'New Labour, New Christian Democracy?' *Political Quarterly*, 73(1), pp. 44–50.

Husson, M. (2002), 'Cette mortelle fascination du dollar', *Le Monde diplomatique*, February.

Hutchinson, F., Mellor, M., and Olsen, W. (2002), *The Politics of Money: Towards Sustainability and Economic Democracy*, London: Pluto.

IDA (International Development Agency) (2001), *Poverty Reduction Strategy Papers and IDA 13*, Washington, DC: IDA, May, pp. 11–13.

IFC (International Finance Corporation) (2002), *Investing in Private Health Care: Strategic Direction for IFC*, paper prepared for joint World Bank/IFC Topical Briefing on Health and Investing in Private Health Care, March.

ILO (International Labour Organization) (1978), *Yearbook of Labour Statistics*, Geneva: ILO.

Inman, R. P., and Rubinfeld, P. L. (1997), 'The Political Economy of Federalism', in D. C. Mueller (ed.), *Perspectives on Public Choice: A Handbook*, Cambridge: Cambridge University Press, pp. 73–105.

Iriart, C., Merhy, E., and Waitzkin, H. (2001), 'Managed Care in Latin America: The New Common Sense in Health Policy Reform', *Social Science and Medicine*, 52(8), pp. 1243–53.

Iriart, C., Waitzkin, H., and Trotta, C. (2002), 'Global Policies, Health Care Systems and Social Movements in Latin America: A Lesson from Argentina', *Global Social Policy*, 2(3), pp. 245–8.

Isenman, P. (1980), 'Basic Needs: The Case of Sri Lanka', *World Developments*, 8(3), pp. 237–58.

Iversen, I., and Wren, A. (1998), 'Equality, Employment and Budgetary Restraint: The Trilemma of the Service Economy', *World Politics*, 50(4), pp. 507–46.

Jackson, T. (2002), 'Quality of Life, Sustainability and Economic Growth', in T. Fitzpatrick and M. Cahill (eds), *Environment and Welfare*, Basingstoke: Palgrave.

Jones, A. (1992), 'Civil Rights, Citizenship and the Welfare Agenda for the 1990s', in T. Harding (ed.), *Who Owns Welfare?*, London: NISW.

Jones, H., and Findlay, A. (1998), 'Regional Economic Integration and the Emergence of the East Asian International Migration System', *Geoforum*, 29, pp. 1–18.

Jones, K., and Buckingham, D. (2000), 'Cultural Dilemmas in English Education Policy', paper presented to Young People and the Media International Forum, Sydney, November.

Jordan, B. (1996), *A Theory of Poverty and Social Exclusion*, Cambridge: Polity.

Jordan, B. (1998), *The New Politics of Welfare: Social Justice in a Global Context*, London: Sage.

Jordan, B. (2004), *Sex, Money and Power: The Transformation of Collective Life*, Cambridge: Polity.

Jordan, B. (2005), 'Social Theory and Social Policy: Individualism, Choice and the Social Order', *European Journal of Social Theory*, 8(2), pp. 149–70.

Jordan, B., and Düvell, F. (2002), *Irregular Migration: The Dilemmas of Transnational Mobility*, Cheltenham: Edward Elgar.

Jordan, B., and Düvell, F. (2003), *Migration: The Boundaries of Equality and Justice*, Cambridge: Polity.

Jordan, B., and Forsythe, B. (2002), 'The Victorian Ethical Foundations of Social Work in England: Continuity and Contradiction', *British Journal of Social Work*, 32, pp. 847–62.

Jordan, B., with Jordan, C. (2000), *Social Work and the Third Way: Tough Love as Social Policy*, London: Sage.

Jordan, B., and Travers, A. (1998), 'The Informal Economy: A Case Study in Unrestrained Competition', *Social Policy and Administration*, 32(3), pp. 292–306.

Jordan, B., Agulnik, P., Burbidge, D., and Duffin, S. (2000), *Stumbling Towards Basic Income: The Prospects for Tax–Benefit Integration*, London: Citizens' Income Trust.

Jordan, B., Redley, M., and James, S. (1994), *Putting the Family First: Identities, Decisions, Citizenship*, London: UCL Press.

Kahneman, D. (1999), 'Objective Well-Being', in D. Kahneman, E. Diener and N. Schwartz (eds), *Well-Being: The Foundations of Hedonic Psychology*, New York: Russell Sage Foundation, pp. 3–14.

Kahneman, D., Diener, E., and Schwartz, N. (eds) (1999), *Well-Being: The Foundations of Hedonic Psychology*, New York: Russell Sage Foundation.

Kant, I. (1970 [1801]), 'Perpetual Peace', in *Kant: Political Writings*, ed. H. Reiss, Cambridge: Cambridge University Press.

Kearney, B., Boyle, G., and Walsh, J. A. (1994), *EU LEADER Initiative in Ireland: Evaluation and Recommendations*, Dublin: Department of Agriculture, Food and Forestry.

Kelly, A. (1991), 'The New Managerialism in the Social Services', in T. Carter, P. Jeffs and M. Smith (eds), *Social Work and Social Welfare Yearbook 3*, Milton Keynes: Open University Press.

Kelly, G., and Lissauer, R. (2000), *Ownership for All*, London: Institute for Public Policy Research.

Kelly, P. (2002), 'Ideas and Policy Agendas in Contemporary Politics', in P. Dunleavy et al. (eds), *Developments in British Politics*, 7, London: Palgrave.

Kelsey, J. (1995), *Economic Fundamentalism: The New Zealand Experiment – a World Model for Structural Adjustment*, London: Pluto.

Keynes, J. M. (1957 [1936]), *A General Theory of Employment, Interest and Money*, London: Macmillan.

Kidron, A., and Segal, C. (1981), *The State of the World Atlas*, London: Pluto Press.

Kindleberger, C. (1967), *Europe's Postwar Growth: The Role of Labour Supply*, Cambridge, MA: Harvard University Press.

Kindleberger, C. (1969), *American Business Abroad: Six Lectures on Direct Investment*, New Haven, CT: Yale University Press.

Kuehn, L. (1997), *Schools for Globalized Business: The APEC Agenda for Education: A Commentary on the 'Concept Paper' for the APEC Human Resources Ministerial Meeting*, www.ven.be.ca/edgesea/carry/html

Kwon, S. (2002), 'Globalization and Health Policy in Korea', *Global Social Policy*, 2(3), pp. 279–94.

Land, H. (1978), 'Who Cares for the Family?', *Journal of Social Policy*, 7(3).

Landers, R. M., Rebitzer, J. B., and Taylor, L. J. (1996), 'Rat Race Redux: Adverse Selection in the Determination of Work Hours in Law Firms', *American Economic Review*, 86(3), pp. 329–48.

Lane, R. E. (1991), *The Market Experience*, Cambridge: Cambridge University Press.

Lane, R. E. (2000), *The Loss of Happiness in Market Democracies*, New Haven, CT: Yale University Press.

Langan, M., and Clarke, J. (1994), 'Managing the Mixed Economy of Care', in J. Clarke, A. Cochrane and E. McLaughlin (eds), *Managing Social Policy*, London: Sage, pp. 73–92.

Layard, R. (2003a), 'What is Happiness? Are We Getting Happier?', Lecture 1, Lionel Robbins Memorial Lectures, London School of Economics, 3 March.

Layard, R. (2003b), 'Income and Happiness: Rethinking Economic Policy', Lecture 2, Lionel Robbins Memorial Lectures, London School of Economics, 4 March.

Layard, R. (2005), *Happiness: Lessons from a New Science*, London: Allen Lane.

Le Grand, J. (1989), 'Markets, Welfare and Equality', in J. Le Grand and S. Estrin (eds), *Market Socialism*, Oxford: Oxford University Press.

Leibfried, S., and Pierson, P. (1994), 'Prospects for Social Europe', in A. de Swaan (ed.), *Social Policy Beyond Borders*, Amsterdam: Amsterdam University Press.

Leira, A. (2002), *Working Parents and the Welfare State*, Cambridge: Cambridge University Press.

Leonard, M. (1999), 'Informal Economic Activity: Strategies of Households and Communities', paper presented at the 4th ESA conference, 'Will Europe Work?', Amsterdam, 18–21 August.

Leonard, M. (2004), 'Bonding and Bridging Social Capital: Evidence from Belfast', *Sociology*, 38(5), pp. 927–44.

Leparmentier, A. (2005), 'La Directive Bolkestein ou le malaise européen', *Le Monde*, 11 March.

Lethbridge, J. (2002), 'International Finance Corporate (IFC) Health Care Policy Briefing', *Global Social Policy*, 2(3), pp. 349–53.

Lewis, J. (1982), *The Politics of Motherhood: Child and Maternal Welfare in England, 1900–1939*, London: Croom Helm.

Lewis, J. (1992), 'Gender and the Development of Welfare Regimes', *European Journal of Social Policy*, 2(3), pp. 159–73.

Lewis, J. (2001), *The End of Marriage? Individualism and Intimate Relations*, Cheltenham: Edward Elgar.

Lewis, J. (2003), 'Feminist Perspectives', in P. Alcock, A. Erskine and M. May (eds), *The Student's Companion to Social Policy*, Oxford: Blackwell.

Lewis, W. A. (1954a), 'Economic Development with Unlimited Supplies of Labour', *Manchester School*, XXII, pp. 139–91.

Lewis, W. A. (1954b), *The Theory of Economic Growth*, London: Allen & Unwin.

Lipson, R., and Pemble, L. (1992), 'China's Medical Equipment Purchases', *China Business Review*, 19(4), pp. 18–21.

Lister, R. (1997), *Citizenship: Feminist Perspectives*, Basingstoke: Macmillan.

Lister, R. (2000), 'To Rio via the Third Way: New Labour's "Welfare" Reform Agenda', *Renewal*, 4(3), pp. 9–20.

Luttwak, E. (1999), *Turbo-Capitalism: Winners and Losers in the Global Economy*, New York: Weidenfeld & Nicolson.

Lynn, P., and Smith, J. D. (1991), *The 1991 National Survey of Voluntary Activity in the UK*, Berkhamstead: Volunteer Centre.

Lyotard, J.-F. (1983), *The Postmodern Condition: A Report on Knowledge*, Manchester: Manchester University Press.

Macadam, E. (1945), *The Social Servant in the Making*, London: Allen & Unwin.

Macmillan, H. (1938), *The Middle Way: A Study of the Problem of Economic and Social Progress in a Free and Democratic Society*, London: Macmillan.

Maglajlic, R., Brandon, D., and Given, D. (2000), 'Making Direct Payments a Choice: A Report on Research Findings', *Disability and Society*, 15(1), pp. 99–113.

Mandel, E. (1972), *Late Capitalism*, London: New Left Books.

Manow, P., and Seils, E. (2000), 'Adjusting Badly: The German Welfare State, Structural Change and the Open Economy', in F. W. Scharpf and V. A. Schmidt (eds), *From Vulnerability to Competitiveness: Welfare and Work in the Open Economy*, Oxford: Oxford University Press.

Marshall, T. H. (1950), *Citizenship and Social Class*, Cambridge: Cambridge University Press.

Marshall, T. H. (1963), *Sociology at the Crossroads, and Other Essays*, London: Heinemann.

Marshall, T. H. (1970), *Social Policy*, Cambridge: Cambridge University Press.

Marshall, T. H. (1981), *The Right to Welfare, and Other Essays*, London: Heinemann.

Martin, H. P., and Schumann, H. (2000), *Le Piège de la mondialisation*, Arles: Actes Sud.

Marx, K. (1978 [1867]), *Capital*, vols 1–3, Harmondsworth: Penguin.

Marx, K., and Engels, F. (1967 [1848]), *The Communist Manifesto*, London: Penguin.

Matthews, R. (1983), *The Creation of Regional Dependency*, Toronto: University of Toronto Press.

Maurin, E. (2004), *Le Ghetto francais: enquête sur le separatisme social*, Paris: Editions du Seuil.

Merton, R. (1949), 'The Self-Fulfilling Prophecy', in *Social Theory and Social Structure*, New York: Free Press, pp. 475–90.

Milanovic, B. (2003), 'Two Faces of Globalization: Against Globalization as We Know it', *World Development*, 31(4), pp. 657–83.

Milburn, A. (2005), Interview on BBC Radio 4, *Today* programme, 12 February.

Mill, J. S. (1965 [1860]), 'Principles of Political Economy, with Some of their Applications to Social Philosophy', in *Collected Works*, ed. J. M. Robson, vols 2 and 3, Oxford: Oxford University Press.

Mises, L. von (1966), *Human Action*, Chicago: Contemporary Books.

Mishan, E. (1967), *The Costs of Economic Growth*, London: Staples Press.

Mishel, L., Bernstein, J., and Schmitt, J. (2000), *The State of Working America, 1998–9*, Ithaca, NY: Economic Policy Research Institute, ILR Press.

Möhle, M. (2005), 'Shifting Frameworks of Welfare, Shifting Needs of Welfare Recipients', paper given at a seminar on Social Exclusion, University of Plymouth, 11 March.

Moore, M. (2003), *A World Without Walls*, Cambridge: Cambridge University Press.

Mouffe, C. (1993), *The Return of the Political*, London: Verso.

Mueller, D. C. (1989), *Public Choice II*, Cambridge: Cambridge University Press.

Musgrave, R. A. (1959), *The Theory of Public Finance*, New York: McGraw Hill.

Myers, D. G. (1999), 'Close Relationships and Quality of Life', in D. Kahneman, E. Diener and N. Schwartz (eds), *Well-Being: The Foundations of Hedonic Psychology*, New York: Russell Sage Foundation, pp. 374–91.

Nash, K. (1998), *Universal Difference: Feminism and the Liberal Undecidability of Women*, Basingstoke: Macmillan.

Neef, R. (1992), 'The New Poverty and Local Government Policies. A West German Perspective', *International Journal of Urban and Regional Research*, 16(2), pp. 202–21.

Nelson, B. (1984), 'Women's Poverty and Women's Citizenship: Some Political Consequences of Economic Marginality', *Signs*, 10(2), pp. 209–31.

NESS (National Evaluation of Sure Start) (2004), *The Impact of Sure Start Local Programmes on Child Development and Family Functioning*, Preliminary Report, Guildford: Surrey.

Newman, A. L. (2003), 'When Opportunity Knocks: Economic Liberalisation and Stealth Welfare in the United States', *Journal of Social Policy*, 32(2), pp. 179–98.

Niskanen, W. A. (1975), 'Bureaucrats and Politicians', *Journal of Law and Economics*, 18, pp. 617–43.

Nissan, D., and Le Grand, J. (2000), *A Capital Idea*, London: Fabian Society.

Nordhaus, W., and Tobin, J. (1972), *Is Growth Obsolete?*, New York: NBER/Columbus University Press.

Oates, W. E. (1972), *Fiscal Federalism*, New York: Harcourt Brace Jovanovich.

Oates, W. E. (1985), 'Searching for Leviathan: An Empirical Study', *American Economic Review*, 75, pp. 748–57.

Oates, W. E. (1999), 'An Essay on Fiscal Federalism', *Journal of Economic Literature*, 27, pp. 1120–49.

Oates, W. E., and Schwab, R. M. (1990), 'The Theory of Regulatory Federalism: The Case of Environmental Management', in W. E. Oates (ed.), *The Political Economy of Fiscal Federalism*, Lexington, MA: Heath-Lexington, pp. 275–355.

OECD (Organization for Economic Co-operation and Development) (1970), *Labour Force Statistics, 1958–69*, Paris: OECD.

OECD (Organization for Economic Co-operation and Development) (1988), *OECD Economic Surveys, Australia*, Paris: OECD.

OECD (Organization for Economic Co-operation and Development) (1995), *Governance in Transition: Public Management Reform in OECD Countries*, Paris: OECD.

Offe, C. (1992), 'A Non-Productivist Design for Social Policies', in P. Van Parijs (ed.), *Arguing for Basic Income: Ethical Foundations for a Radical Reform*, London: Verso, pp. 61–86.

Okun, A. (1975), *Equality and Efficiency: The Big Trade-off*, Washington, DC: Brookings Institution Press.

Oldman, C. (1991), *Paying for Personal Care: Personal Services and Funding of Care*, York: Joseph Rowntree Foundation.

Oliver, J. (1999), 'The Effects of Metropolitan Economic Segregation on Local Civic Participation', *American Journal of Political Science*, 43(1), pp. 186–212.

Oliver, M. (1990), *The Politics of Disability*, London: Macmillan.

Oliver, M. (1992), 'A Case of Disabling Welfare', in T. Harding (ed.), *Who Owns Welfare?*, London: NISW.

Olson, M. (1965), *The Logic of Collective Action: Public Goods and the Economics of Groups*, Cambridge, MA: Harvard University Press.

O'Neill, O. (2000), 'Agents of Justice', in T. W. Pogge (ed.), *Global Justice*, Oxford: Blackwell.

Ostrom, E. (1990), *Governing the Commons: The Evolution of Institutions for Collective Action*, Cambridge: Cambridge University Press.

Oxfam (2002), *Rigged Rules and Double Standards*, Oxford: Oxfam.

Panayotou, T. (1995), 'Environmental Degradation at Different Stages of Development', in I. Ahmed and J. Doelman (eds), *Beyond Rio*, London: Macmillan.

Paranagua, P. (2005), 'Le Nouveau Patron des patrons brasiliens défend les partenaires public-privé', *Le Monde* (Economie), 22 February, p. v.

Parker, H. (1988), *Instead of the Dole: An Enquiry into Integration of the Tax and Benefit Systems*, London: Routledge.

Parton, N. (2006), *Safeguarding Childhood: Early Intervention and Surveillance in a Late Modern Society*, Basingstoke: Palgrave.

Pateman, C. (1988), *The Sexual Contract*, Cambridge: Polity.

Peacock, A. I. (1979), *The Economic Analysis of Government*, Oxford: Martin Robertson.

People and Planet (2000), *The Threat to Higher Education: A Briefing on Current World Trade Organisation Negotiations*, October.

People's Daily (2001), 'China Strives to Ensure Medical Care of Rural People', 28 June.

Pettersen, T., and Geyer, K. (1992), *Värderings görändingar i Sverige: den svenska modellen, individualismer och rätvisan*, Stockholm: Brevskolan.

Phillips, A. (1993), *Democracy and Difference*, Cambridge: Polity.

Pieke, F. (2002), 'Fujianese Migration to the UK', paper presented to a seminar at IPPR, 15 March.

Pierson, C. (1991), *Beyond the Welfare State? The New Political Economy of Welfare*, Cambridge: Polity.

Pierson, P. (1994), *Dismantling the Welfare State*, Cambridge: Cambridge University Press.

Pierson, P. (2000), 'Post-Industrial Pressures on Mature Welfare States', in P. Pierson (ed.), *The New Politics of the Welfare State*, New York: Oxford University Press, pp. 1–28.

Pigou, A. C. (1920), *The Economics of Welfare*, London: Macmillan.

Pilger, J. (2002), *The New Rulers of the World*, London: Verso.

Plummer, K. (1995), *Telling Sexual Stories: Power, Change and Social Worlds*, London: Routledge.

Pogge, T. (1994), 'Cosmopolitanism and Sovereignty', in C. Brown (ed.), *Political Restructuring in Europe: Ethical Perspectives*, London: Routledge.

Pogge, T. (2002), *World Poverty and Human Rights*, Cambridge: Polity.

Polanyi, K. (1944), *The Great Transformation: The Political and Economic Origins of our Times*, Boston: Beacon Press.

Psimmenos, I., and Kassimati, K. (2003), 'Immigration Control Pathways: Organisational Culture and Work Values of Greek Welfare Officers', *Journal of Ethnic and Migration Studies*, 29(2), pp. 337–72.

Pusey, M. (2003), *The Experience of Middle Australia: The Dark Side of Economic Reform*, Cambridge: Cambridge University Press.

Putnam, R. D. (1993), *Making Democracy Work: Civic Traditions in Modern Italy*, Princeton, NJ: Princeton University Press.

Putnam, R. D. (2000), *Bowling Alone: The Collapse and Revival of American Community*, New York: Simon & Schuster.

Putnam, R. D. (ed.) (2002), *Democracies in Flux: The Evolution of Social Capital in Contemporary Society*, Oxford: Oxford University Press.

Ramchandran, V. K. (1996), 'On Kerala's Development Achievements', in J. Drèze and A. Sen (eds), *Indian Development: Selected Regional Perspectives*, Oxford: Oxford University Press.

Rawls, A. W. (1989), 'Language, Self and Social Order: A Reformulation of Goffman and Sacks', *Human Studies*, 12, pp. 147–72.

Rawls, J. (1971), *A Theory of Justice*, Oxford: Blackwell.

Rawls, J. (1993), *Political Liberalism*, New York: Columbia University Press.

Rawls, J. (1996), *Political Justice*, New York: Columbia University Press.

Rawls, J. (1999), *The Law of Peoples*, Cambridge, MA: Harvard University Press.

Reich, R. (1993), *The Work of Nations: Preparing Ourselves for Twenty-First Century Capitalism*, New York: Knopf.

Reich, R. (1997), 'New Deal and Fair Deal', *The Guardian*, 4 July, p. 16.

Ricard, P. (2005), 'Comment la directive Bolkestein mis le feu aux poudres: les clivages sont nombreux autour de la liberalisation des services', *Le Monde* (Economie), 22 February, p. ii.

Richling, B. (1985), 'You'd Never Starve Here: Return Migration to Rural Newfoundland', *Canadian Review of Sociology and Anthropology*, 22(2), pp. 236–49.

Rivais, R. (2005), 'Les Socialistes européens veulent la révision de la "directive services"', *Le Monde* (International), 18 February, p. 3.

Robbins, L. (1932), *The Nature and Significance of Economic Science*, London: Allen & Unwin.

Roberts, K. (1983), *Automation, Unemployment and the Distribution of Income*, Maastricht: European Centre for Work and Society.

Roche, B. (2000), 'UK Migration in a Global Economy', speech at a conference on Migration in a Global Economy, Institute for Public Policy Research, 11 September.

Rodrik, D. (2001), 'The Global Governance of Trade as if Development Really Mattered', www.undp.org/bdp

Roemer, J. (1983), 'Unequal Exchange, Labour Migration and International Capital Flows: A Theoretical Synthesis', in P. Desai (ed.), *Marxism, the Soviet Economy and Central Planning: Essays in Honor of Alexander Erlich*, Cambridge, MA: MIT Press, pp. 34–60.

Rose, N. (1996), *Inventing Ourselves: Psychology, Power and Personhood*, Cambridge: Cambridge University Press.

Rose, N. (1999), 'Inventiveness in Politics', *Economy and Society*, 28(3), pp. 470–86.

Rothschild, M., and Stiglitz, J. (1976), 'Equilibrium in Competitive Insurance Markets: An Essay in the Economics of Incomplete Information', *Quarterly Journal of Economics*, 90, pp. 629–49.

Rothstein, B. (2002), 'Sweden: Social Capital in the Social Democratic State', in R. D. Putnam (ed.), *Democracies in Flux*, Oxford: Oxford University Press, pp. 289–332.

Rothstein, B., and Stolle, D. (2001), 'Social Capital and Street-Level Bureaucracy: An Institutional Theory of General Trust', paper presented at the conference 'Social Capital', Exeter University, 15–20 September.

Ruddick, S. (1983), 'Maternal Thinking', in J. Trebilcot (ed.), *Mothering: Essays in Feminist Theory*, Totowa, NJ: Rowman & Allanfeld.

Ruggie, J. (2003), 'Taking Embedded Liberalism Global: the Corporate Connection', in D. Held and M. Koenig-Archibugi (eds), *Taming Globalization*, Cambridge: Polity.

Rupesinghe, K. (1986), 'The Welfare State in Sri Lanka', in E. Øyen (ed.), *Comparing Welfare States and their Futures*, Aldershot: Gower.

Rutter, M., and Smith, D. (1995), *Psychosocial Disorders in Young People*, Chichester: Wiley.

Rutter, M., Giller, H., and Hagell, A. (1998), *Antisocial Behaviour in Young People*, Cambridge: Cambridge University Press.

Salt, J. (1988), 'Highly-Skilled International Migrants, Careers and Internal Labour Markets', *Geoforum*, 19, pp. 387–99.

Salt, J., and Clarke, J. (2001), 'Foreign Labour in the United Kingdom: Patterns and Trends', *Labour Market Trends*, October, pp. 473–83.

Sanders, D. (2000), 'Primary Health Care 21: "Everybody's Business" ', paper for WHO conference, Alma Ata, 27–8 November.

Sanders, D. (2002), 'Globalization, Health and Health Services in Sub-Saharan Africa', *Global Social Policy*, 2(3), pp. 255–9.

Sassen, S. (1988), *The Mobility of Labor and Capital: A Study in International Investment and Labor Flow*, Cambridge: Cambridge University Press.

Sassen, S. (1991), *The Global City: New York, London, Tokyo*, Princeton, NJ: Princeton University Press.

Sassen, S. (1998), *Globalization and its Discontents: Essays on the Mobility of People and Money*, New York: New Press.

Saunders, P. (1993), 'Longer-Run Changes in the Distribution of Incomes in Australia', *Economic Record*, 69(207), pp. 353–66.

Saywell, T. (1999), 'Strong Medicine', *Far Eastern Economic Review*, 162(34).

Scharpf, F. W. (1997), *Employment and the Welfare State: A Continental Dilemma*, Working paper 9/97, Cologne: Max-Planck Institute for the Study of Societies.

Scharpf, F. W. (1999), *The Viability of Advanced Welfare States in the Global Economy: Vulnerabilities and Options*, Working paper 99–9, Cologne: Max-Planck Institute for the Study of Societies.

Scharpf, F. W., and Schmidt, V. A. (eds) (2000a), *Welfare and Work in the Open Economy*, Vol. 1: *From Vulnerability to Competitiveness*, Oxford: Oxford University Press.

Scharpf, F. W., and Schmidt, V. A. (eds) (2000b), *Welfare and Work in the Open Economy*, Vol. 2: *Diverse Responses to Common Challenges*, Oxford: Oxford University Press.

Schor, J. (1998), *The Overspent American*, New York: Basic Books.

Schumpeter, J. (1961 [1934]), *The Theory of Economic Development: An Inquiry into Profits, Capital, Interest and the Business Cycle*, Oxford: Oxford University Press.

Schumpeter, J. (1994 [1954]), *History of Economic Analyses*, London: Routledge.

Sciortino, G. (2004), 'When Domestic Labour is Not Native Labour: The Interaction of Immigration Policy and the Welfare Regime in Italy', in P. Ruspini and S. Gorny (eds), *East–West Revisited: Migration in the New Europe*, Basingstoke: Palgrave.

Seeleib-Kaiser, M., Van Dyk, S., and Roggenkamp, M. (2005), *What Do Parties Want? An Analysis of Programmatic Social Policy Aims in Austria, Germany and the Netherlands*, Working paper 01/2005, Bremen: Centre for Social Policy Research.

Self, P. (2000), *Rolling Back the Market*, Basingstoke: Palgrave.

Sen, A. (1981), *Poverty and Families: An Essay in Entitlement and Deprivation*, Oxford: Clarendon Press.

Sen, A. (1985), *Commodities and Capabilities*, Oxford: Elsevier Science.

Sen, A. (1999), *Development as Freedom*, Oxford: Oxford University Press.

Sevenhuijsen, S. (2000), 'Caring in the Third Way: The Relation between Obligation, Responsibility and Care in Third Way Discourse', *Critical Social Policy*, 20(1), pp. 5–37.

Sevenhuijsen, S. (2002), 'A Third Way? Moralities, Ethics and Families: An Approach Through the Ethic of Care', in A. Carling, S. Duncan and R. Edwards (eds), *Analysing Families: Morality and Rationality in Policy and Practice*, London: Routledge.

Sinclair, S. (2000), *Comment les nouvelles négociations sur les services à l'OMC menacent la democratie*, Quebec: Centre Canadien des Politiques Alternatives, April.

Singh, A. (2000), 'Liberalisation: Globalisation, Employment, Work and Insecurity', paper presented at ILO seminar, Bellagio, Italy, March.

Smart, C., Neale, B., and Wade, A. (2001), *The Changing Experience of Childhood: Families and Divorce*, Cambridge: Polity.

Smith, A. (1976 [1776]), *An Inquiry Concerning the Nature and Causes of the Wealth of Nations*, ed. R. H. Campbell and A. S. Skinner, Oxford: Clarendon Press.

Solnick, S. J., and Hemenway, D. (1998), 'Is More Always Better? A Survey on Positional Concerns', *Journal of Economic Behaviour and Organisation*, 37, pp. 373–83.

Solow, R. (1990), *The Labour Market as a Social Institution*, Oxford: Blackwell.

Spencer, H. (1969 [1860]), *The Man Versus the State*, ed. D. MacRae, Harmondsworth: Penguin.

Spruyt, H. (1994), *Nation States and their Competitors*, Princeton, NJ: Princeton University Press.

Squires, J. (2000), 'The State in (and of) Feminist Visions of Political Citizenship', in C. McKinnon and I. Hampsher-Monk (eds), *The Demands of Citizenship*, London: Continuum, pp. 35–50.

Stalker, P. (2000), *Workers without Frontiers: The Impact of Globalization in International Migration*, Geneva: International Labour Organization.

Standing, G. (1991), *In Search of Flexibility: The New Soviet Labour Market*, Geneva: International Labour Organization.

Standing, G. (1996), 'Social Protection in Central and Eastern Europe: A Tale of Slipping Anchors and Torn Safety Nets', in G. Esping-Andersen (ed.), *Welfare States in Transition*, London: Sage, pp. 225–55.

Standing, G. (1999), *Global Labour Flexibility: Seeking Distributive Justice*, Basingstoke: Macmillan.

Standing, G. (2002), *Beyond the New Paternalism: Basic Security as Equality*, London: Verso.

Starrett, D. A. (1988), *Foundations of Public Economics*, Cambridge: Cambridge University Press.

Steiner, H. (1992), 'Three Just Taxes', in P. Van Parijs (ed.), *Arguing for Basic Income: Ethical Foundations for a Radical Reform*, London: Verso, pp. 81–92.

Stiglitz, J. (2002), *Globalization and its Discontents*, London: Allen Lane.

Stocker, K., Waitzkin, H., and Iriart, C. (1999), 'The Exportation of Managed Care to Latin America', *New England Journal of Medicine*, 340(14), pp. 1131–6.

Swaan, A. de (1988), *In Care of the State: Health Care, Education and Welfare in Europe and the USA in the Modern Era*, Cambridge: Polity.

Swaan, A. de (1994), *Social Policy Beyond Borders: The Social Question in Transnational Perspective*, Amsterdam: Amsterdam University Press.

Swank, D. (2001), 'Mobile Capital, Democratic Institutions, and the Public Economy in Advanced Industrial Societies', *Journal of Comparative Policy Analysis, Research and Practice*, 3.

Tachibanaki, T. (ed.) (1994), *Labour Market and Economic Performance: Europe, Japan and the USA*, New York: St Martin's Press.

Tawney, R. H. (1931), *The Acquisitive Society*, London: Allen & Unwin.

Thompson, D. (1996), 'Fetishing the Family: The Construction of the Informal Carer', in H. Jones and J. Millar (eds), *The Politics of the Family*, Aldershot: Avebury.

Tiebout, C. (1956), 'A Pure Theory of Local Expenditures', *Journal of Political Economy*, 42, pp. 416–24.

Titmuss, R. M. (1968), *Commitment to Welfare*, London: Allen & Unwin.

Tocqueville, A. de (1968 [1836]), *Democracy in America*, ed. J. P. Mayer, and M. Lerner, London: Collins.

Tomlinson, R. (1997), 'Health Care in China is Highly Inequitable', *British Medical Journal*, 315(7112), p. 835.

Touraine, A. (1997), *What Is Democracy?*, Oxford: Westview.

Triandafyllidou, A. (2003), 'Immigration Policy Implementation in Italy: Organisational Culture, Identity Processes and Labour Market Control', *Journal of Ethnic and Migration Studies*, 29(2), pp. 257–98.

Tronto, J. (1994), *Moral Boundaries: A Political Argument for an Ethic of Care*, London: Routledge.

Tugendhat, N. (1973), *The Multinationals*, London: Eyre & Spottiswoode.

Tullock, G. (1980), 'Rent Seeking as a Negative Sum Game', in J. M. Buchanan, R. D. Tollison and G. Tullock (eds), *Towards a Theory of a Rent Seeking Society*, College Station: Texas A & M University Press, pp. 13–29.

UNDP (United Nations Development Programme) (1992), *Human Development Report, 1992*, New York: UNDP.

UNDP (United Nations Development Programme) (1993), *Human Development Report, 1993*, New York: Oxford University Press.

UNDP (United Nations Development Programme) (1995), *Human Development Report, 1995*, New York: Oxford University Press.

UNDP (United Nations Development Programme) (1999), *The China Human Development Report*, New York: Oxford University Press.

Unger, R. (1987), *False Necessity*, Cambridge: Cambridge University Press.

Ungerson, C. (1987), *Policy Is Personal: Gender and Informal Care*, London: Tavistock.

UNHCR (United Nations High Commission for Refugees) (2001), *UNHCR Population Statistics (Provisional)*, Geneva: UNHCR.

UNHCR (United Nations High Commission for Refugees) (2003), *Asylum Levels and Trends*, Geneva: UNHCR.

UNICEF (2000), *The State of the World's Children, 2001*, Oxford: Oxford University Press.

United Nations (2001), *The Global Compact: Corporate Leadership in the World Economy*, New York: United Nations.

United Nations (2002), *Final Outcome of the International Conference on Financing for Development* (Monterrey Consensus), http://www.un.org/esa/ffd/aac257L13-E.doc

Van de Ven, W. P. M. M., and Ellis, R. P. (2000), 'Risk Adjustment in Competitive Health Plan Markets', in J. P. Newhouse and A. J. Culyer (eds), *Handbook of Health Economics*, Vol. 1A, Amsterdam: North Holland, ch. 14.

Van Kersbergen, K. (1995), *Social Capitalism: A Study of Christian Democracy and the Welfare State*, London: Routledge.

Van Parijs, P. (1989), 'A Revolution in Class Theory', *Politics and Society*, 15, pp. 453–82.

Van Parijs, P. (1992), 'Commentary: Citizenship Exploitation, Unequal Exchange and the Breakdown of Popular Sovereignty', in B. Barry and R. E. Goodin (eds), *Free Movement: Ethical Issues in the Transnational Migration of People and Money*, University Park: Pennsylvania University Press, pp. 155–66.

Van Parijs, P. (1995), *Real Freedom for All: What (if Anything) Can Justify Capitalism?*, Oxford: Clarendon Press.

Van Trier, W. (1995), *Every One a King*, PhD thesis, Department of Sociology, University of Leuven, Belgium.

Veenhoven, R., et al. (1994), *World Database of Happiness: Correlates of Happiness*, Rotterdam: Erasmus University Press.

Verhoogen, E. (1999), 'Trade Pressures and Wage Convergence', University of Massachusetts, Amherst, and Brookings Institution.

Voet, R. (1998), *Feminism and Citizenship*, London: Sage.

Vogel, D., and Cyrus, N. (2003), 'Work Permit Decisions in the German Labour Administration: An Exploration of the Implementation Process', *Journal of Ethnic and Migration Studies*, 29(2), pp. 225–56.

Waddan, A. (1997), *The Politics of Social Welfare: The Collapse of the Centre and the Rise of the Right*, Cheltenham: Edward Elgar.

Walzer, M. (1983), *Spheres of Justice*, New York: Basic Books.

Watts, J. (2004), 'A Tale of Two Countries', *The Guardian* (G2), 9 November, pp. 6–7.

Webb, B., and Webb, S. (1911), *Industrial Democracy*, London: Bell.

Weinstein, M. C., and Fineberg, H. V. (1980), *Clinical Decision Making*, Philadelphia: W. B. Saunders.

Whitfield, D. (2001), *Public Services or Corporate Welfare?*, London: Pluto Press.

Wicksell, K. (1958 [1896]), 'A New Principle of Just Taxation', in R. A. Musgrave and A. T. Peacock (eds), *Classics in the Theory of Public Finance*, London: Macmillan, pp. 72–116.

Wigley, V., Fisk, M., Gisby, B., and Preston-Shoot, M. (1998), 'Older People in Care Homes: Consumer Perspectives', Liverpool: John Moores University.

Williams, C. C., and Windebank, J. (1999), *Empowering People to Help Themselves: Tackling Social Exclusion in Deprived Neighbourhoods*, Leicester: Leicester University, Department of Geography.

Williams, F. (1989), *Social Policy: A Critical Introduction*, Cambridge: Polity.

Williams, F. (1998), 'New Principles in a Good-Enough Welfare State in the Millennium', paper delivered at the World Congress of Sociology, Montreal, 26–31 July.

Williams, F. (2001), 'In and Beyond New Labour: Towards a New Political Ethics of Care', *Critical Social Policy*, 21(4), pp. 467–93.

Williams, F. (2005), 'Practical and Political Ethics of Care and Implications for Child Welfare', paper presented at the Centre for Applied Childhood Studies, Huddersfield University, 27 February.

Wilson, E. (1977), *Women and the Welfare State*, London: Tavistock.

Wilson, W. J. (1989), *The Truly Disadvantaged: Public Policy and the Ghetto*, Chicago: University of Chicago Press.

Wilson, W. J. (1996), *When Work Disappears: The World of the New Urban Poor*, London: Vintage.

Wood, G. (2004), 'Informal Security Regimes: The Strength of Relationships', in I. Gough et al., *Insecurity and Welfare Regimes in Asia, Africa and Latin America*, Cambridge: Cambridge University Press, pp. 49–87.

Woods, L., Makepeace, G., Joshi, H., and Galinda-Raeda, F. (2003), 'The World of Paid Work', in E. Ferri, J. Bynner and M. Wadsworth (eds), *Changing Britain, Changing Lives: Three Generations at the Turn of the Century*, London: Institute of Education, pp. 71–104.

Woolhandler, S., and Himmelstein, D. U. (1999), 'When Money Is the Mission: The High Cost of Investor-Owned Care', *New England Journal of Medicine*, 5, August.

World Bank (1982), *Economic Adjustments of Sri Lanka: A World Bank Report*, Washington, DC: World Bank.

World Bank (1985), *World Development Report, 1985*, Washington, DC: World Bank.

World Bank (1999), *World Development Report, 1998/9*, Washington, DC: World Bank.

World Bank (2000), *World Development Report, 2000*, Washington, DC: World Bank.

World Bank (2001), *World Bank Development Report 2000/2001: Attacking Poverty*, Washington, DC: World Bank.

World Bank (2002), *World Development Indicators, 2002*, Washington, DC: World Bank.

World Values Study Group (1994), *World Values Survey 1990–93*, Ann Arbor: University of Michigan, Institute for Social Research.

World Values Study Group (1998), *World Values Survey 1995–8*, Ann Arbor: University of Michigan, Institute for Social Research.

Wright, K. G. (1985), *The Application of Cost–Benefit Analysis to the Care of the Elderly*, York: University of York.

Xing, L. (2002), 'Shifting the "Burden": Commodification of China's Health Care', *Global Social Policy*, 2(3), pp. 248–52.

Young, I. M. (1990), *Justice and the Politics of Difference*, Princeton, NJ: Princeton University Press.

Zhan, S. K., Tang, S. L., and Quo, Y. D. (1997), 'Drug Prescribing in Rural Health Facilities in China: Implications for Service Delivery and Cost', *IDS Bulletin*, 28(1), pp. 66–70.

Zhu, L. (2000), 'Investing in Rural Health in Western China', *China and World Economy*, 8(4), pp. 44–9.

Zolo, D. (1997), *Cosmopolis: Prospects for World Government*, Cambridge: Polity.

Zweifel, P., and Breuer, M. (forthcoming), 'The Case for Risk-Based Premiums in Public Health Insurance', *Journal of Health Insurance*.

Index